LEADING
AND
MANAGING
ARCHIVES
AND
RECORDS
PROGRAMS
STRATEGIES
FOR SUCCESS

Edited by

Bruce W. Dearstyne

NEAL-SCHUMAN PUBLISHERS, INC.
NEW YORK   LONDON

Published by Neal-Schuman Publishers, Inc.
100 William St., Suite 2004
New York, NY 10038

Printed and bound in the United States of America

The paper used in this publication meets the minimum requirements of American National Standard for Information Sciences—Permanence of Paper for Printed Library Materials, ANSI Z39.48-1992.

Library of Congress Cataloging-in-Publication Data

Leading and managing archives and records programs : strategies for success / edited by Bruce W. Dearstyne.
    p. cm. — (The archivist's & records manager's bookshelf ; no. 3)
    Includes bibliographical references and index.
    ISBN 978-1-55570-615-9 (alk. paper)
    1. Archives—United States—Administration. 2. Records—United States—Management. I. Dearstyne, Bruce W. (Bruce William), 1944-

CD3021.L43 2008
027.073—dc22   2008008747

Contents

Foreword   ix
    Gregory S. Hunter
Preface   xi
Acknowledgments   xvii

**1. Setting the Stage: Challenges and Opportunities
in Leading Archives and Records Programs**   **1**
    Bruce W. Dearstyne
    Introduction   1
    The Tenor of the Times: State Archives and
       Records Programs   4
    Challenges and Opportunities   7
    Perspectives on Building Strong Archives and
       Records Programs   21

2. The Records Management Leader   **25**
    Eugenia K. Brumm
    Introduction   25
    Contextual Leadership   27
    Playing a Leadership Role   31
    Strategy   35
    Vision, Innovation, and Risk-Taking   36
    Building and Managing Relationships   40
    Conclusion   43

**3. Records Management Standards: What They Are
and Why They Are Important**   **45**
    Diane K. Carlisle
    Laying the Foundation   45
    Definitions   47
    Types of Standards   50
    Who Does the Work?   53
    Evaluating a Standard for Potential Use   55

Ways to Use Standards   56
ISO Standards for Records Management   58
Electronic Records Management Applications   61
Process-oriented Standards   62
Process-oriented Technical Reports/Guidelines   64
Summary   66
Helpful Web Sites for Records and Information
    Management Standards   66

4. **Leading a Successful Records Management Program**   **69**
    Carol E. B. Choksy
Introduction: The Key Role of Leadership   69
Communication   71
Relationships   74
Strategy   78
Records Management Program Planning   81
Employee Development and Leadership   83
Project Management   86
Organizational Environment   87
Concluding Observations   88

5. **From Cultural Luxury to "The Way We Do Things . . . ?"**
    The Influence of Leadership in Archives and
    Records Management   **91**
    Peter Emmerson
Introduction   91
In the Beginning . . .   92
The Challenge of Constant Change   94
Trimming to New Business Realities   96
Learning from Experience   98
Engaging with Reality   98
Seizing the Opportunities   101
Serving the "Doers"   102
Entrepreneurial Approaches   106
The Human Factor   107
Setting People Free   109
Managing the Future   110
Conclusion   112

6. **Competing for Relevance: Archives in a Multiprogram Organization**   **115**
    James E. Fogerty
    "Opportunity and Adaptation"—The Archivist's Mantra   115
    Institutional Context   116
    Identifying Internal Needs and Objectives   117
    Identifying External Needs and Objectives   119
    Why Business?   120
    Creating the Mind-set   127
    Seizing Opportunity—Examples from the Real World   128
    Conclusion   133

7. **Trying to Lead from Good to Great and Some Reflections on Leadership at All Levels**   **137**
    Mark A. Greene
    Introduction   137
    The Leadership Challenge at AHC   138
    Creating a Vision for the Program   141
    Identifying and Managing Change at AHC   144
    Making Decisions and Taking Responsibility   149
    Leadership at Other Levels in the Hierarchy   153
    Dealing with Challenges   156
    Conclusion   157

8. **Meeting Leadership Challenges: Lessons from Experience**   **163**
    Edie Hedlin
    Support the Goals of the Parent Organization   164
    Define and Constantly Articulate Your Mission   166
    Seek and Work with Allies to Advance Your Program   168
    Develop Careful Plans and Set Priorities   170
    Focus on Staff Productivity   173
    Evaluate Your Leadership or Management Style   175

9. **Stranger in a Strange Land: The Archivist and the Corporation**   **183**
    Philip F. Mooney
    Introduction: Growing Numbers of Corporate Archives   183
    Why Corporate Archival Programs Begin   184
    Why Coporate Archival Programs Fail   186

Selling History to Management   187
Integrating Archives into the Business Plan   189
Marketing the Archives   190
The Importance of Relationships   198
Measuring the Value   199
The Leadership Factor   201
Conclusion: Leadership Is the Key   203

10. **Managing Change at the Vermont State Archives:**
    A Continuing Issue   **207**
    Gregory Sanford and Tanya Marshall
    Introduction   207
    History of the Vermont State Archives   209
    Reintroducing the Evidentiary/Accountability
        Function of Archives   212
    Presenting Records-based Information to Decision Makers 217
    Gaining Statutory Authority to Actively Manage
        Records and Information Across Government   220
    Integrating Records and Archival Management Functions 222
    Lessons Learned   224

11. **Appraising, Transferring, Preserving, and**
    Making Available Born-Digital Records from
    Central Government Departments ("Seamless Flow")   **227**
    Kelvin Smith
    Background   227
    The Business Change and Training Project   231
    Project Teamwork   235
    Redaction of Digital Records in Response to Requests
        Under the Freedom of Information Act   236
    Pilot Transfers   238
    Benefits Analysis   239
    Conclusion   240

12. **Leading from the Middle: Building a**
    University Archives   **243**
    Leon Stout
    Introduction: My Route to Penn State Archivist   243
    Assessing the Archives Program   245
    Taking Advantage of Opportunities   247

Records Management and University Archives   250
Opportunities in Electronic Records   252
Promoting Awareness of Archives   254
Is It Me or Is It the Archives? Institutionalizing
    Archival Success   255
Conclusion   263

13. **The State Archives, Education, and Politics in
New York**   **269**
    Christine Ward
Introduction   269
The New York State Archives and Education   273
New Opportunities: Education Policy Change in
    New York State   283
New Opportunities: Leadership Change in
    New York State   286

14. **Leading Archives and Records Programs:
Perspectives and Insights**   **291**
    Bruce W. Dearstyne
The Essential Role of Leadership   291
Varieties of Leadership   294
Three Models for Developing Strong Programs   301
Identifying and Implementing Successful Strategies   303

15. **Leading Archives and Records Programs: Issues
and Sources**   **313**
    Bruce W. Dearstyne
Looking Toward the Future   313
Some Issues for Future Consideration   314
Sources   316

About the Editor and Contributors   327
Index   335

Foreword

Leadership is an elusive thing. We know it when we see it, but it can be difficult to quantify or emulate. Yet, as a society we long for true leaders in various spheres: politics, business, education, etc. We do not just want managers who can crunch numbers and execute business plans. Rather, we want leaders with inspiring visions and the motivational skills to help us achieve more than we thought possible both individually and collectively.

Leadership also is important in the world of archives and records management. Programs have risen and fallen based largely upon the leadership of a dedicated professional who has earned the respect of his or her colleagues in the parent organization. We sometimes mistakenly believe that archives and records management are all about the records; in reality they are all about the people we serve. Outstanding leaders have internalized this view and make it the hallmark of all they do.

Despite this success, we are at a professional crossroads. Many of the outstanding leaders of archival and records management programs are nearing retirement. This leads to some key questions: Can the archives and records management programs they built survive past their own retirement? Are there lessons we can learn from the success of the current generation? And, ultimately, how do we develop the next generation of archives and records management leaders?

Bruce Dearstyne has taken an important step in answering these questions by editing the volume you now are reading. Bruce is an internationally recognized leader in his own right, making distinguished contributions in archives, records management, and professional education. He well could have written the entire volume on leadership. However, Bruce chose to approach some of his professional colleagues in the United States and the United Kingdom to share their insights as well. The result is an all-star lineup of archives and records management leaders sharing stories of success and failure.

Because leadership is always dependent upon context, many of the stories are personal. Each author has been careful, however, to draw general principles from his or her experiences and to relate them to archivists and records managers from other types of institutions. The result is a balanced, very readable text that includes both personal anecdotes and universal insights.

This volume is an excellent example of Neal-Schuman's purpose in establishing the series *The Archivist's and Records Manager's Bookshelf*. The authors in this volume recognize that archivists and records managers have much to learn from one another. They also recognize that technological imperatives and organizational realities are bringing the two professions closer together. Finally, they appreciate that we learn from one another's stories as well as from more formal educational structures.

I hope you will be both inspired by these stories of leadership and motivated to bring your own programs in archives, records management, or another discipline to even greater heights.

Gregory S. Hunter, PhD, CA, CRM
Palmer School of Library and Information Science
Long Island University
Series Editor

Preface

Leading and Managing Archives and Records Programs: Strategies for Success provides insights into strategies for leading, developing, and managing effective archives and records management programs. It reflects the experiences and insights of some of the most accomplished leaders in the fields who have established track records developing and applying strategic approaches and building and sustaining successful programs over the course of several years.

These chapters are written by individuals who provide their own perspectives about what they *did*; they are not case studies prepared by external observers. In short, the book offers accumulated experience and wisdom that can be considered and applied by others. The authors not only relate their experiences but also reflect on why things happened, what they learned in the process, and how the developments in their programs related to broader trends in the field.

These wonderfully wide-ranging accounts share common themes. Each chapter reveals the hard work required to achieve sustained program success, to construct and nurture a program, to deal with challenges, and to keep the program fresh and responsive. The chapters also reveal the importance of developing skills and applying leadership approaches that fit the individual program and its organizational environment, and that are responsive to the challenges of the times.

THE AUTHORS

The authors of the following chapters include Eugenia K. Brumm, Diane K. Carlisle, Carol E. B. Choksy, Peter Emmerson, James E. Fogerty, Mark A. Greene, Edie Hedlin, Tanya Marshall, Philip F. Mooney, Gregory Sanford, Kelvin Smith, Leon Stout, and Christine Ward. They express multiple perspectives and insights. They include two program directors from Great Britain, thus bringing an international perspective. Each uncovers the secrets of his or her success and lays out what it takes to build and manage a dynamic, high-achieving program.

THE AUDIENCE

These essays have been written primarily for:

- people who lead or manage archives, records, and related programs;
- professionals who aspire to such leadership;
- executives who are interested in strengthening the leadership of archives and records programs in their organizations;
- students in archives and records programs;
- information professionals in related fields; and
- others who want to understand successful leadership and management techniques.

THE CHAPTERS

Chapter 1, "Setting the Stage: Challenges and Opportunities in Leading Archives and Records Programs," provides context for the essays in the subsequent chapters by discussing some of the issues, challenges, and opportunities faced by leaders and managers of archival and records management programs.

In Chapter 2, "The Records Management Leader," Eugenia K. Brumm examines the role and importance of leadership in successful, high-achieving records management programs, and describes the skills sets and the behaviors that are most often associated with such leadership.

In Chapter 3, "Records Management Standards: What They Are and Why They Are Important," Diane K. Carlisle focuses selectively on the standards and best practices in the field of records and information management, concentrating on standards and best practices that are developed through a formal standards body, such as the American National Standards Institute (ANSI), or the International Organization for Standardization, or through professional associations.

In Chapter 4, "Leading a Successful Records Management Program," Carol E. B. Choksy discusses experiences, insights, and observations on excellence in records management programs. She describes and analyzes the skills needed by successful records managers today, including skills in communication, relationship management, strategy development and execution, employee development and leadership, project management, and negotiating in the environment of the industry and the organization.

In Chapter 5, "From Cultural Luxury to 'The Way We Do Things . . . ?': The Influence of Leadership in Archives and Records Management," Peter Emmerson draws upon his experience as head of Barclays Bank's Records Services operation and as a consultant, and discusses how important it is for records management to be responsive to, and aligned with, the changing circumstances and strategic objectives of the wider business. He examines what this means in practice and draws out the strategic and leadership points.

In Chapter 6, "Competing for Relevance: Archives in a Multiprogram Organization," James E. Fogerty uses his experiences directing archives and oral history programs to examine the importance of supporting the organization's goals and, at the same time, identifying and meeting the expectations of external constituencies. He describes strategies for dealing with business records and for capitalizing on opportunities to strengthen the program and raise its profile.

In Chapter 7, "Trying to Lead from Good to Great and Some Reflections on Leadership at All Levels," Mark A. Greene reflects on his experience in playing a leadership role in a variety of settings, and notes the important role leadership plays at all levels of an organization. He focuses on three important components of leadership: "defining, disseminating, and implementing a vision; defining and managing change; and making decisions."

In Chapter 8, "Meeting Leadership Challenges: Lessons from Experience," Edie Hedlin shares the insights gained and the lessons learned from her varied archival career. These include supporting the goals of the parent organization; defining and constantly articulating your mission; seeking and working with allies; developing careful plans and setting priorities; focusing on staff productivity; and evaluating your leadership/management style.

In Chapter 9, "Stranger in a Strange Land: The Archivist and the Corporation," Philip F. Mooney discusses the unique opportunities and challenges faced by corporate archivists. He examines why corporations begin archival programs; why corporate archival programs sometimes do not succeed; how to sell history to corporate management; how to integrate archives into the business plan; how to market the archives; why forming relationships with other operating units is important; how to measure the value of the archives; and leadership's role in administering an archival program.

In Chapter 10, "Managing Change at the Vermont State Archives: A Continuing Issue," Gregory Sanford and Tanya Marshall examine the evolution of the Vermont State Archives over the past quarter century. They describe strategic approaches that have helped in its development "from a small, outdated office to a modern, robust program," including making records-based information useful to decision makers, expanding statutory authority, and integrating records and archives management.

In Chapter 11, "Appraising, Transferring, Preserving, and Making Available Born-Digital Records from Central Government Departments ('Seamless Flow')," Kelvin Smith describes the Seamless Flow Programme of the National Archives of the United Kingdom, an Internet-based delivery system for digital records. The Programme is divided into projects, eight of which are summarized. The ninth, the Business Change and Training Project, is discussed in detail because it is central to the Seamless Flow Programme and presents some of the most complex management challenges.

In Chapter 12, "Leading from the Middle: Building a University Archives," Leon Stout reflects on his leadership experience and describes his work as the University Archivist at Penn State University. He provides insights about leadership at the middle level, where one serves as a program manager but must also answer to executives higher in the institution's leadership hierarchy, and examines qualities that were important to him in his leadership work over the years.

In Chapter 13, "The State Archives, Education, and Politics in New York," Christine Ward examines the New York State Archives' strategic approaches to supporting the mission of its parent organization, the State Education Department, and the goals of state government. She describes the leadership work involved in expanding the program, campaigning for program resources, and tailoring the archives program to changing institutional priorities.

Chapter 14, "Leading Archives and Records Programs: Perspectives and Insights," places the essays in this book into perspective by considering interpretations of leadership that have been advanced in recent literature and by examining how these insights may apply to archives, records, and related information programs.

Chapter 15, "Leading Archives and Records Programs: Issues and Sources," suggests topics for further attention, as well as sources with which to explore them, and delves further into some of the issues raised by the authors of the other chapters.

Acknowledgments

I am very grateful to all the authors in *Leading and Managing Archives and Records Programs: Strategies for Success* for sharing their ideas with us. They all took time from busy schedules and other priorities to organize and share their best thoughts on leadership and management techniques. Each did so in the hope that the information and experience will be useful to many others in their own leadership and management endeavors. It is often the case that the people who are the busiest achieving program breakthroughs and impact have the least time to write about what they have done.

I would also like to express my appreciation to the people who supported, guided, and fostered the production of the book. Dr. Gregory Hunter, professor at the Palmer School of Library and Information Science, Long Island University, who is the editor of the series, of which this volume is a part, *The Archivist's and Records Manager's Bookshelf*, encouraged and helped shape the original proposal. Several people at Neal-Schuman provided the guidance and support essential to get the book done. Charles Harmon reviewed and strengthened the initial proposal and got the project started; Elizabeth Lund and Paul Seeman, the editors for the book, were immensely helpful as the chapters were developed; Amy Rentner, production editor, managed the final revisions and the process of getting the book completed and published.

Finally, I would like to thank my wife, Susan, for all her patience, support, encouragement, and wisdom with many projects over many years, including this book. She read all of the chapters and prepared the index for the book. Without her, none of this would be possible.

Chapter 1

Setting the Stage: Challenges and Opportunities in Leading Archives and Records Programs

Bruce W. Dearstyne

INTRODUCTION

This chapter sets the stage for the rest of the volume by describing some of the issues, challenges, and opportunities that leaders and managers of archival and records programs face. Some of these issues appear in one form or another in some of the chapters in this book; in other cases, as the chapters illustrate, programs face unique problems and opportunities that seldom turn up elsewhere. The chapters have been written by some of the most accomplished leaders in the archives and records management fields; they illustrate a broad array of applications of leadership principles to particular programs and circumstances. The programs they describe are broad ranging but fit within working definitions, outlined below, from two of the leading professional organizations in the field—the Society of American Archivists and the Association of Records Managers and Administrators (ARMA International):

> *Archives* are the "non-current records of individuals, groups, institutions, and governments that contain information of enduring value;" the primary work of archivists is to establish and maintain

control, both physical and intellectual, over records of enduring value; and archival repositories and programs vary greatly in size and level of support and exist in governments, universities, colleges, businesses, religious institutions, historical societies and other settings where there is a recognized importance "to retain the records of people or organizations." (Society of American Archivists, 2003)

Records are "the evidence of what the organization does. They capture its business activities and transactions such as contract negotiations, business correspondence, personnel files, and financial statements. . . ." Records are important, come in many formats, and are used daily by the employees in organizations that create them. Records management is "the systematic control of records throughout their life cycle." (ARMA International, 2005)

Leadership—shaping, directing, and changing programs and, overall, ensuring effectiveness, progress and success—matters a great deal in these fields. Whatever their setting, leaders develop vision, direction, and priorities. They appeal to and bring out the best in people and programs. They help link their programs to larger goals and priorities of the programs' parent organizations. To some degree, they personify and represent the program to the outside world. Moreover, since both archives and records management are fields in flux, program leaders also affect and influence the development of their fields by what they do in their individual programs.

Chapter 14 of this book discusses leadership styles and program development strategies and compares the insights in this book to the recommendations in recent leadership and management literature.

Applying leadership principles in archives and records programs requires imagination, creativity, and improvisation. Leaders need to develop themselves, through study, practice, and trial and error. Moreover, leadership is not something that resides solely at the top; in fact, people at just about any level in the program can play a leadership role. Like any other advanced skill, leadership is likely to improve the more you work on it, the more you apply it, and the more your self-confidence improves.

Leadership styles, approaches, and successes depend to a significant degree on program settings and issues. Leadership in archives and records presents some special challenges. A study of archival leadership issues, based on the results of a survey of the profession carried out during 2003–2006 by the Society of American Archivists (the "A*CENSUS"), noted that archives is a field in the process of evolution.

If we look at professions as being "in process"—as shifting and adjusting to jurisdictional and other challenges—then the concept of leadership must reflect the ability to navigate that unpredictable terrain. Leaders emerge according to their ability to carry out activities that move the profession forward. (Davis, 2006: 408)

Archivists need to exert leadership and influence in their workplaces but, because of their relative isolation in their organizations, tend also to have a strong sense of identification with the profession at large and with archival organizations. Archivists often pursue opportunities for participation and leadership in professional organizations, including holding office. The "A*CENSUS" study also noted:

Leaders are those who contribute toward the growth and progress of a profession and support that profession's ability to meet challenges. Leaders, by word and action, set examples for their colleagues to emulate or follow. . . . Attitude also plays a major role. . . . The interest and willingness to put in the effort required by leadership suggest a strong bond with the profession and its goals. An individual has to be inclined to see the big picture and capable of wearing the multiple hats of individual archivist, institutional employee, and member of a profession. (Davis, 2006: 417)

On the other hand, the "A*CENSUS" revealed a surprising lack of concern among archivists about leadership as a field. One question asked respondents to cite the three most important issues that they and their programs faced. Only 1 percent listed "Leadership." However, program issues and skills related to leadership scored far higher; for instance, about 23 percent listed "Funding" as one of their top three issues, and about 26 percent included "Advocacy." Successfully confronting these issues requires, by implication, strong leadership skills. Another factor is that as archivists think about the issues they face, important technical ones loom large—for instance, 39 percent included technology (e.g., electronic records) among their top three choices, and around 27 percent identified "Access, Arrangement, and Description" (Walch, 2006, "A*CENSUS: A Closer Look": 341).

THE TENOR OF THE TIMES: STATE ARCHIVES AND RECORDS PROGRAMS

This is a time of challenge and change for archives and records programs. Both fields seem to be expanding, though the lack of hard-and-fast standards for programs makes quantification difficult. Funding and resources seem to be a perpetual problem, but in some areas, there is notable program expansion. Digital information technology is both an opportunity (e.g., easier access and quicker transfer of documents) and a challenge (e.g., preserving e-mail and other electronic records). The tenor of the times, and the leadership and management challenges program directors face, are well-reflected in a 2006 survey of state archival and records management programs (Council of State Archivists, January 2007, *The State of State Records*). The oldest state archival programs are around 100 years old; the most recent dates from the 1970s. Their administrative settings include state libraries, historical societies, secretaries of state, and other locations. State records management programs are sometimes in the same office as archives or may be housed in a separate agency such as administration, management, and general services. Several factors have supported positive change in state records programs over the past couple of decades: new program directors, strategic assessment and planning projects, new and growing professional associations, support via competitive grants from a federal funding agency (the National Historical Publications and Records Commission), a professional development institute in the 1990s (co-sponsored by the National Association of Government Archives and Records Administrators and the University of Pittsburgh), and clarification (and in some cases expansion) of statutory mandates. The report describes core program responsibilities: managing the documentation of state government, providing stewardship for the records of key values of state government, supporting access to and use of records of continuing value, providing records management advice and services, advising local governments and issuing retention/disposition schedules covering their records, and, in some cases, leading the state's historical records community. There was lots of good news to report in this survey—growing accessions, escalating numbers of researchers (many via the Web), and several new or renovated buildings. Clearly, the collective leadership of the nation's state archival and records management agencies have achieved some notable progress over the past several years. The report makes clear that it is an exciting time to be the director of a state archival or records program (Council of State Archivists, January 2007, *The State of State Records*: 1–7).

On the other hand, the survey also discussed several issues and concerns, indicative of the continuing leadership challenges. These include (Council of State Archivists, January 2007, *The State of State Records*: 7–21, 115–123):

Leading in an institutional setting. Program setting helps determine program robustness, but no single placement emerged as the best in all circumstances. For instance, programs in historical societies may find strong support for archival work but less interest in records management and therefore may be regarded as a low funding priority for state government, particularly in hard budgetary times. The report emphasized the advantages of jointly administered records/archives programs (which exist in 37 states), including better coordinated advisory services to state agencies, streamlined retention/disposition scheduling and more certain identification of archival records; economies of scale in storing inactive and archival records, and more efficient approaches to electronic records.

Meeting changing expectations. Expectations within state governments are rising and changing; for instance, archives and records programs need to develop working relationships with state Chief Information Officers, whose authority for information resources is increasing in many states.

The adequacy of legal authority. Most state programs reported having adequate legal authority to carry out their work. But in most states, the definition of "record" is based on a 1943 federal statutory definition with a phrase "regardless of physical form or characteristics," a catchall term meant to encompass electronic records but one that does not clearly distinguish between record and nonrecord electronic information. Moreover, the report documents a gap between program authority and program resources, the wherewithal to actually carry out the statutory responsibilities.

Managing and reporting on impact. Genealogists are the single largest group of users. But just reporting the numbers may underreport the significance of the State Archives. For instance, the use of Archives' holdings to shed light on a social or environmental issue, determine the outcome of important litigation, or document how a policy was developed, may count as only a single "use" but one of transcending importance. This, in turn, illustrates the leadership challenge of how to report on the impact of the program.

Managing in hard budgetary times. Budgetary resources vary greatly but budgets for archives/records programs are less than one tenth of one percent of total expenditures of state governments across the board, raising the question of whether state support is even close to commensurate with the function's importance. Many programs were hurt by the budgetary reductions that occurred in many states during the past few years. Reductions to records management programs, particularly critical for electronic records, make meeting that challenge all the more difficult and the "catch-up" burden all the greater. It takes a long time to recover from staff layoffs, particularly given the learning curve of new professional employees before they become fully proficient.

Finding new revenue sources. New revenue sources, e.g., fees from document filings, provided income boosts in several states. On the other hand, state budget offices and legislatures may consider diverting such funds to other purposes; in New York, for instance, state library and museum programs were shifted to the fee-based source.

Dealing with electronic records. The volume of paper records held by the state archival programs continues to grow. On the other hand, most states have not begun to accession significant quantities of electronic records. Digital technologies present enormous and as yet unresolved preservation and access problems.

Ensuring adequate storage facilities. Several states reported new or expanded facilities, as noted above. However, cramped facilities and lack of space continued to plague programs in other states.

Serving distant researchers. Reference numbers are increasing; but most of this increase is in the form of e-mail, visits to websites, and over-the-Web interactions with researchers rather than traditional phone, mail, or walk-in reference traffic. This presents the challenge of finding new ways to service and interact with researchers at a distance. The volume of reference traffic is rising faster than the budgetary resources to take care of it. Several of the states reported another impediment to full use: a backlog of holdings that are undescribed and therefore inaccessible.

CHALLENGES AND OPPORTUNITIES

Following is a more detailed look at some challenges for leaders of archival and records management programs.

Dealing with the Pace of Change

One of the challenges (which may also be one of the opportunities) is the pace of change in the field, particularly in records management. There, new laws, such as Sarbanes-Oxley, which sets requirements for record keeping in companies to help ensure accountability, and older but changing laws such as privacy, copyright, and data protection, create a constantly changing setting. The expectations of executives for what records managers should be able to accomplish also continue to evolve. Natalie Ceeney, chief executive of the National Archives in Great Britain, has noted:

> [Records managers are now] required to evaluate records management procedures, develop business cases for change, while adapting to rapidly evolving and changing IT processes. On top of this record managers often have to champion the benefits of e-investment when integrating sophisticated electronic records management systems into common work practices . . . [at the same time] record managers struggle to have the support of the whole organization. If we are to do it effectively we need long-term strategies in corporate plans as well as total buy in from managers and the resources to train staff. Records management needs to be recognized as a key corporate activity. . . . Moving to electronic records management is not just about installing new software. It is fundamentally about changing how an organization works and how it will operate and deliver its services in the future. (Ceeney, 2006: 22–23)

Need for a Skilled, Experienced Workforce

Both the archives and the records management fields need a skilled workforce comprised of people who are not only technically proficient but also have other, "softer" skills of communication, teamwork, adaptiveness, and a commitment to personal growth. These needs mirror the needs of the programs where these people work—the programs also need to do their work to a high degree of excellence while at the same time surviving and prospering in their institutional settings. Communication skills, particularly the ability to dramatize and make clear the importance of archives and records management work, are particularly important, and are a factor in just about all the essays in this book. Versatility and an inclination to learn and grow over time are essential to keeping people—and the programs where they work—fresh and responsive.

A related issue is how to retain accumulated know-how and wisdom in programs as people leave for other jobs or, more important in the coming years, retire in large numbers. The "A*CENSUS" found that the so-called "Baby Boomer" generation is present in great numbers in the archives field: nearly half of all respondents were 50 years old or older. Many of these professionals can be expected to retire in the next several years, introducing a need to capture their knowledge and experience and transfer it to the next generation of archivists. Of course, it's relatively easy to learn the fundamentals of some skills from reading and courses. But others are developed over time and best transferred to younger people through the process of younger and more experienced employees working side by side over time. These include, for instance, insight into how the program really gets things done in its parent institution, e.g., the budget and personnel office; the best way of interacting with "customers" whose needs may be difficult for even the customers themselves to articulate; the skill of appraising records; and the knack of working with researchers. Transfer of such skills over time is an important management challenge (Walch, 2006, "The A*CENSUS: Call to Action": 311–319).

The demographic makeup of the workforce is also an issue. Only a small percentage of the people who responded to the "A*CENSUS" questionnaire—8 percent—are members of minority groups; only about 10 percent of Society of American Archivists' members are minorities. This represents a challenge at a time when the U.S. population is becoming more diverse, and the archival field is increasingly concerned with documenting minority groups. The "A*CENSUS" also revealed that for nearly two—thirds of today's archivists, archives is actually a second career. Many were first in some other field, often closely related, such as history or library work. All of this shows the need for more emphasis on diversity, for leadership development opportunities for younger members of the field to ensure continuity of leadership, and for development opportunities for people entering the archives field from other fields (Walch, 2006, "A*CENSUS: Call to Action": 312–317 and "A*CENSUS: A Closer Look": 330–348).

Alignment with Organizational Priorities

Several of the chapters in this book demonstrate strategies for keeping archives and records programs relevant to and aligned with the priorities of the parent organization while, at the same time, following recognized archives and records management principles and practices. Alignment is important because it is a measure of how much and how well the archives or records program is contributing to the "bottom line" of the parent organization. That, in turn, is a major determinant of the organization's funding and support for its archives/ records program. In difficult budgetary times—which seem to recur frequently—organizational executives and budget analysts turn a sharp eye toward what programs contribute to the organization's priorities. The degree of alignment is just as important when more resources are available, and helps determine what areas are identified for enrichment or expansion. The degree of alignment is often reflected in the program's mission or vision statement, which may contain an allusion to its support for the organization's goals and indicate how its work supports them. The Georgia State Archives (2007), for instance, declares its vision: "We support the Secretary of State's vision to become the most customer-friendly agency in state government. We strive to provide innovative, efficient, accurate, and professional service to the citizens of Georgia" (Georgia State Archives, n.d.). The National Archives of the United Kingdom went through a major redefinition of its mission and role in 2006. In addition to a commitment to guaranteeing the survival of today's information for tomorrow's users and a promise to "bring history to life for everyone"—fairly traditional archival functions—the Archives asserted a major role in assisting government-wide digital information management (National Archives of the UK, 2006: 4):

> *Challenge 1*: We've moved from a predictable world of paper to a volatile world of information of all kinds. Government and the wider information sector need better information management to strengthen accountability and get the most from their assets.
> *Vision*: Lead and transform information management.
> *We will*:

- Shape future government information policy, from information creation to re-use
- Show leadership in helping the public sector understand the importance of good information management
- Create a common infrastructure of service and guidance to support these aims.

A Balanced, Complete Record

Records managers often focus on the business aspects of records, retention/disposition, legal admissibility, and related issues. Archivists have more long-term considerations in mind: how well do records document certain people, groups, and functions; who is likely to want to use them, and for what purposes, in the future? Archivists are also concerned with the completeness and objectivity of the records. Records are important in documenting and recalling major developments in human affairs and institutional history. Helen Forde, president of the Society of Archivists in Great Britain, noted in an article a few years ago that government archives may document human rights issues; oppressive regimes may deliberately destroy records to cover up misdeeds. Even if the records survive, issues of privacy, access, and use inevitably arise. "Issues of access loom large in situations where information is power, and where the owners may be extremely wary of permitting the use of such information," she notes, adding that sensitivity to such records and the issues surrounding them helps us all "to remember the past so that we do not repeat it" (Forde, 2004: 119, 121).

Dramatizing the Case

Records management and archival administration are extraordinarily important but it is sometimes difficult to make the case to busy executives, resource allocators, and the public. "The archives is a place of knowledge, memory, nourishment, and power," said Randall Jimerson in his 2005 SAA Presidential Address. "Archives at once protect and preserve records; legitimize and sanctify certain documents while negating and destroying others; and provide access to selected sources while controlling the researchers and conditions under which they may examine the archival record" (Jimerson, 2006: 20). Three years earlier, in *his* presidential address, Steve Hensen asserted that "'being archival' means taking a methodological and conscientious approach to the stewardship of information; it means maintaining its context and authenticity... and it means (or *should* mean) providing open and democratic access to that information.... What a time to be an archivist!" (Hensen, 2002: 172, 175). Archivists and records managers are proud of what they do and the importance of the function seems self-evident; but archives and records program leaders often struggle to get that point across to decision makers and resource allocators. Ian E. Wilson, archivist and librarian of Canada, has noted that this is an issue for libraries, archives, and other repositories of cultural information (Wilson, 2005):

> In addition to the traditional uses of libraries and archives, it is important to keep in mind that information supports the public good; social inclusion, democracy and citizens's rights, universal access and literacy. Libraries and archives are an integral part of the supporting fabric for these public objectives. But how do we influence public policy? If libraries and archives are important to society, we need to build capacity for leadership and innovation.... Libraries and archives can advance nation-building and community development, contribute to a sense of identity and make a real and significant difference to the quality of life of all Canadians.
>
> The documentary heritage in the custody of LAC [Library and Archives of Canada] is the most valuable asset owned by the people of Canada—more valuable than our resources, our national parks, our very sovereignty. It does not belong to librarians or archivists, it was created by and belongs to the people of Canada. And it is this that we hold in trust for all Canadians ... archives [are] a precious asset for here one finds the fundamental documents of our democracy, records that establish our borders, that protect our rights, that tell our story across the centuries as a nation, as communities and as individuals. We are the stewards of these priceless and authentic records, these are the archives that we maintain for future generations. Knowledge—as found in our libraries and archives—is essential because it helps us to understand our past, it informs our present and prepares us for the future; it is the intellectual capital of a modern society.

Many studies and reports on archival issues over the past few years have emphasized the need for advocacy for the importance of archives.

One of the best advocacy publications, developed by the Society of American Archivists for celebrations of "Archives Month" (October of each year), includes these "Talking Points" on the value of Archives (Society of American Archivists, n.d.: 3):

- An archives serves to strengthen collective memory by creating a reliable information bank that provides access to an irreplaceable asset—an organization's, government's, or society's primary sources.
- Archival records are essential to support society's increasing demand for accountability and transparency in government and public and private institutions.
- Archival records protect the rights, property, and identity of our citizens.
- Archival records play a key role in ensuring that the digital records being created today will be accessible when needed in the future.

Capitalizing on New Issues

Several of the chapters that follow describe how program leaders reacted to and dealt with issues, challenges, and opportunities that they did not expect, or where the development had a much larger impact than they anticipated. Often the choice needs to be made among avoiding the issue, trying to minimize its impact, or embracing it head-on but, in the process, risking skewing the program toward the issue. The records management field has been one of the most interesting arenas for observing the impact of such issues over the past few years, particularly in two related areas: (1) legal record-keeping requirements in the wake of the Enron, Arthur Andersen, and other scandals, and (2) the need for making electronic records available in the discovery phase of litigation. The Sarbanes-Oxley Act, passed in 2002, mandated more transparency in company operations, tightened audit requirements, and imposed other documentation requirements. Some records management programs were marginalized as legal offices took the lead. But dynamic records management program directors responded by seeking the authority and resources to implement the requirements, working closely with corporate IT, legal, audit, and program offices. In effect, they used Sarbanes-Oxley to strengthen sound records management practices. Implementation steps include setting up or strengthening the corporate records retention program; reviewing and improving file plans, data structures, indexing, and nomenclature; and documenting certification and compliant processes (Montaña et al., 2006).

The process of legal "discovery"—the opening phase of litigation when parties to litigation are required to turn over documents to their opponents—is not a new one. But the proliferation of electronic documents such as e-mail and the scattering of electronic information in databases, electronic files, servers, and individual employees' desktop computers, vastly complicate the challenge. Changing requirements (e.g., revised federal rules of evidence that went into effect late in 2006), and changing case law via judge's decisions, also keep things in motion. As with Sarbanes-Oxley compliance, in some companies, records managers are secondary players in all of this. But in other cases, progressive records management program directors used the challenge of "e-discovery" to introduce better records management practices, particularly developing legally compliant systems, focus on retention/disposition schedules, and classification/retrieval systems. The leading professional association, ARMA International, shifted considerable attention to this issue over the years; this is both a reflection of how a professional association responds to its members' needs and how, in turn, professionals draw on their associations for inspiration and guidance (Cogar, 2005, and ARMA International Standards Task Force, 2007, are good examples).

Disaster preparedness is another example. The terrorist attacks of 9/11/01, the devastation wrought by Hurricane Katrina four years later, and other disasters in recent years have raised public awareness of the potential for more destruction, either natural or man-made. That, in turn, has led to many archives and records management programs giving renewed attention to disaster planning and, perhaps more important, urging their parent organizations to include provisions for protecting records in their broader disaster preparedness and response planning. State archives, for instance, have stepped up their work with state emergency planning offices, and the Council of State Archivists has produced very effective guidelines that reinforce why records are important, explain the impact on government if they are lost, and outline action steps to ensure their preservation (Council of State Archivists, 2006).

Limited Program Standards and Models

Both the archives and the records management fields have mecha-nisms for certifying professionals (though certified people are still a minority in each field). There are guidelines, but not hard-and-fast standards, for education in the archives field and, to some degree, in the records management field. These are helpful, but they need fur-ther development. There is an impressive array of standards for vari-ous aspects of archives and records management work (records management standards are covered by one of the chapters in this book). But as a professional field, we seem to underestimate or at least not fully appreciate the importance of leadership, program develop-ment strategies, and standards or benchmarks for *program success.* The factor of limited standards for programs also complicates the work of the program director in securing resources and support from CEOs and boards of directors. Having a standard to point to is often (though not always) useful, particularly in making the case for program expan-sion or greater budgetary resources. Something nearly as useful as standards, *canons of best practice* for programs, is also underdeveloped. In the absence of standards, executives in organizations may turn to what they regard as more standards-based offices—for instance, coun-sel, the auditing office, or the IT shop—for guidance on records is-sues, rather than to records professionals.

In the same vein, there are few professional forums that concen-trate on *leadership* and *program development* issues as opposed to issues pertaining to the care and management of materials. Publications (e.g., this book), university courses, and even short seminars on leadership and strategies in the archives and records management fields are rare (though the literature on issues, methods, and techniques is robust and growing). Informal mechanisms—for instance, discussions at profes-sional conferences—fill part of the gap, but more is needed.

Underdeveloped Leadership Skills

Too often, people are promoted to leadership positions because of their technical proficiencies, achievements, and seniority. Promotion to a management or leadership position is the only option for advance-ment. In these cases, people may assume leadership positions for rea-sons unconnected with a real desire to lead or well-developed leadership skills. They may lack the time, the inclination, or the confidence to learn to be good leaders. Facing the challenges of their new positions, they find it difficult to devote time to reading leadership books, taking courses, working with mentors, or taking other paths to development. Learning "on the job" is more of a challenge than they anticipated. In other cases, people become very effective managers but can't find a way to go one step further and *develop leadership* skills. They may excel at getting work done through others on a day-to-day basis but are not as adept at envisioning the future or lifting the program to new heights. In still other cases, they become discouraged after too short a time, settle into a pattern of moderate effort and attainment, and never rise beyond mediocrity as leaders. A final, common pattern, particularly in small- to modest-sized programs, is the lack of clear delineation of roles. Individuals find the need to do some of the more complex work themselves, to carry out some day-to-day management functions, and also to act as the leader in keeping the program fresh, resilient, and moving. In those cases, it is often the leadership function that languishes. On the other hand, of course, there are many people in leadership positions in both the archives and records management fields who achieve notable success and attainment as program leaders; some of the best examples are presented in this book.

While leadership and management concerns have not been a top priority in either the records management or archival arenas, in both areas there is some focused attention and concern, particularly on including at least some understanding of management in the preparation of new professionals. The Society of American Archivists includes a short section on management in its archival graduate education guidelines (Society of American Archivists, 2002):

Management. Archivists should understand how to manage resources and to make decisions based on systematic analysis. They often must demonstrate programmatic vision and innovation. Thus, archivists need to know the fundamental principles related to organizational management, strategic planning, administrative leadership, human resources management, financial management, resource allocation, fundraising, and facilities management.

The Academy of Certified Archivists (ACA) includes a set of expectations for its Managing Archival Program in its examination for certified archivists; it also includes educational requirements (master's degree) and an experience requirement. This "domain" includes an expectation that archivists will know and can apply knowledge about several management challenges and that they are proficient in the following tasks (Academy of Certified Archivists, 2003, Domain 6):

Task 1. Participate in the development of a strategic vision for an archival program, establish priorities, continually assess progress toward that vision, and make adjustments as environments and resources change.

Task 2. Assess staffing needs, recruit appropriate personnel, and train staff; support professional development; and ensure that the staff works together to fulfill the archives' mission.

Task 3. Plan, gain approval of, and administer a budget; assess financial performance; and monitor progress.

Task 4. Identify facility and equipment needs and prepare and implement plans to meet those needs.

Task 5. Create policies, standards, and procedures that facilitate the range of activities in archival programs.

Task 6. Use appropriate technologies to manage an archival program.

The Institute of Certified Records Managers (ICRM) places heavier emphasis on program management. The ICRM requires three years' experience for candidates with a bachelor's degree (two years with a graduate degree) to qualify to take the Certified Records Manager exam; one of the areas of qualifying experience may be management of a records management program. The exam itself is comprised of five parts; the first one is "Management Principles and the Records and Information (RIM) Program." The handbook for candidates (Institute of Certified Records Managers, 2006: Part 1) outlines several areas for study and preparation including: principles of management, human resources/staffing, financial management, developing a RIM program, planning a RIM program, organizing a RIM program, legal and ethical considerations, and other elements. This part of the exam covers management and some aspects of leadership. Under "Principles of Management," the discussion of "Organizational Mission, Goals, and Objectives" states:

Goals and objectives help to formulate decision making, establish consistency, and facilitate teamwork. Review how organizational, departmental, and individual goals (MBOs) and objectives are interrelated. Identify the goals and objectives of a RIM program. Be able to identify what responsibilities RIM managers have when designing programs to fit into the culture, mission, and goals of the organization. Identify how a RIM program fits into the overall goals and objectives of an organization if the organization is growing, stabilizing, retrenching, or downsizing.

There is also provision for recertification for certified archivists and certification maintenance for records managers. In any case, certified professionals are, at least at present, a minority in both the archives and records management fields. This increases the need for postappointment development opportunities in leadership and management. It also increases the likelihood that archivists and records managers will learn for themselves, on their own, through their own educational work and experience, how to be good managers and leaders when they reach that stage in their careers. The chapters in this volume illustrate several leaders' experience in this regard.

Shifting Contexts for Archives and Records Work

The dramatic upsurge in the volume of digital information over the past few decades has made archives and records work more complicated. The importance of *information* is now recognized in the fields of leadership and management, though it often misconceptualized as *information technology* and the central place of *records* is often overlooked. Information is of central importance in businesses and other organizations for several reasons:

A *basis for leadership and decision making.* CEOs and other executives and managers need fresh, reliable, consistent information on a regular basis to assess the environment in which their program is operating, to make decisions on resource allocation, to determine how well the program is achieving objectives, to assess customer reactions, and generally to keep the enterprise moving ahead.

The fuel and substance for information/knowledge workers. Productive workers need access to information—about their institutions, about customers, about their settings, and about other topics—in order to do their work well. "More than anything else, information is the top necessity for every employee" in the most successful organizations. (Coffman and Gonzalez-Molina, 2002: 82–83)

The sustainer of business or service priorities. It is information that forms the basis for design, research, marketing, supply chain management, and other aspects of manufacturing and commerce. A book based on review of RAND Corporation studies noted that "high performance thrives on information" and that most successful companies "saturate themselves with information" that is carefully organized and analyzed to keep them agile and adaptable. (Light, 2005: 82–85)

A basis for interactions and transactions. People who conduct online banking, access government web sites to check policies or to conduct transactions, buy books on Amazon.com or buy or sell on e-Bay, or otherwise use the Internet and the Web, are in reality dealing with information. This use of information is rapidly expanding as people's use of the Web grows.

The source of documentation. Information of transcending importance needs to be systematically kept, organized, and accessible for as long as needed for administrative, fiscal, legal, research, historical, or other purposes.

A measure of accountability. Information is the basis for asserting and measuring the accountability of organizations. Government Freedom-of-Information laws, use of records in government investigations and court proceedings, tobacco company files on the hazards of smoking, and corporate documentation of personnel practices, are a few examples.

The importance of digital information is evidenced by the rise in status and influence of chief information officers (CIOs). Increasingly, CIOs are broadening their role well beyond information technology and are becoming, in effect, chief information managers and strategists for their organizations. Records—recorded *information*—are a central component of any information universe, and archives are records of transcending/enduring value. But the prominence of the records management and archives fields has not risen in a commensurate fashion. Awareness of importance, and policies to deal with electronic records, are lagging. A recent survey of records/information professionals in companies and other institutions found that nearly one-third rated their records management programs as "marginal" or "fair"— the two lowest categories in a five-point semantic scale; 29 percent said their organizations adhered to retention schedules "not regularly" or "when time permits"; 43 percent do not include electronic records in their schedules; and 49 percent have no formal e-mail retention policies (Williams and Ashley, 2005: 9). These figures represented modest progress from previous years, but also demonstrated the gap that still exists. Organizations often make decisions about information technology applications and the development of information systems without consulting records or archives professionals or factoring in the need for recordkeeping systems. SAA identifies the electronic information/records issue as a strategic priority: "Rapidly changing information technologies challenge archival principles and practices, and demand increasingly effective leadership from the archival community to prevent loss of records and improve preservation of and access to modern archival records in all formats" (Society of American Archivists, 2006).

One of the central challenges for the leader of a records or archives program is to educate the organization to differentiate between records and nonrecord information, and to treat records in an appropriate fashion. This requires an ability to gain the attention and support of higher level executives; an ability to negotiate with CIOs, information technology experts and others to build recordkeeping capacity into information systems; an understanding of the need to build professional development opportunities for archives and records management program staff so that they can keep up with the technology; and a need to balance attention, with the resources and expertise available, to both paper and electronic records.

Inadequate Resources

Issues relating to budget strategies, program development, warding off reductions, and other resource questions emerge in one form or another in just about all the chapters that follow. One of the constant challenges for the director of an archives or records program is securing adequate resources. These programs are often underresourced or modestly resourced. It is easy for fiscal officers and other executives to underestimate the amount of work required for an archives, records, or related information program to handle its very important responsibilities. To the uninformed, it may look like a relatively unchallenging matter of moving and storing electrons, files, and cartons. This, in turn, leads to underappreciation of the level of personnel and other resources needed to do the work. Multiple surveys and studies over the past several years have documented this problem. A recent report based on a national survey of state archives and records management programs (Council of State Archivists, *Report of the Blue Ribbon Panel,* January 2007: 4–5) indicated a lack of resources and a commensurate gap between what is expected and what the program can actually deliver:

> State archives and records management programs have insufficient resources to fulfill their responsibilities. Funding and staffing levels are chronically low and many have been further downsized in response to state budget reductions. Facilities are too small to accommodate the volume of incoming records. Although a number of state archives and records management budgets appear to have increased at a rate that exceeds the inflation rate, in most cases those funds now cover expanded responsibilities, so there is no actual net gain. . . . There is a gap between the authority to act and the ability to act effectively. While most state archives and records management programs have sufficient authority in law or regulation to establish policies and procedures for current records and to ensure that those of long-term significance are preserved, most do not have commensurate resources, enforcement mechanisms, or mandates to assert this authority effectively.

The lack of adequate resources also demonstrates the need for more sustained attention to advocacy and educational efforts. It points to the need to make a business case about why records and archives are a good investment for the organization. In addition, measures need to be developed; leaders need to report on *inputs* (resources used) and *outputs* (direct, visible things such as a new e-mail system set up) but also, and more important, on *outcomes* and *impacts*—the ultimate benefit of what the program is doing and contributing. This may be difficult to measure, in part because the benefit comes some time after the work, e.g., scheduling records, describing archival materials, or developing an information portal, has concluded.

PERSPECTIVES ON BUILDING STRONG ARCHIVES AND RECORDS PROGRAMS

The archives and records management literature abounds with articles, reports, and manuals on principles, techniques, approaches, and professional issues, but coverage of management, leadership, and program development issues is much rarer. A couple of recent examples provide helpful insights and also exemplify the type of literature that needs expanding in both the archives and records fields. Richard Cox, a professor at the University of Pittsburgh, carried out a study supported by the ARMA International Education Foundation to identify the factors that account for sustained records/information (RIM) programs. He presented his findings in a report (Cox, 2005) and an article (Cox, 2006). He identified seven factors that are present for most strong programs; some of these have reverberations in the chapters in this book. The seven factors are (Cox 2005; Cox 2006):

1. Often, programs are established because of an impending anniversary or some other commemoration which calls attention to the organization's history and possibly leads to a written commemorative history or a celebratory event. Initiating a program to organize records and archives is a natural outcome of this attention.

2. Probably the most common factor in the establishment of strong RIM programs is the presence of a champion—someone in the organization (other than the director of the archives or records program) who understands the importance of records or archives and works actively to promote them.

3. Standards are critical in helping others understand what RIM professionals do; the argument that an organization needs to adhere to RIM standards can be persuasive in building programs. Legal requirements such as the Sarbanes-Oxley Act of 2002 are powerful incentives for the establishment of RIM programs because they impose recordkeeping requirements or increase the likelihood that records will be needed for accountability or audit purposes.

4. Recognition by the organization's executives of the administrative, fiscal, legal and research value of records can lead to RIM programs.

5. Recognition of how records management can support organizational priorities is particularly useful.
6. Disasters and crises, such as the 9/11 terrorist attacks and Hurricane Katrina, can spark interest in records management, particularly the need to protect vital records.
7. Selected records may be helpful in marketing and public relations; and a policy of allowing access to open, well-organized records may itself be a good public relations tool.

Another particularly useful model is the management book written by Assistant Archivist of the United States, Michael J. Kurtz, for the Society of American Archivists (Kurtz, 2004). It covers all aspects of managing an archival program including planning and reporting, project management, human resources, communication, facilities, and other topics. But it is even stronger in its discussion of management theory and leadership. Kurtz maintains that archival program directors must have both leadership (e.g., communicate, motivate, inspire) and management (plan, organize, and direct) skill sets. His list of "Archival Leadership Skills" is particularly useful (Kurtz, 2004, 23):

1. Leaders develop the team concept, choosing people with varying talents and allowing them to do what they do best, while simultaneously moving them toward an assigned goal.
2. Leaders think of renewal, developing strong values, new skills, and new leaders within the staff.
3. Leaders have good motivational skills and encourage their subordinates.
4. Leaders have good political skills and are able to resolve or reconcile conflicts and satisfy constituencies both inside and outside the repository.
5. Leaders seek to influence people outside the archives. They communicate not only the archives' intrinsic importance and purpose, but also its value to the larger organization.
6. Leaders see difficult situations not as problems, but as opportunities for seeking solutions.
7. Leaders are calm in the face of adversity. When faced with a challenge, they look for solutions rather than scapegoats.

Mike Kurtz's list of leadership traits is an appropriate way to conclude this introductory chapter and an excellent lead-in to the following chapters.

REFERENCES

Academy of Certified Archivists. 2003. *The 2003 Role Delineation Statement Revision.* Available: www.certifiedarchivists.org (accessed August 1, 2007).

ARMA International. 2005. *What Is Records Management? Why Should I Care?* Available: www.arma.org (accessed August 1, 2007).

ARMA International Standards Task Force. 2007. *Records Management Responsibility in Litigation Support.* Lenexa, KS: ARMA International.

Ceeney, Natalie. 2006. "The Changing Face of Records Management." *RecordKeeping.* (Spring): 22–24.

Coffman, Curt and Gabriel Gonzales-Molina. 2002. *Follow This Path: How the World's Greatest Organizations Drive Growth by Unleashing Human Potential.* New York: Grand Central Publishing.

Cogar, Rae N. 2005. "Legal 101 for RIM Professionals." *Information Management Journal* 39 (November/December): 49–54, 56.

Council of State Archivists. 2006. *Safeguarding a Nation's Identity.* Available: www.statearchivists.org/prepare/epireport_all.pdf (accessed August 1, 2007).

Council of State Archivists. 2007. *Report of the Blue Ribbon Panel Convened to Evaluate and Make Recommendations on Archives and Records Management in State Government.* January. Available: www.statearchivists.org/reports/2007-ARMreport/BRPreport-final.pdf (accessed August 1, 2007).

Council of State Archivists. 2007. *The State of State Records: A Status Report on State Archives and Records Management Programs in the United States.* January. Available: www.statearchivists.org (accessed August 1, 2007).

Cox, Richard. 2005. *A Minor Nuisance Spread Across the Organization: Factors Leading to the Establishment and Support of Records and Information Management Programs.* October. Available: www.armaedfoundation.org (accessed August 1, 2007).

Cox, Richard. 2006. "7 Paths to Developing or Sustaining RIM Programs." *Information Management Journal* 40 (March/April): 48–50, 52–55.

Davis, Susan E. 2006. "Part 7. A*CENSUS: Report on Archival Leadership." *American Archivist* 69 (Fall/Winter): 407–418.

Forde, Helen. 2004. "'We Must Remember Our Past So That We Do Not Repeat It.'" *Journal of the Society of Archivists* 25: 117–122.

Georgia State Archives. n.d. *Who Are We?* Available: http://sos.georgia.gov/archives/who_are_we/default.htm (accessed August, 2007).

Hensen, Steven L. 2002. "Revisiting Mary Jane, or Dear Cat: Being Archival in the 21st Century." *American Archivist* 65 (Fall/Winter): 168–175.

Institute of Certified Records Managers. 2006. *Certified Records Management Examination Outline*. October. Available: www.icrm.org/outline.pdf (accessed August 1, 2007).

Jimerson, Randall J. 2006. "Embracing the Power of Archives." *American Archivist* 69 (Spring/Summer): 19–32.

Kurtz, Michael J. *Managing Archival and Manuscript Repositories*. 2004. Chicago: Society of American Archivists.

Light, Paul C. 2005. *The Four Pillars of High Performance*. New York: McGraw Hill.

Montaña, John C., J. Edwin Deitel, and Christine S. Martins. 2006. "Strategies for RIM Program Compliance with Sarbanes-Oxley. *Information Management Journal* 40 (November/December): 55–58, 60.

National Archives of the UK. 2006. *A New Vision for the National Archives, 2006–2011*. October. Available: www.nationalarchives.gov.uk/documents/vision.pdf (accessed August 1, 2007).

Society of American Archivists. n.d. *American Archives Month, October 2006: Celebrating the American Record*. Chicago: Society of American Archivists. Available: www.archivists.org/archivesmonth/ArchivesKit.pdf (accessed August 1, 2007).

Society of American Archivists. 2002. *Guidelines for a Graduate Program in Archival Studies*. Available: www.archivists.org/prof-education/ed_guidelines.asp (accessed August 1, 2007).

Society of American Archivists. 2003. *So You Want to Be an Archivist: An Overview of the Archival Profession*. Available: www.archivists.org/prof-education/arprof.asp (accessed August 1, 2007).

Society of American Archivists. 2006. "SAA's 2006–2007 Strategic Priorities." *Archival Outlook*. July/August. Available: www.archivists.org/governance/strategic_priorities.asp (accessed August 1, 2007).

Walch, Victoria, 2006. "A*CENSUS: Call to Action." *American Archivist* 69 (Fall/Winter): 310–326.

Walch, Victoria, 2006. "A*CENSUS: A Closer Look." *American Archivist* 69 (Fall/Winter): 327–348.

Williams, Robert F. and Lori J. Ashley. 2005. "2005 Electronic Records Survey: A Renewed Call to Action." Chicago: Cohasset Associates. Available: www.merresource.com/pdf/survey2005.pdf (accessed August 1, 2007).

Wilson, Ian E. 2005. Speech at Ontario Historical Society. May 7. Available: www.collectionscanada.ca/about-us/012-203-e.html (accessed August 1, 2007).

Chapter 2

The Records
Management Leader

Eugenia K. Brumm

INTRODUCTION

Records management (RM) is becoming high profile and organizations are seeking records management professionals at director levels and above who can function strategically in leading, developing, and managing comprehensive RM programs. Records management knowledge and experience now includes electronic records, e-mail, imaging, document conversion, instant messaging and installing, configuring and deploying RM applications. This is in addition to expertise in all facets of traditional records management and working knowledge of regulatory requirements that impact the industry of the company. Job descriptions for corporate records managers specify strong leadership skills and emphasize strategy development, change management, initiating and developing professional relationships, establishing trust, continuing to stay abreast of developments in the field, and being able to develop innovative solutions. Increased requirements and expectations are resulting in increased compensation for experienced records managers, with six-figure salaries not uncommon. Organizations are recognizing that records management is pivotal to the information management structure of the organization and that records managers must function at a senior level in developing and implementing RM programs.

The appearance of senior-level positions results, in part, from recently instituted government regulations that demand accountability and transparency in operations and processes and establish new requirements for management of the records that are created in those processes. Implementing and leading a front office RM function is not a simple process, especially at the senior management level. It demands knowledge, skills, competencies, and behaviors that enable the RM professional to work in an integrated way with key players to develop a coherent infrastructure for delivering the organization's RM strategy.

This chapter focuses on the role and importance of leadership in successful, high-achieving records management programs. Since leadership itself remains an elusive concept, this will not attempt to define leadership. Instead, this is a discussion of those behaviors most often associated with leadership and how they are manifested in a records management setting. It will present the ideas that leadership in records management requires skill sets and behaviors beyond those required in other professions and that records managers, by definition, are innovative change agents and risk takers.

More so than other functions, records management programs tend to be personality-dependent. Whether RM operations are successful or not is directly attributable to the individual who is responsible for administering those operations. The reasons for this are complex; not the least is that records management, as a profession, does not have a standard university degree associated with it. People enter the profession through various channels, come from various educational and work backgrounds, and may or may not have experience in or knowledge about the field prior to being responsible for developing and managing a records management program. Even though the trend is for organizations to be more RM aware, many still have limited knowledge of what comprises records management and the value that it brings to the organization, resulting in divergent views regarding the need for appropriate levels of education and experience. Individuals who have had little or no experience in the field, and who may not hold a four-year college degree, may be appointed to RM positions. Recently a large, global pharmaceutical company promoted an employee with no previous exposure to records management and no college degree from a manufacturing supervisory position to the director of records management, including oversight of a 60-person, multimillion-dollar function. The likelihood of this happening in another function, e.g., finance, would be slim to none.

The perception of records management and how it should be practiced is often dependent on the first person to manage that function in the organization. That first individual puts a stamp on the expectations of the organization regarding the breadth and depth of records management and how it should be practiced. Where initial exposure to records management has been limited to offsite records storage, conducted by an administrative assistant, records management is perceived as a clerical and tactical operation. Elevating that perception in such an environment is difficult.

Successful records management programs are comprehensive, strategic, dynamic, and effective, resulting from a combination of factors, the most important one being the records manager who is leading the program. They exist on a higher plane than mediocre programs, which are characterized by being tactical, stagnant, and limited in scope to perhaps one records management component. The high-performing RM professional intentionally and instinctively brings to bear leadership skills, business acumen, and relationship skills. Knowledge, expertise, and conduct coalesce, positioning the RM leader to make unique and valuable contributions to the information infrastructure of the organization.

CONTEXTUAL LEADERSHIP

Unlike other professions that comprise organizational operations, RM suffers from preconceived notions that it is a narrowly defined, tactical operation, or from complete ignorance about it. In most instances, where some awareness exists, records management is narrowly defined as a "retention program." This is not the case with other operations in the organization. As mentioned earlier, records management does not have a standard university degree or program associated with it. Undergraduate degrees exist in finance, human resources, logistics, information systems, packaging, and other areas. Formalized, institutionalized degree programs provide legitimacy to those other professions, making them accepted and welcome at the senior management table.

Since, most frequently, other leaders and department heads have had little exposure to records management, the RM leader carries an increased responsibility of serving as a spokesperson for the profession, educating others about the field, informally as well as in structured ways. This is a records-management-specific leadership competency that, typically, is not required of other professionals in the workplace. The RM leader must possess a keen awareness of the acceptance of RM in the organization and of the misunderstanding that is detected in meetings and individual discussions. Being a leader in records management means working around and overcoming misconceptions about the field and turning condescending, negative, and even aggressive comments and questions into opportunities to educate colleagues, superiors, and subordinates about the RM field. The most common misconceptions that the records manager should be poised to address are:

- Retention schedules comprise the entirety of records management.
- Records management is a project—once it is developed and implemented, it can run by itself without staff or a department.
- Records management is paper centric—it has little or nothing to do with electronic records.
- Records management consists of administering hard-copy records stored offsite.

In addition, the RM leader functions as a role model for the field at large, so he or she should pay attention to behavior, bearing, communication, and even attire. The leader manifests emotional maturity by exhibiting confidence in the role and the value that he/she brings, and at the same time, addressing doubts about the legitimacy of the profession. Furthermore, because other leaders in the organization are not cognizant of the possible contributions that records management can make, it is often up to the RM leader to create a vision for them of what can be done in their own areas. This is unlike competencies and behaviors required of leaders in other professions.

Demonstrate Mastery of the Field

The RM function is often small in size and number of staff. The RM leader is the spokesperson for the field, the sole source of knowledge about it, the authority on how to operate and what resources are needed, and the "answer man/woman" for all things pertaining to records management. For this reason, it is more important for RM leaders to demonstrate mastery of their field than it is for leaders of other functions. Whereas leaders in other functions are surrounded by knowledgeable people in their own field, RM professionals often have no one or only a few colleagues with whom they can brainstorm and discuss relevant issues. This increases their responsibility to have true mastery of the field and their need to be in a continual learning mode. This proves to be a burden and a benefit at the same time.

It is a burden because records managers are forced to go outside of the organization to learn about and remain current in the field. Only by being involved in the profession, attending conferences, participating in seminars and Webinars, and staying abreast of the literature can the RM leader remain current. Yet, organizations must be convinced that there is value in paying for professional dues, participation in professional education, and allowing time for that participation. Records managers must justify the expenditure and time in order to remain knowledgeable about their field.

However, going external provides benefits, since the education includes information about what other companies are doing, new ideas, and breakthrough technologies and best practices, resulting in a richer knowledge base. An important side benefit is networking with other professionals. Over the years, this benefit has proven to be critically important in my career and professional growth. Because they are not forced to go external to learn about their field and to network with other professionals, other leaders tend to have a more myopic view of their field that revolves around organization-specific practices. These leaders may know their jobs and how to perform them extremely well, but there is a difference between knowing the job and knowing the field. The records management leader is required to know both—the job and the field.

Mastery of the field is a leadership competency that manifests itself as a foundational element for other RM leadership skills and behaviors. This mastery enables the RM leader to educate others about the field and to recognize shifts in the landscape before they occur, precipitating future-oriented, innovative thinking and problem-solving outside of the proverbial "box." Such behaviors are often associated with risk-taking. The professionally engaged records manager benefits by exposure to best practices and new models, and is in a better position to develop programs for benchmarking and ascertaining the state of technology within his/her own operating environment.

Visibly Seek to Teach, Visibly Seek to Learn, Be a Presence

Having *presence* in the organization includes teaching and learning, which are intertwined and mutually interdependent. Because RM programs are personality-dependent, the visibility of the program is a direct result of the visibility of the RM leader. Every action to educate others about RM increases awareness in the organization and helps establish a presence for the RM leader and the program. Educating others is a daily occurrence for records management leaders—casually, during conversations in the hallways, on elevators, at lunch, over a cup of coffee, and during staff meetings. I have often explained the same concepts of records management to different individuals on the same day, or, perplexingly, to the same individual on different occasions. Using ad hoc, informal opportunities as well as formal settings leads to greater understanding and appreciation and raises the visibility of the program.

Whenever the RM leader has assembled an audience or a project group, there exists an opportunity to teach aspects of records management. For example, a departmental or building-focused session for rollout of a retention schedule initiative can present the entire retention process within the context of a complete records management program. This provides the records manager with an opportunity to define the components of a complete RM program, emphasizing that retention is but one such component, albeit a foundational one and usually the first one to be implemented. Emphasis can be placed on the holistic nature of an RM program that requires the inclusion of all elements because of their interdependency.

Visibility resulting from RM training establishes presence for the RM leader and the RM department and program. Today, training can be offered through face-to-face classes as well as online through electronic courses that can be taken at the individual's convenience. Training can be offered on a broad range of RM topics, including those that are:

1. specific to the operations within the organization, such as how to read and apply the retention schedule;
2. helpful to end-users in their daily work, such as how to organize desktop files, and set up effective paper file systems; and
3. provide specific instructions, for example, how to comply with the records destruction procedure, including which documentation to create and how to fill out that documentation.

Short notices that appear in the organization's electronic newsletters describing activities in the records management department and new elements of the RM program also serve an educational role. Newsletters can also be used to provide handy tips about a variety of RM topics, such as how to save e-mails to folders. Records and Information Management (RIM) Month, sponsored by ARMA International, provides opportunities for promoting the profession in creative ways, and RIM Month activities can be advertised in the e-newsletters. Too often, RM programs are not high profile because information about them is not publicized.

Visibly seeking to learn also provides opportunities for the RM leader to establish presence. Similar to the "learning organization," the RM leader lives in a continual learning mode, "continually expand[ing] their [sic] capacity to create the results [they] truly desire . . ." (Senge, 1990: 3). Records managers who aspire to leadership need to know the following:

- The RM field
  —What comprises the field
  —Emerging components and practices
  —Changes in the field
  —Learning about forces and trends external to the field that can impact and shape the field
- The organization where the RIM program is situated
- The industry or line of business
- Executive skills and behaviors, such as leadership and strategy
  —Skills and behaviors that need to be mastered to effectively perform as a leader, such as connecting with and empowering others
  —Getting commitment and buy-in from staff
  —Being authentic
  —Emotional intelligence

PLAYING A LEADERSHIP ROLE

Becoming a leader of an RM program, or a leader in the RM professional arena, requires organizational skills, perceptiveness, vision, and a strong desire to shape and strengthen the field. In my own career, for instance, keeping my finger on the pulse of forces that impact the

RM field enabled me to anticipate the impact that the ISO 9000 Standards were going to have, as they became more widely required as a precondition to conducting business. ISO 9000 is a family of standards for quality management systems developed by the International Organization for Standardization (ISO) to promote quality services and products. Requirements include procedures for key processes, checking products for defects and taking corrective action, facilitating continual improvement, and several other provisions, including keeping appropriate records. In 1993, I introduced ISO 9000 to ARMA leadership, emphasizing the connection between the standards and records management and stressing the importance of the profession being fluent in ISO 9000. Even though ARMA was initially disinterested, I persisted. I participated in forming an ARMA ISO 9000 Task Force and arranged for the first meeting between representatives of American Society for Quality (ASQ) and ARMA. A relationship was formed that led to the first joint conference hosted by ARMA and ASQ in 1997, with me as chairperson. My book *Managing Records for ISO 9000 Compliance* (Brumm, 1995) became a standard text for organizations seeking ISO 9000 registration.

I cross-pollinated RIM and the quality arena by introducing one to the other through magazine and journal articles, workshops at George Washington University, quality meetings and conferences, and RIM meetings and conferences. ARMA established a position to focus on standards development, and became active in the records management standards development processes at ISO and ANSI (American National Standards Institute). My work in this area illustrates how a RIM professional can change and broaden the field and connect records management with other important management practices.

It is important, as well, to demonstrate an eagerness to learn about the organization where the RM program is situated. Presentations about specific operations—marketing, for example—should be attended by RM leaders for the following reasons:

- They provide face time which cannot be overestimated.
- They provide opportunities for networking across functions.
- They provide opportunities for others in the organization to see that the RM leader is interested in learning about the company.
- Knowledge about that function can generate ideas about the value that RM can bring to the function in improving processes or operations.

RM leaders also continue to learn about the industry in which they are operating.

I have worked in three heavily regulated industries: nuclear, environmental, and pharmaceutical. To perform at the level I desired, I became intimately familiar with the laws, regulations, and standards of those industries. The Code of Federal Regulations (CFR) titles for those industries are highly prescriptive, delineating not only the records to be created and retained and the records management activities that must be conducted, but also defining operating processes. RM leaders need to expand their industry knowledge by talking to experienced employees in mission-critical areas, reading industry professional and trade journals, and being alert to news events about the industry. Industry knowledge combined with records management knowledge results in effective, successful records management programs that go beyond compliance and risk mitigation, by promoting productivity and process improvement.

Functioning as a leader also requires learning about leadership. Leadership is a skill whose mastery is preceded by the recognition that it can be learned and by the desire to learn it. My first position in records management, in 1979, ignited a keen interest to learn about management and leadership. I reported to an individual who was reputed to be "the best manager in the company," who made a concerted effort to manage people effectively. I was determined to learn how he accomplished this, and thus began my education in management and leadership. At that point, I was managing eight people, and felt that I needed to develop management skills to function more effectively. I realized that an advanced degree placed me in a management position, and most likely, I would continue in that capacity for the remainder of my professional life. I have been a constant student ever since. Many seminars, lectures, courses and conferences later, I have arrived at the following: Learning to become a leader is an ongoing, never-ending process of moving toward a goal, but never quite achieving it. The lessons are cumulative and evolutionary, changing with each new experience and affiliation.

Since then, I have observed excellent leaders as well as those whose behaviors bordered on the satanic; good mentors who took the time to patiently coach versus those who are obsessed with themselves; those who are interested in growing their people versus those who are so interested in playing politics that they focus on the next job over the current one; those who are living examples of the "Peter Principle";

and those who are threatened by growth and the manifestation of excellence in their people.

A common mistake for those aspiring to leadership is to emulate others who hold positions of power and authority in an organization, under the assumption that their behavior comprises leadership. Negative behaviors, such as aggressiveness, belligerence, and authoritarianism are the antithesis of leadership. Leadership is born of trust and empowerment of, concern for, and belief in subordinates. It does not exist when people are threatened, belittled, or coerced. Good leadership is present only when people are willing, eager, and enthusiastic to follow. Lessons of leadership, once learned, must be practiced, for without being applied, they will atrophy, just like any other skill. "You can be many things without dedicated followers, but not a leader" (Dodd, 2004: 62).

Be a Presence, Take the Initiative

Presence is also a function of taking initiative. RM leaders seek out and request avenues to present information about the RM program and ongoing or new initiatives. They request a time slot, at least annually, to present an update to the senior executive staff, summarizing what has been accomplished, benefits that have accrued to the organization and future plans for the program. They also request invitations to attend key staff meetings, such as those in the Information Systems Department, where information is both gathered and shared. Periodically, they attend functional or departmental management meetings, i.e., Finance Department, where they discuss information that is relevant to that level of staff and operations. For example, after a multiyear project to address uninventoried offsite stored records, I was able to methodically destroy several thousand boxes, in compliance with a newly developed retention schedule. I presented the annual cost savings to the departmental budgets and the reduced risk that resulted from destroying records that should have been destroyed 40 years ago.

Creating a records management annual report and distributing it to key stakeholders also establishes a presence and demonstrates initiative. It provides information that had not been required, such as cost savings, productivity and process improvements, all supported by sound metrics that have been collected on a regular basis throughout the year.

RM leaders become a presence in the organization by taking the initiative to discuss RM-related issues with business unit leaders individually, and by making appointments with vice presidents and senior vice presidents. Knowing the field enables identification of significant problems that might exist in the business unit around information retrieval—the number one records problem in organizations. This leads to intelligent discussions about the impact on their operations emanating from the inability to retrieve information in a timely manner, and more importantly, what the RM function can do to ameliorate the issue by developing organizing architectures and standardized terminology.

Being a leader in records management includes being a presence in the profession, where opportunities abound for participation at the chapter, regional, and national levels. Applying to serve on committees and to speak at conferences; attending meetings, seminars, and conferences; and writing for the chapter newsletter and ARMA International's *Information Management Journal* are some ways that RM leaders have established themselves in the profession.

STRATEGY

Every organization has strategies to provide direction and focus, and knowing and understanding these strategies is mandatory in shaping and developing a records management program. The lesson in this arena is simple: Clearly and overtly align RM program goals and objectives with the strategies of the organization by mapping RM initiatives to the key strategies.

Beyond strategic alignment, the high-performing RM leader has learned how to formulate strategy—to develop a long-term plan of action, designed to achieve a specific goal. Strategy formulation involves a propensity for risk, since choices seldom are obvious and the reasons for selecting a specific strategy often fall outside the realm of purely analytical considerations. Formulating strategy in the RM arena is an outgrowth of knowing the organization, knowing the field, and having one's finger on the pulse of emerging trends in the field and the industry. Strategy is future-oriented, based on what the RM leader anticipates or forecasts, rather than what is known; it incorporates vision and a proactive stance toward change. A records management strategy is most often formulated at the business unit or functional level rather than corporate level, but it is linked to corporate strategy and translates it into action. Business unit and functional strategies operationalize the corporate strategy and provide a game plan for the RM area within the company. Formulating a records management strategy involves the following elements:

1. Developing a mission statement for the records management function.
2. Developing objectives and short-term strategies that are compatible with long-term corporate strategy objectives.
3. Reviewing and evaluating the success of the strategies to serve as a basis for control, to monitor and measure, and for future decision making.

VISION, INNOVATION, AND RISK-TAKING

Vision, innovation, and risk-taking are intertwined and inextricably linked with change and challenging the status quo. One of the main reasons that records managers encounter resistance is because they introduce change. Most records managers enter established organizations with pre-existing work methods and mind-sets and begin designing, creating, and introducing concepts, practices, methods, and procedures that did not exist or were performed differently. The very nature of records management requires that people work differently with their records and think differently about them. By definition, a records manager is a change agent and innovator, since developing and implementing previously nonexisting programs and practices is commonplace in the RM field. The most challenging level of managing change is being the leader of change, introducing new ways of working and thinking, and obliterating previously held beliefs and long-term practices.

The Emmett Leahy Award recipients present examples of innovation, vision, and risk-taking. The award is presented annually at the Institute of Certified Records Managers meeting at the ARMA International conference. The criteria for this award focus around innovative, pioneering work with a major impact on the field, moving it in a direction that, otherwise, it might not have gone. Recipients are the visionaries and prophets of records management, and in reviewing their accomplishments it becomes evident that vision, innovation, risk-taking, and change have been their operating trademarks. Some representative examples are:

- *Robert Williams*, for his pioneering work in bringing a high-profile focus to the topic of managing electronic records, and by establishing high-caliber conferences and producing literature and conducting studies on the topic.
- *Donald Skupsky*, for his groundbreaking work in applying legal requirements for managing records and developing awareness, publications, and an entire industry that, heretofore, had not existed.
- *Luciana Duranti*, for her work in commandeering financial and human resources to successfully spearhead the multinational effort to preserve electronic records, known as the INTERPARES project.

(A complete listing can be seen on the Leahy Web site: www. leahyaward.com.)

RM leaders who manage successful programs work to continuously refine and improve their programs, their organizations, and the RM field. They are people of vision and they work to make that vision a reality. In so doing, they play a significant role in shaping and directing the future not only of operations in the organization, but also the future of the field. Those who are exposed to an excellent RM program and those who hear of it carry a different perception of records management. Program excellence in one organization, therefore, elevates the entire field. Refining and improving programs requires a passion for excellence, a passion for the field, knowledge of the field, and knowledge of the organization.

Whether it is examining a records management problem, championing a new technology, or advocating cleaning up shared computer drives, I have found myself repeatedly formulating vision, providing a sense of purpose, influencing, negotiating, inspiring, and driving people and the organization outside of their comfort zones. Often, it has been necessary to challenge paradigms and thought processes in other functions in order to accomplish a records management goal. This was the case in one company where I was spearheading an initiative to bring content management technology into the organization.

One of the roadblocks to this initiative came from the Finance Department, which had been using an ROI (return on investment) cost justification model that measured only tangible items and was rooted in the Industrial Age. Current information age costing elements used by other organizations were not included in the model, such as productivity measures and quantifying lost information.

In addition to spearheading the technology, I found myself in the position of introducing new ROI concepts to the chief financial officer, who had been working for the company over 25 years, since college graduation, and who was schooled only in the company model. Bringing to bear current thinking and examples of other cost justification models, I succeeded in enlightening him about alternative approaches. Although he could not disregard the long-esteemed company model, he worked with me to create an ROI percentage that was an acceptable threshold for new projects. It is often necessary to step outside well-worn pathways to move the organization forward.

My willingness to pursue unorthodox approaches stems from early professional experiences. My first position in records management, in 1979, laid the groundwork for how I would practice records management for the rest of my career. Because I was among the first people hired into a start-up company, I was expected to create, design, develop, introduce, and manage a records management program and all records pertaining to the processing and fabrication of zirconium and hafnium—two metals that are used in the core of nuclear reactors (zirconium tubes house the uranium pellets while hafnium rods comprise the control rods). Guidelines for records and for the RM program were stringent because of Nuclear Regulatory Commission (NRC) requirements. In 1979, only two other companies in the world manufactured zirconium and hafnium; both companies were soon to be competitors thus making it impossible to elicit advice from them regarding NRC requirements and records that needed to be created. The position called for a high degree of creativity, inventiveness, improvisation, and management skills, and I became accustomed to creating, designing, and developing not only records and components of records management, but also solutions to problems that fell under my area of responsibility. I was assigned duties and responsibilities not normally associated with records management, such as the following:

- Developing and managing a records management program that complied with 10 CFR50—Nuclear Regulatory Commission requirements for construction of nuclear power plants
- Developing and managing a material certification process for the zirconium and hafnium
- Developing and managing a document control center
- Developing and managing an internal quality audit function

This proved to be advantageous since these initial experiences provided me with an expanded viewpoint of what can and should fall under the purview of records management. In addition, I grew accustomed to solving unusual records-related problems with novel approaches, such as identifying and retaining thousands of metal samples that had undergone a variety of tests for tensile strength, corrosion, chemistry, hardness, and others characteristics.

At a time when word processing systems were new in the business world and mainframes were the technology of the day, I learned how to utilize these systems to create material certification data packages and database reports to manage the controlled documents and to monitor and control over 10,000 calibrated items. I learned how to apply early technology to RM problems, champion necessary technology, garner support, and tap into financial resources that were available outside traditional channels. In so doing, I was able to purchase and incorporate the latest content management technology, a CAR (Computer-Assisted Retrieval) system, to enable rapid access and retrieval of all records associated with the processing and manufacture of the materials, a necessary requirement because of frequent NRC and customer process and records audits.

Risk-taking is an anticipated outcome from introducing change and bringing innovation into an organization. The risk can be political in nature; well-entrenched and powerful individuals can oppose the change, their opposition having nothing to do with the merit of the initiative or the value of the change to the organization. There is also the risk of failure—that the initiative will not succeed on some level, or will take longer or be more expensive than anticipated, with the sponsoring individual suffering adverse consequences.

A good RM leader identifies the areas that provide great leverage and focuses vigorously on them. Incorporating knowledge of the field with knowledge of the organization, having ability to identify problems, and possessing a passionate zeal and an understanding of the strategy of the organization enables the RM leader to craft a vision. These skills also help the leader state it in a way that is meaningful to the specific circumstances of the moment and the culture. The interplay of professional expertise, determination, optimism, competence and demeanor enable the RM leader to craft a clear and compelling vision, not allowing the ambiguities of how it will be accomplished to dampen that vision.

BUILDING AND MANAGING RELATIONSHIPS

Leaders have a knack for establishing relationships and they do so long before those relationships are needed. Building relationships is a process—slowly formed on a daily basis, through consistent, predictable behavior and actions, acting with integrity, honoring confidences, and following through on promises. Good relationships are important for the RM leader in order to have support for future initiatives and to be able to receive honest, candid information about records-based operating problems. Identifying problems in a process is complex and incomplete analysis can lead to misdiagnosis. Identifying the root cause of problems is even more difficult, especially when that root cause is records related, since often only the RM leader may recognize and understand it. Problems can involve records about the activities, procedures surrounding them, faulty or nonexistent organizing schemes, and so forth.

This was brought home to me during the days that I was heavily involved with the ISO 9000 quality standards—writing, lecturing, and consulting. During the rigorous ISO 9000 registration process, most questions posed by auditors revolved around the recorded information about the activities that took place in regard to product and service quality. About 60 percent of companies failed to win immediate recommendation for ISO 9000 certification, with most problems centering on document control and records.

Organizations may mistakenly name the activity or process as the problem, when the records pertaining to the activity are the true problem. Until RM exists in an organization, no one has looked at records and their management as a separate area of focus. This is compounded by the fact that executives and upper management, for the most part, do not have an awareness of how people actually work to get their jobs done. A solution can be devised only when there is an accurate and truthful description of the problem, and this is where personal relationships, built on long-term commitment and trust, enter the picture.

In one company, I had learned of a records-based problem associated with contract renewals and changes. Because I had a pre-established relationship with the directors and the vice president of those areas, I received permission to interview the analysts who actually worked with the contracts and supporting documentation. This enabled an accurate diagnosis of the root cause, leading to an effective series of solutions.

Leadership Case Study

The following case study describes how the ingredients and character traits associated with RM leadership worked in an integrated way to change operations and mind-sets and to drive the strategy of the organization.

I entered an organization that had been functioning without records management since its inception over 100 years ago. My initial intensive activities in developing a records retention schedule involved interviewing representatives from each department to gather information about the records that they created and used in their processes. As I was documenting this information, I noticed that a pattern was emerging—almost every department revealed that employees had difficulty getting their work done because of records retrieval issues. Each time this was mentioned, I documented the situation in my notes, recording the circumstances and scenarios that were being described.

I gathered the problem instances on spreadsheets that identified the issue, the department, and the contact person and I added the impact on the department, the company, and the strategy of the organization. I brought my knowledge of industry statistics to bear, regarding the amount of time that knowledge workers spent looking for information. I then established relationships with department leaders and senior executives, discussing with them my intention to focus on solving these problems, sharing a vision that was still in its embryonic stage. I requested and set up monthly informal lunch meetings with key leaders, such as the VP of IT and the CFO, and during those lunches, I laid the groundwork for what I was about to propose. I met numerous times with employees in the problem work areas, who had revealed their frustrations with records and information as impediments to their jobs. It was necessary to educate them about RM during these discussions, and simultaneously define those RM-related issues that were crippling their work areas. I identified the percentage of time that individuals were spending looking for information and gathered anecdotal evidence, quotes from employees and information about workarounds that people had resorted to simply to get their work done. In addition to collecting factual information, I gathered information about the demoralizing effects on employees that these problems had created.

In some departments, the time spent looking for information exceeded the cited industry percentages of 15 to 20 percent and went as high as 50 to 60 percent. Astoundingly, this percentage was reported among the most highly educated and highly paid employees—scientists in the R&D areas.

Based on average salaries in the functions, I calculated the cost of employees looking for information to do their jobs. As high as this cost was, however, I emphasized that it represented only part of the story, since it did not measure the following:

- What is the increase in creativity and original thinking that might be unleashed if knowledge workers had more time to think and were not frustrated looking for and not finding information?
- How do you know that a project has taken twice as long as it should have for lack of good access to information?
- How do you compare the value of a good decision to a bad one?

I was able to gather dollar costs of research and marketing studies that had to be repeated because of the inability to find the previous work that employees knew had been done on specific topics. The annual total spent on repeat work was well into the six figures. The good rapport that I had established with a senior vice president enabled me to get on the agenda of an executive committee meeting, where I presented my findings and pitched my proposal before the president and his executive staff. Prior to my presentation, I met with each vice president who would attend the meeting to discuss my findings and proposal, with the intention of preselling the ideas, allowing them an opportunity to express questions and concerns and I requested their support. I also discussed my presentation with the vice president of IT, the CFO, and my senior vice president contact. The careful preparation paid off, and the executive staff meeting approved my proposal.

While I gathered information internally, I simultaneously launched a fact-finding mission to seek out vendors that could provide the content management technology to address the document-intensive problems. Having learned about the organization, its regulatory requirements, its IT infrastructure and its operations, I was able to quickly narrow down potential vendor candidates. Knowledge of the field enabled me to further narrow the candidates, since I was intimately familiar with key players in this arena as well as the functionalities of their product offerings.

I invited the selected vendors to present in-house demos of their solutions, making certain that key stakeholders were in attendance: IT, finance, and departmental representatives from each department who could benefit from this technology and/or serve as the initial implementation area. Inviting these functions was calculated to educate the attendees about solutions with which they were unfamiliar and to create enthusiasm and excitement that would be shared with their colleagues, leading to easier approval of my proposal.

After executive-staff approval of my proposal, I actively pursued the next steps, seeking financing of the project and selecting a vendor. Because of the long lead time in the budgetary process, it was already too late to insert this new technology initiative into the budget for the next calendar year and this posed a new challenge.

Because of the enthusiasm among employees that had been engendered by the product demos, it was clear to me that I had to act quickly. I began to work under the radar screen, tapping into relationships that I had established. Eventually I learned about a project that had been funded but had fallen through, making that money available without having to go through a formal budgetary approval process. Getting the finances transferred from one department to another, from one project to a new one, required meeting with all of the players involved, including the departmental financial representatives. Numerous discussions later, after completing many forms, the funding had been allocated to the content management technology project. The entire process from beginning to ordering spanned a two-year timeframe, during which I relied on many of the lessons that I had learned over the years in my management and leadership education—both formal and self-study.

CONCLUSION

Beyond developing retention schedules, twenty-first-century records management leaders are dedicated to bringing added value to the organization's operations, promoting effectiveness and profitability by identifying problems and implementing solutions that often involve changing thought processes and behaviors. Driven by a commitment to excellence, and exhibiting a passion for the field, they provide a sense of purpose, and inspire confidence and trust because of their technical competence and personal character. They are people of conviction, understanding that if they don't believe what they are doing is important, no one else will either. They often force others out of their comfort zones. They possess an unwarranted degree of optimism, expecting success and anticipating positive outcomes that help generate energy and commitment necessary to achieve desired results. In my estimation, becoming a leader is a lifelong, maturity-building pursuit, a process of personal, social and emotional growth, coupled with character development. As such, it is never completed.

"... becoming a leader is synonymous with becoming yourself. It's precisely that simple, and it's also that difficult." (Bennis, 1994: 9)

REFERENCES

Bennis, Warren. 1994. *On Becoming a Leader.* Reading, MA: Perseus Books.

Brumm, Eugenia. 1995. *Managing Records for ISO 9000 Compliance.* Milwaukee: American Society for Quality.

Dodd, David. "On the Road of Experience: Seven Observations on Leadership" *Educause Quarterly* 27, no. 4, (2004): 61–63. Available: www.educause/edu.pub/eq/eqm04/.

Senge, Peter Michael. 1990. *The Fifth Discipline: The Art and Practice of the Learning Organization.* New York: Doubleday.

Chapter 3

Records Management Standards: What They Are and Why They Are Important

Diane K. Carlisle

LAYING THE FOUNDATION

Chapter Scope

This chapter has a select focus on standards and best practices that are directly relevant to the field of records and information management. Even with this as the focal point, it is impossible to provide comprehensive coverage of *all* the relevant standards. Therefore, the author has further narrowed the scope by concentrating on standards and best practices that are developed through a formal standards body, such as the American National Standards Institute (ANSI), ISO (International Organization for Standardization), or a member of these standards bodies. The standards discussed have broad applicability across a variety of organizations; there is no attempt to cover state, local, industry-specific, or organization-specific standards.

Why Standards Are Important

Standards and best practices foster program excellence by providing a baseline of generally accepted principles, methods, and tools that can be relied upon to produce desirable results. A standard usually synthesizes or summarizes the most critical requirements for the topic at hand. This is particularly useful for individuals who may not have had much prior experience before establishing a program. Likewise, it is useful for those who want to enhance existing programs. The baseline provided in the standard is also useful to those who are working in a multinational organization where differing records management practices have been established. The standards provide a common benchmark of expectations and outcomes that can be used to forge consistency out of the varying practices. They can help to identify mandatory elements of a records management program or software application that all sectors of the organization must complete.

Another reason formal standards are important lies in the fact that they are objective. Objectivity primarily arises from the controlled development process which engages a variety of individuals and organizations. These individuals and organizations have expertise in the area and generally have either professional or commercial interests in the topic area. The sponsoring organization is responsible to ensure the work is not dominated by any one set of interests. Closely linked to the objectivity of standards is the fact that they are viewed as authoritative. The authority comes from the fact they are developed by experts in the field.

All of these factors lend credibility to the individual records manager's efforts when those efforts are guided by a formal standard. Relying on relevant standards and best practices results in more credible, defensible records management programs. When a practitioner bolsters a recommendation by use of a formal standard, explains the development process and explains how experts participate in the development, managers can not easily dismiss the recommendation.

Let's Not "Reinvent the Wheel"

Whether a person is seeking *standards* or *best practices*, a common theme underlies each quest: "I don't want to waste time trying to invent something that already exists. I want to learn from others who have had more experience. Why should I 'reinvent the wheel'?" Over the past 50–60 years, a number of techniques and records management program components have come to be accepted as the body of knowledge for a records management professional. And yet, this knowledge is generally dispersed across a variety of textbooks, journal articles, and workshop or seminar materials. Authoritative materials can be difficult and time-consuming to locate—if one is able to locate them at all. Seminar materials are generally only accessible to seminar attendees. Books go out of print. Professional journals usually cannot be found in public libraries. Even the Internet falls short, since Web site addresses change and links to materials are often broken. The end result? The reader is left without access to valuable material or faces a daunting and time-consuming task of trying to find materials through obscure sources.

From a formal education standpoint, generally accepted practices can be taught in community colleges, universities, or by correspondence course. Unfortunately, the records management professional in the United States has few options for formal college or university level programs. The Internet has opened up a number of online programs. However, access to those materials is usually limited to formally enrolled students. Some online programs include a requirement to attend certain classes or events in person—limiting the reach of an online program to individuals who are still within traveling distance.

In general, the person seeking guidance on the creation and maintenance of a successful records management program can be frustrated by the difficulties in accessing authoritative, objective advice. Standards can alleviate this frustration because they are generally more available to the public than some of these other sources. In addition, the standards process has synthesized the core requirements for the topic at hand. The new-comer does not have to rely on individual judgment to decide what is most important.

DEFINITIONS

What is a standard? The Merriam-Webster Online Dictionary provides this definition: "something established by authority, custom, or general consent as a model or example" (www.m-w.com/dictionary/standard). The standards organizations themselves can't agree on one definition. Following are a few examples:

ARMA International: Standards create a professional environment of "best practice" procedures. They enable organizations to confidently create systems, policies and procedures, maintain autonomy from vested interest groups and assure high operational quality that leads to exceptional records and information management performance. (www.arma.org)

American National Standards Institute: A standard is a document, established by consensus that provides rules, guidelines or characteristics for activities or their results. (*as defined in ISO/IEC Guide 2:1996*) (www.ansi.org)

British Standards Institute: A standard is an agreed, repeatable way of doing something. It is a published document that contains a technical specification or other precise criteria designed to be used consistently as a rule, guideline, or definition. (www.bsi-global.com)

Even this small sampling of definitions begins to introduce the nuances in a formal standards development process. These definitions are more specific than what we learn from *Merriam-Webster's*; they begin to highlight different features of a formal standard, or the process by which they are developed. The ARMA International description focuses on how the standards are used and what results should be expected when they are used. The American National Standards Institute (ANSI) definition refers us to the International Organization for Standardization (ISO) definition, and introduces a new concept—*consensus*. The British Standards Institute (BSI) emphasizes the use of standards as rules or guidelines.

There are definitely common themes in how organizations and individuals define standards. For our purposes, I will use this definition: A model method, material or practice, which is developed through consensus, created by experts in the field, and leads to results that are consistent, predictable, and desirable. This definition comprehensively captures the key elements of why we want to rely on standards. We are looking for a model that will help achieve a level of excellence, or at the very least, a level of quality that is considered minimally acceptable. The word *consensus* signals that the interests of more than one individual or organization have been considered. The inclusion of *experts* indicates that standards are informed by contributions based on extensive knowledge and experience. Most of all, we want to be assured of predictable and desirable results when we implement standards.

Compliance with standards is largely voluntary, at least when they are initially issued. The authority they have comes from the rigorous and carefully monitored development process that governs their creation and the fact that knowledgeable experts have contributed to their development. It is this authority that encourages the adoption and use of standards. Those who choose to adopt standards do so because they want to rely on an objective, credible authority as the foundation for the work they are doing. This foundation can be important if the records management practices are being challenged by either internal or external authorities. It is better to say that the practices are based on requirements in a formal standard, than to have to confess that it "just seemed like a good idea."

Although compliance with standards is initially voluntary, there are ways to make compliance with standards more mandatory. One way is for them to be adopted into legislation or regulations. Legislators and/or regulators do not develop the standards, but bring them into the legislation as a required element. This enhances the authority of a given standard, which can be useful. However, if/when the standard changes, it can be problematic if the legislation refers to a specific edition of the standard.

Sometimes an industry will adopt a standard in such an overwhelming manner that it becomes a de facto mandatory requirement in order for an organization to remain competitive. The ISO 9000 series of standards is one example of this phenomenon. Though the standard may not be well understood by the layperson, most businesspeople are aware that being "ISO 9000-certified" can boost their reputation and their ability to compete in their industry.

This leads us to a final way in which the authority level of a standard can be enhanced—development of a formal certification process. As the business world has become more focused on compliance issues and ways to demonstrate that they are a good corporate citizen, many organizations strive to develop a formal certification process by which organizations can demonstrate that they meet certain requirements. Certification is not automatically developed for all standards, but is a frequent topic of conversation when standards committees discuss how to promote the standards they have developed.

Formal standards bodies such as ANSI and ISO also distinguish standards from other types of documents that provide guidance or suggestions for the best methods to accomplish certain ends. Terms such as *technical reports*, *technical specifications*, *recommended practices*, or *guidelines* generally indicate that, for a variety of reasons, the organization was unable to develop a formal standard. In a rapidly changing field, a standards body may choose to issue a technical report or guideline, in order to respond more quickly to changes in the marketplace. Sometimes the committee drafting the document believes that the nature of the material does not meet the mandatory nature of a standard, but feels that the contents merit distribution. These other documents can be valuable to the practitioner and should not be dismissed. However, it is important to understand how they have been developed, who sponsored their development, and how the balloting requirements for these documents differ from those for a standard. This is the caveat emptor in standards—understand the process so you can determine how "fit" that guidance is to your own organization and environment.

TYPES OF STANDARDS

Standards can be characterized in a number of different ways, most often, by *development process* and by *scope*.

Development Process

With the imprimatur of ISO, ANSI or other national standards organizations, the user understands that the standard was developed under a set of formal procedures that were approved by a nationally recognized standards oversight body. Members of a formal standards body are required to develop operating procedures that will direct their standards development activities. These procedures protect the objectivity of the standard by addressing two key principles in standards development—balance and consensus.

BALANCE

Balance refers to the composition of the group that wrote and voted on the standard. Formal standards bodies must prevent commercial interests from dominating the process and the resulting standards. They are committed to open and transparent processes so that any person or organization with an interest in the work can easily participate, or at least have a better understanding of how the work was conducted. ISO and ANSI protect the need for balance by requiring that a standards developer actively solicit participation from multiple interest categories throughout the standards development process. In addition, balance is protected by requiring standards developers to conduct both public review and appeals processes.

CONSENSUS

Consensus refers to the process of deliberation that is pursued in each standards development committee. It is not enough to conduct a vote and have the majority win—consensus requires that issues be debated and the participants find a compromise or position on the issue that will satisfy all of the contributors. Each view has equal standing in the process. The vote of a large organization or country is no more significant than the vote of any other participant. Voting and standards development under these criteria is usually an iterative process and can be time-consuming. However, standards developers feel the resulting work is worth the time and effort involved, since it results in impartial standards that should be applicable to a broader range of organizations and entities.

Some organizations do not choose to be officially accredited by a national standards organization. Instead, they may follow ISO or ANSI principles of balance, consensus, transparency, etc., in the development of their standards. They may have an oversight board, but it may not be independent of the parent organization developing the standard. Such organizations may still refer to their "standards." ISO and ANSI do not have a copyright on the word "standard." It does not always refer to what we understand as a formal standards process.

Finally, some organizations determine their own standards, based on their own criteria. Those criteria may not include balance, consensus, or openness. An organization may develop its standards in response to commercially driven factors that members believe are more important.

In any case, it is prudent to understand both the organization that is endorsing and/or promoting a standard, and the processes used in its development. The potential user can then make a judgment call regarding the applicability of the standard and its usefulness for their purposes.

Differentiated by Scope

The intended scope of the standard is also important to understand. Do the developers intend for the standard to be used by a particular industry segment, or is it intended to have a broader scope? Do the

developers intend to develop a national standard, or do they anticipate that it will be adopted internationally? Is the standard a highly
technical standard, or is it a process-oriented standard?

Having an understanding of all these factors gives the records and
information management professional the appropriate context within
which to understand the standard's content and requirements. This
type of information is usually found in the introduction or preface to
a published document. Based on an understanding of the context, it
is easier to determine which sections of the standard are of greatest
importance to any particular organization.

Standards are sometimes found to be useful beyond the scope initially defined when the standard was created. A good example is DoD
5015.2-STD *Design Criteria Standard for Electronic Records Management
Software Applications.* This standard was designed specifically for use in
the U.S. Department of Defense. The foreword to the 2002 edition
of the standard states, "This Standard applies to the Office of the Secretary of Defense, the Military Departments, the Chairman of the Joint
Chiefs of Staff, the Combatant Commands, the Inspector General of
the Department of Defense, the Defense Agencies, the DoD Field Activities, and all other organizational entities within the Department of
Defense (hereafter referred to collectively as 'the DoD Components')"
(U.S. Department of Defense, 2002). Initially introduced in 1997, the
standard was mandatory only for Department of Defense agencies.
Approximately a year later, the National Archives and Records Administration (NARA) endorsed both the standard and the JITC (Joint
Interoperability Test Command) records management application testing process for use in other federal agencies. This government standard became the object of much professional interest as
nongovernment records management professionals sought any guidance they could obtain in managing electronic records. Now, vendors
in the marketplace have JITC testing conducted on their software and
use the compliance certification they receive as a key part of their marketing materials. DoD 5015.2 has helped to standardize practices in
the management of electronic records, both in the United States and
abroad. Many private organizations have adopted the standard as a
basis for their electronic records management efforts. The standard
gives them confidence that what they are doing can be defended as
appropriate and reasonable. Vendors now look to developments in this
standard as one factor in their own development plans for software
and hardware developments.

A similar process occurred in Europe in the development of MoReq (Model Requirements for the Management of Electronic Records). MoReq was initially commissioned by the DLM Forum, which was a part of the European Council's efforts to encourage greater cooperation in the area of archives. The intended scope of MoReq was to be for both public and private organizations and its focus is on the functional requirements for the management of electronic records by an Electronic Records Management System (ERMS). Again, records managers look to this standard for guidance, even if they are not a part of the European Council.

Both MoReq and DoD 5015.2 are being updated at this time. It would be misleading to imply that these are the only two electronic records management standards. Australia has been a leader in developing standards for records management and many other countries have developed standards as well. You can find electronic records management standards at the state and local levels in many countries. In the United States, NARA is in the midst of an ambitious electronic archives project, Electronic Records Archives (ERA). The goal of ERA is: "The Electronic Records Archives (ERA) will be a comprehensive, systematic, and dynamic means for preserving virtually any kind of electronic record, free from dependence on any specific hardware or software" (U.S. National Archives and Records Administration). Clearly, records managers across the globe will be looking to this project as another source of standards and best practices.

WHO DOES THE WORK?

In a formal standards program, an array of individuals and organizations are involved. Each has a distinct role and set of responsibilities. The following overview discusses the roles and complementary responsibilities throughout the standards process.

The Accrediting Body

The accrediting body is the organization that provides oversight to the development of formal standards within its jurisdiction. At the international level, the predominant organization is the International Organization for Standardization (ISO). ISO is made up of the national standards institutes of approximately 157 countries. In the ISO hierarchy, each country is entitled to one member and the balloting process for proposed standards is conducted through these national members. ISO is administered through the Central Secretariat, located in Geneva, Switzerland. ISO establishes the rules for the standards development process when the intended scope of the standard is international.

There are also accrediting bodies at the national level. These bodies have two primary responsibilities:

1. Represent their country's interests and facilitate participation from their country in the development of ISO standards.
2. Provide oversight for the development of their country's national level standards. In this role, they establish the essential requirements that a standards developing organization (SDO) must meet in order to be formally accredited.

Standards Developing Organizations (SDOs)

The SDO is the organization that undertakes the work to develop a standard. An SDO may be an association, a trade organization, a government entity, or a corporation. It is an organization that has an interest in seeing that standards are developed in a particular area. For example, ARMA International develops standards that are related to processes and methods necessary for effective records management. AIIM develops standards to ensure the effective use of technology in managing and protecting records. Both ARMA and AIIM participate in ISO committees that are parallel to their national level work, but are intended for international use. Corporations such as Oracle or Microsoft are also ANSI members, and participate in related technical work.

It is up to the SDO to determine the organizational structure and processes it will use to get standards written. The SDO submits its procedures to the accrediting body for approval, but then guides its own standards development activities based on those procedures. When the text is considered complete, they submit the standard and a summary of the balloting they conducted to the accrediting organization for approval as an official standard. The summary shows evidence that the SDO met its procedural requirements to be approved as a standard. If the accrediting body agrees, the document can be published as a standard.

Subject Matter Experts

The standards development process would not be possible without the scores of individual professionals who devote time and resources to the development of standards. Many of these individuals receive financial support from the organizations they work for and represent. They are the ones who debate the content of the standards, draft the text that makes up the standard, and provide input to the SDOs and national members of ISO regarding whether a standard should be approved or rejected. This work ensures that standards have depth, breadth, and relevance, and is one of the reasons that standards have authority and credibility.

Complementary Roles

The accrediting organization and the SDO have complementary roles and shared responsibility in the development of these formal standards. Since the accrediting organizations do not maintain a stable of experts to weigh the relative merits of a proposed standard, they rely on the professional judgment of the subject matter experts, the deliberative process that requires each viewpoint to be carefully considered and resolved, and the SDO's adherence to their approved procedures. To this end, they certify the procedures of the developers and require evidence that the voting standards and requirements were met in each standard the SDO submits for approval. The SDO oversees the development process for each standard they initiate and ensures that they are following their own procedures. The SDO must ensure that no one interest group unfairly dominates the development process and the resulting standard. The accrediting organization and the SDO share responsibility for ensuring there is a process for the resolution of negative ballots and adjudication of appeals that may be made regarding a particular standard.

EVALUATING A STANDARD FOR POTENTIAL USE

Once the records manager has identified a standard for potential use in a records management program, the following characteristics should be assessed as a part of the adaptation process.

1. *Who is the creator of the standard?* Is the organization an accredited SDO? How similar are the interests of that organization to the interests of my own organization? This can help determine whether to adapt the standard full-scale, or whether to make alterations.
2. *What is the intended level of authority of the standard?* If it has been developed as a standard, it intends to be authoritative. However, even an accredited SDO sometimes develops technical reports, recommended practices, or guidelines that have been vetted, but are not intended as mandatory requirements.
3. *How mature is the field of study I am exploring?* If it is a discipline that is fully mature, it is reasonable to expect that standards have been developed. However, if it is a field of emerging study or rapid change, it may only be possible to find best practices or technical reports. Perhaps the issues have not been debated sufficiently to determine what the mandatory requirements should be.
4. *How mature is my own organization in the implementation of records management disciplines?* An organization that is relatively new into developing records management processes may need to establish a foundation of the records management basics: a records management policy and a records retention and disposition program. A more mature records management program may need to move into the management of electronic records and associated metadata, long-term preservation issues in electronic records, and management of e-mail.

WAYS TO USE STANDARDS

Standards provide a foundation of credibility for work that is pursued in records management. But, there are additional reasons that a records management professional would want to implement standards.

Authoritative Foundation for New Program Development

Basing a records management program element or service on an established standard provides a foundation of credibility that might be difficult to achieve as quickly without the standard. Management concerns that a program is either too restrictive or not rigorous enough are often alleviated if the program was based on a standard developed by experts in the field and vetted through a formal standards process.

Consistency in Practice Across Business Units

Records professionals in multinational organizations may be asked to harmonize the differing records management practices in a variety of geographic regions. Corporations often are looking for cost efficiencies that can be gained by using a common process and technology. Standards provide a common foundation for meeting a variety of needs within an organization.

Continuous Improvement of an Existing Program

With the new requirements for responsible handling of records and information, corporations are increasingly interested in knowing whether their records management processes are providing adequate protection in the event of litigation, government investigation, and regulatory compliance. Standards can provide the baseline against which current practices can be evaluated. The standards that ARMA International develops can be particularly useful in this regard, as many of them are process-oriented standards. The records professional can implement these steps as presented in the standard, or can adapt them to his or her own organization.

A good example is the ISO 15489-1 standard, *Records Management— Part I*. This international standard defines 11 key elements that are required for a comprehensive records management program. When used together, these 11 elements provide a solid foundation for the program, and ensure that the organization's records are appropriately captured and identified, protected, and eventually destroyed in accordance with predefined rules. The standard is *results-oriented*. In other words, it defines the results or outcomes that the organization should achieve through implementation of a records management program. It is a relatively simple matter for professionals to identify the major requirements of the standard, and then compare their own policies, procedures, and use of technology against those requirements.

Develop Policies and Procedures

Standards can be useful for developing the policies and procedures that an organization must implement. Some of the standards are very

specific about clauses or issues to address in a policy or to incorporate in a procedure. Other times, the policies and procedures can be
derived from the requirements in the standard, even if they are not
explicitly stated.

ISO STANDARDS FOR RECORDS MANAGEMENT

Two ISO Technical Committees (TC46 and TC171) are the primary
sources for records management standards within ISO.

ISO 15489-1; ISO 15489-2

ISO standards for records management are developed by a subcommittee known as TC46/SC11. In 2001, this subcommittee released its
first landmark work—ISO 15489-1 *Information and Documentation—
Records Management—Part I: General*. This publication is informally referred to as "the international records management standard." This
standard is an outgrowth of an Australian National Standard that was
published as AS 4390. When Standards Australia approached ISO
about adopting their national standard as an ISO standard, the members of ISO were asked to vote on the proposal. ISO's members
thought an international standard would be useful, but were not entirely comfortable with the specifics of AS 4390. Therefore, ISO formed
a new subcommittee for records management issues. The committee's
first major effort was to "internationalize" the Australian standard so
that it would be more broadly applicable to a broader range of national traditions. The subcommittee drafted two ISO documents to establish a high-level framework for records management. It is
subsequently at work on a number of additional standards for the
records management profession. These additional standards expand
upon themes and/or requirements contained in ISO 15489 and provide more specific requirements for implementation.

The chief value of ISO 15489 is that it establishes a strong foundation for a records management program. The standard applies equally
to electronic and hard-copy records. It recommends that records management be embedded in the business processes that generate the
records to begin with. The committee recognized that upper management needs to be convinced of the value of records management, and
to that end, identified 13 benefits or outcomes to be achieved through
a records management program. These range from operational con-

cerns with the efficiency and effectiveness with which records are managed, to managerial concerns with accountability and risk management, to a concern for protecting future needs for research.

The framework also includes establishing a records management policy, designating the responsibilities all levels of employees have toward the creation of authentic records and allocating authority to ensure the program can be implemented, designing the system and the records management tools to be used in administering records management requirements, protection of records for business continuity purposes, storage and maintenance of records, disposition of records, and monitoring records management programs. The standard does not go into great detail about each of these elements. But it does state that you should *have* each of these elements in order to have a complete program.

The subcommittee also developed a technical report to accompany the standard. Part I contains the requirements; Part II contains guidelines and common practices that can help in the implementation of Part I. The subcommittee states that the technical report represents one methodology, but that other factors may need to be considered in implementation. These factors include national standards and national legislation or regulation.

ISO 23081 Information and Documentation—Records Management Processes—Metadata for Records—Part I: Principles

The subcommittee has embarked on an ambitious effort to address the issue of metadata related to records and records management requirements. This is expected to be a multipart document, and the committee has issued Part I, which identifies the principles behind metadata and metadata management. This part does not identify metadata elements, but rather explains how to determine which metadata elements are needed. Parts II and III are expected to be technical reports, and will address more practical aspects of implementing the principles identified in this standard.

In this and in the other standards and technical reports that the subcommittee is developing, they have been conscientious to ensure that the work ties back to the relevant sections of ISO 15489-1. If ISO 15489-1 is the "umbrella" standard, the others all have a place underneath it. The additional standards delve into another layer of detail and implementation that was not possible to achieve in the initial standard.

Other Work of ISO

ISO TC 171 is another subcommittee that develops standards related to records and information management. Its particular scope of work focuses on document management applications (including imaging and microfilming). AIIM is the association that coordinates the U.S. position on proposed standards and technical reports in this field of study. This committee supports a number of related documents and has work in progress, as well as finalized standards/technical reports. In order to stay current with this work, it is best to check the ISO Web site from time to time. Table 3-1 is a brief overview of the subcommittee's current work. Detailed information regarding this committee's work is available on the AIIM standards Web page.

Table 3–1. ISO Standards

Document Name	Sponsor / Identifier	Short Description
Microfilm standards developed and maintained by ISO TC171	ISO / Various	The topics address a wide array of issues, among them: microfilming processes, terminology, quality standards and processes; equipment and supply specifications, processes for preparing documents for filming, and inspection procedures.
Imaging standards developed and maintained by ISO TC171	ISO / Various	The topics addressed include: test targets, media error monitoring, image compression, forms for optimal, image management, and human/organizational issues for implementation of document management systems.
Electronic document file format for long-term preservation: Part 1 Use of PDF 1.4 (PDF/A-1)	ISO 19005-1: 2005	Specifies the use of Portable Document Format (PDF) 1.4 for long-term preservation of electronic documents. It is applicable to documents containing combinations of character, raster and vector data.

ELECTRONIC RECORDS MANAGEMENT APPLICATIONS

Many federal governments have undertaken extensive work in defining electronic records management specifications and functionality. The select listing in Table 3-2 represents those that have achieved the widest distribution and use.

Table 3–2. Electronic Records Management Standards

Document Name	Sponsor / Identifier	Short Description
Design Criteria Standard for Electronic Records Management Software Applications	U.S. Department of Defense DoD 5015.2 –STD	Contains mandatory and nonmandatory baseline requirements deemed desirable for Records Management Application (RMA) software. Written specifically for the DoD and other federal agencies, it is sometimes used by the private sector as well.
MoReq	European Council	Contains functional requirements for the management of electronic records by an Electronic Records Management System (ERMS). It is intended for use by both the public and private sectors.
Victoria Electronic Records Strategy (VERS)	Public Record Office of Victoria, Australia PROS 99/007	A series of standards focused on the cost-effective, long-term preservation of electronic records that must be retained in the Victoria State Archives.
Functional Requirements for Electronic Records Management Systems	Public Record Office, U.K.	Contains a set of baseline functional requirements for use by government agencies and departments that are the minimum necessary to undertake credible electronic records management. The standard identifies minimum mandatory elements and a set of desirable elements that will enhance the quality of the management of these records.

PROCESS-ORIENTED STANDARDS

Table 3-3 contains the primary standards for processes in records management that were complete and published at the time of this writing.

Table 3–3. Process-oriented Standards

Document Name	Identifier	Short Description
The Digital Records Conversion Process: Program Planning, Requirements, Procedures	ARMA International ANSI/ARMA 16-2007	Provides requirements for ensuring that electronic records remain authentic and trustworthy as they are converted from one digital recordkeeping system to another. Though it does not address digital preservation, there is a substantial link between conversion and digital preservation, as many preservation strategies involve some type of conversion process. Part I of the standard addresses the decisions relating to program planning and recordkeeping issues. Part II discusses the actual conversion process.
Establishing Alphabetic, Numeric, and Subject Filing Systems	ARMA International ANSI/ARMA 12-2005	Provides requirements for the standardization of various types of filing systems. Includes considerations in selecting a filing system, based on criteria such as records volume, the type of record being filed, the available metadata for classification and implementation.

Table 3–3. Process-oriented Standards *(Continued)*

Document Name	Identifier	Short Description
Legal Acceptance of Records Produced by Information Technology Systems	AIIM ANSI/AIIM TR31-2004	Addresses fundamental legal principles and expectations for records that were initially recorded on paper and then entered into an IT system. Organized in three parts: (I) overview of U.S.-based evidence law; (II) presents a performance guideline for the legal acceptance of records produced by IT systems; and (III) a self-assessment for accomplishment of the performance guideline. Material generally applies to system environments that are entirely digital in format as well as those where a conversion takes place.
Managing Electronic Messages as Records	ARMA International ANSI/ARMA 9-2004	Defines requirements for developing a corporate policy for managing electronic messages as records, according to the **content** of the message. The appendix includes recommended provisions for inclusion in the policy statement.
Retention Management for Records and Information	ARMA International ANSI/ARMA	Provides guidance for establishing and operating a retention and disposition program. It covers general principles, including delegation of authority and responsibility, identification and classification of records for retention purposes, and principles for determining retention periods. It addresses records on all media and in all formats.

Table 3–3. Process-oriented Standards (Continued)

Document Name	Identifier	Short Description
Vital Records: Identifying, Managing, and Recovering Business-Critical Records	ARMA International ANSI/ARMA 8-2005	Contains requirements for establishing a vital records program, including: (I) identifying and protecting vital records; (II) assessing and analyzing their vulnerability; (III) determining the impact of their loss on the organization.

PROCESS-ORIENTED TECHNICAL REPORTS/GUIDELINES

Table 3-4 contains the primary standards for processes in records management that were complete and published at the time of writing.

Table 3–4. Process-oriented Technical Reports

Document Name	Sponsor/Identifier	Short Description
Analysis, Selection, and Implementation Guidelines Associated with Electronic Document Management Systems (an AIIM Recommended Practice)	AIIM ANSI/AIIM ARP 1-2006	Contains a set of procedures and activities which should be considered and/or performed during all aspects of analyzing, selecting, and implementing an EDMS. Also contains an extensive bibliography of various standards and guidelines (ISO, ANSI, and other industry groups) relevant to document management systems.
Framework for Integration of Electronic Document Management Systems and Electronic Records Management Systems	AIIM ARMA International ANSI/AIIM/ARMA TR48-2004	This report addresses requirements for EDMS and ERMS to ensure they can integrate and interoperate for more comprehensive management of records.

Table 3–4. Process-oriented Technical Reports *(Continued)*

Document Name	Sponsor/Identifier	Short Description
Procedures and Issues for Managing Electronic Messages as Records	ARMA International ANSI/ARMA TR 02-2007	This report discusses practical managerial issues typically confronted during the implementation and management of any text-based electronic messaging system or communication, such as e-mail or instant messaging (but excluding voice mail). It was developed as an implementation guideline for ANSI/ARMA 9-2004 standard, *Requirements for Managing Electronic Messages as Records.* The technical report addresses issues such as privacy, confidentiality, security, electronic message policy compliance, appropriate use, legal considerations, and disaster recovery.
Records Center Operations	ARMA International ANSI/ARMA TR 01-2002	Designed to assist organizations in designing or selecting an appropriate records center site (whether in-house or commercial). It addresses equipment, staffing needs, operating procedures, vaults, security, protection of records, and records center software.
Records Management Responsibility in Litigation Support	ARMA International	Identifies the steps of a typical U.S.-based litigation and defines the roles the records manager has in the process. It encompasses both law firm and corporate records, and provides checklists of the process as well as an extensive bibliography of resources, Web sites and case law.
Various titles on microfilming/micro-fiche standards	AIIM	

SUMMARY

This chapter is a "scratch on the surface" of the standards world. The phrase "caveat emptor" is a good rule to follow when exploring the world of standards—let the "buyer beware" and gain a substantive understanding of the process by which a standard was developed, as well as its content and anticipated use.

The world of standards and the array of available standards, technical reports, and recommended practices is vast and changes on a daily basis. In addition to the standards organizations listed in this chapter, there are worthwhile standards produced by universities, by special projects supported by grants and scholarships, and work done by individuals. While it may be impossible to remain *fully* informed, the standards provided in this article represent a solid working foundation and beginning.

Records management standards will be sustainable only to the point that individual professionals and their organizations continue to place value on their creation. It is a substantive commitment of time and resources. And yet, the benefits to be gained indicate that working professionals will always be eager to benefit from the work of those who have practical experience they are willing to share in this format.

Records management professionals use standards to enhance and improve the contribution(s) their program makes to an organization's ability to function more effectively and efficiently. Relying on standards gives professionals additional credibility in what they are proposing, and gives the organization greater defensibility if its records management activities are being questioned. The use of standards facilitates cooperation between business units and even between business organizations.

HELPFUL WEB SITES FOR RECORDS AND INFORMATION MANAGEMENT STANDARDS

All of the formal standards bodies mentioned are in the process of developing new standards or revising existing standards. The world of records management is in constant turmoil as new technologies create new sources and formats of records. Those interested in learning more about standards will find the following Web sites of help. Internet searches will reveal numerous additional sources that may prove useful.

AIIM
www.aiim.org and www.aiim.org/standards
ARMA International
www.arma.org and www.arma.org/standards
British Standards Institute
www.bsi-global.com
The National Archives, United Kingdom
www.nationalarchives.gov.uk/electronicrecords
National Archives and Records Administration (NARA)
www.nara.gov
National Information Standards Institute
www.niso.org
Province of Victoria
www.prov.vic.gov.au/vers/standard/version2.htm
Standards Australia
www.standards.org.a

REFERENCES

International Standards Organization. 2001. *ISO 15489.1 Information and Documentation: Records Management, Part I: General.* Geneva: International Standards Organization.
Merriam-Webster Online Dictionary. Available: www.m-w.com/dictionary.htm (accessed February 14, 2007).
National Archives and Records Administration. Available: www.archives.gov/era/ (accessed February 19, 2007).
U.S. Department of Defense. 2002. *Design Criteria for Electronic Records Management Software Applications.* June 19. Available: http://jitc.fhu.disa.mil/recmgt/p50152s2.doc.

Chapter 4

Leading a Successful Records Management Program

Carol E. B. Choksy

INTRODUCTION: THE KEY ROLE OF LEADERSHIP

Managing a records management program is one of the most challenging opportunities in business regardless of the type of organization. Whether the program is in private industry, government, a cultural institution, or a financial services firm, a successful program has several key elements all aligned toward the business needs of the organization. The program must reflect the organization's strategic plan and risk management strategy. It must be led by a creative and articulate manager with a clear understanding of the corporate culture and the peculiar challenges of records management in that organization. The records manager must also have knowledge specific to the organization's industry and the industry's litigation environment.

The records manager faces complex leadership challenges because his or her work spans every part of the organization and deals with an intangible asset that is not well understood outside of the records management field. Other parts of the organization often administer records as liabilities as with litigation, or as "content" to be placed on virtual shelves as with information technology. Communication, employee development, and project management take on a different flavor for records managers because of those peculiarities. We speak with the board and the janitor, our employees are entry level and have advanced degrees, and we deal with million-dollar contracts and receipts for petty cash. No other part of the organization has the same challenges.

Over the past few years some rather spectacular issues such as Bill Gates' e-mail, the Arthur Andersen and Enron scandals, Sarbanes-Oxley, and precedent-setting court decisions such as *UBS Warburg v. Zubulake* have brought what records managers do to the attention of agency directors and boards of directors. The very electronic information technology that was supposed to deliver us from time and space has become the source of disaster for too many organizations. Records managers are now challenged to work with parts of the organization where many staff members may have believed records managers were the people who sent boxes of documents to storage and retrieved them when necessary. These developments have brought new opportunities as records managers assume roles as organizational leaders whose programs can extend from service centers to innovation centers.

In this chapter, I will discuss experiences, observations, and readings on management excellence in records management programs. Much of the work involves communication, advocacy, and education. For example, on my first day as the records manager of a large law firm, I had to write memoranda to influential attorneys saying why the plug should not be pulled on the massive records conversion then taking place in anticipation of a move that would take the firm from a horizontal to a vertical culture, from alphabetic to numerical files, from a card catalog to an electronic catalog, and from departmental to centralized filing. We eventually marched and stumbled our way from a good records management program to a great one, but it took the full support of that firm's leaders, both lawyers and nonlawyers, particularly my then-boss. Since that time, I have had the great opportunity of working with a variety of organizations—for-profits, not-for-profits, nonprofits, NGOs, and governmental organizations—and to have witnessed the myriad ways information can be managed well or poorly. I have seen how programs can be given confidence to improve or a massive infusion of people, money, and time to fail. The key in every case was leadership by both the organization and the records manager. Records managers who viewed themselves as leaders rather than as managers or supervisors, even if all they did was manage a file room, made the difference between a great and a poor program. The great records management leaders garner a set of vital skills in communication; developing and maintaining relationships;

creating, aligning, and executing strategy; developing employees; and encouraging a Drucker-style understanding of leadership, managing projects, and negotiating in the organizational environment.

COMMUNICATION

The most important skill any records manager can have is the ability to communicate (Hamm, 2006). Records managers must be able to communicate with all levels of an organization: from entry-level mailroom workers to the board of directors. Few other employees within any organization are required to do this. This is necessary, however, if the value of filing and finding information and the risks of not doing so are to be articulated well. That challenge is further exacerbated by the fact that records are both tactical and strategic assets. A truly excellent program requires a well-trained records manager who can communicate comfortably with upper-level management, middle management, and line employees. That is a rare skill. The records manager must deal with everyone within an organization. That may include janitorial staff, administrative assistants, manufacturing staff, records room staff, professional staff, and executives. Each requires a different type of communication and listening style. All employees want to believe they are being listened to and their concerns taken into consideration. But the records manager must also communicate what is required of each employee, the importance of those requirements to the organization, and how those requirements can benefit the particular employee. Emphasizing the need to manage information strategically rather than tactically makes it easier for employees to understand and accept the need for sound records management practices.

The greatest communication challenge for every records manager is to recognize and communicate that program responsibilities must extend beyond the narrow definitions of "records" provided by ISO 15489, government statutes and regulations, and many well-known archivists. A litigation subpoena requests "documents" or "electronically stored information," making no distinction between information created for personal use, amusement, or harassment of other employees and that information created to document the long-term decisions and transactions of the organization. At a minimum, the sheer amount of captured "nonrecord" information makes finding "real" records difficult. Even government agencies, having undergone a "do not destroy" litigation order for e-mail, will attest to the nuisance of having e-mail backup tapes in every closet, in boxes behind every door, and under every desk. If a records management program limited itself to managing "records" as defined by ISO, governments, archivists, and organizations would lose many if not all lawsuits . The majority of those lawsuits require the management of documents that are not "records" in any of the above definitions. The size of the damages from *UBS Warburg v. Zubulake* ($38 million) and *Morgan Stanley v. Coleman* ($1.5 billion) stem from not managing e-mail by filing it according to a file plan in a designated repository, storing it in an indexed and accessible form, deleting it according to a retention schedule, or following the organization's e-mail procedure so that employees did not create the e-mails in the first place. If we managed only records and paid no attention to all the other captured information within the organization, we would not be managing a recognized risk. This risk has always existed, but until the magnitude of the electronic data problem created by information technology software applications, IT departments, and complacent leadership became clear through the lawsuits, calls to action by records managers fell on deaf ears (Choksy, 2006, Chapters 2–3).

Communicating this risk is difficult in any organization. Until recently, poor records management was not a major element of risk management or a concern for most executives. Communicating this issue to government and business employees is difficult because of the entrenched ideas of records being only what regulators would ask for, or only in paper form. The problem of copies in many formats, drafts forgotten on local drives, and old versions accessible to people who need only the latest, exacerbate this risk. The solutions are as varied as the programs, but clear and concise communication of the problems and the solutions is a requirement.

Communicating the value of records management is even more challenging. Information is an intangible asset, but it is also a resource. Like most other intangible assets, information cannot be presented on the balance sheet. Yet like a tangible asset, neglecting information creates a risk. If a building is neglected, it becomes dangerous to employees and others, and so becomes the source of potential litigation. When furniture or equipment is neglected it becomes useless, or possibly even dangerous. Likewise, as noted, unmanaged information can become the source of very expensive lawsuits. We hire specialists in maintaining buildings, furniture and equipment, yet many organizations still neglect to hire a records manager to manage their information. Information is like any other resource in that it can be used correctly and harnessed or used poorly and wasted. Like time and money, information must be micromanaged as well as macromanaged. Time must be scheduled for a project, but it must also be managed by the individual employee; information must be managed at the enterprise level, but also by individuals at their desks. Information must be managed on a large scale, such as following a records retention schedule, but also on a micro scale, such as ensuring that each e-mail is deleted or filed appropriately. If the microscale activities are not performed effectively, the macroscale activities cannot be performed at all (Lev, 2004).

The same activities that mitigate the risks of not having managed information properly also create opportunities for more efficient and effective use of information. Mitigating the risks of information turns a liability into an asset and a poorly managed resource into a well-managed one. Continued mitigation of the risk posed by poorly managed information creates opportunities in efficiency, effectiveness, and innovation that were not previously available. Unlike buildings, equipment, and time and money, the appropriate aggregation and sharing of information creates more information and more possibilities for exploiting it. The telephone is a good example: the more people who own a telephone, the more valuable one's own telephone becomes. CNN is another example of how aggregating and sharing information makes more information and makes the original information more valuable. Although sometimes, inadvertently, the opposite is the case because the "instant" information provided by 24-hour news services can be misleading without the context necessary to understand the information, such as the reporting on the Iraqi National Museum at the beginning of the Iraq War (Choksy, 2006, Chapter 6; Gottfreson and Aspinall, 2005).

One of the more difficult concepts to communicate to any organization's directors and employees is the full range of benefits of records management. Few organizations implement and maintain a records management program because the benefits are clear. Most programs were created because the costs for having the records management program were less than continuously paying for the effects of not having one: maintaining organized information reduces the costs of continually responding to litigation and decreases the need to re-create information because it could not be located. Records management in such a light is as much cost avoidance as risk management. Currently, many companies are considering whether to have a retention schedule because of the high-priced and high-profile court cases noted. In light of these court decisions, executives are making prudent, strategic choices to invest in creating and following records schedules. With the creation of a retention schedule being the foundation for a records management program, adding governance, training, policies and procedures, and an audit program are incremental costs that still do not exceed the potential price of litigation. Chief legal counsels at many companies are aware that just the cost of going through the process of litigation can be extreme and that records management can help avoid such processes or at least mitigate the expenses.

One would think that the actual benefits of having organized information that can be accessed easily are obvious. But to date many organizations have not perceived that benefit. Conversations about how documents can be "mined" in a way similar to data often fall on deaf ears. Part of the reason is that many employees believe they have mastered information retrieval. They have scanners at their desks to image documents or they may even know how to change an e-mail into a PDF. The "Google Effect" and the "Folksonomy Effect" have convinced many employees they can find what they want using what used to be called "free text search." Depending upon what role the employee plays and his or her searching skills, this may be a delusion or quite true. When told that employees will have even quicker access to their documents if they would just put them in the correct folder, electronic or otherwise, many managers shoot back that employees cannot be expected to do their own filing. It is now not unusual to find upper-level managers with more than 10,000 e-mails in an e-mail inbox, the excuse being that the e-mails can be sorted by date, title, or author (Peterson, 2006).

RELATIONSHIPS

Records managers rarely manage every document within an organization. The growth of individual employee e-mail "inboxes" is a perfect example. Yet, even in the "paper world," there are department file cabinets, sometimes rather extensive, and not under the records manager's purview. In such situations the records manager becomes a consultant within the organization for individual employees, for workgroups, and for departments. Consultancy is effective, however, only when the records manager is brought in early in the process; it is best if the records manager's involvement occurs even before technology selection.

The preceding points may suggest that the records manager needs to make a strong relationship with the Information Technology Department. However, that strong relationship may be built through a reporting relationship such as when a records manager reports to a "C"-level executive (e.g., the chief executive officer, chief operating officer, or chief fiscal officer) with leverage throughout the organization. With the confidence and support of that executive, the records manager can have a dramatic impact on how information is managed throughout the life cycle, not just when it is subpoenaed, sent to storage, or needs destruction. The records manager's advice and direction may focus on how information is to be captured, organized, or retrieved; what privacy and security is to be applied to the information; how it is to be used and distributed; how long it should stay in primary and secondary storage; and how and when it should be destroyed. As a major part of the enterprise information architecture, these records management principles and guidelines should dictate the technical architecture, not vice versa, as is currently practiced.

When records managers are trusted consultants of the legal office, IT, and line-of-business managers, they can provide a review gate on plans and proposals, including purchasing information technology, whether hardware or software, organizing information, or creating security, privacy, or FOIA plans. The review provided by the records manager can be the difference between a tactical improvement in services and a strategic innovation. In addition, a records manager should be providing advice on change management, and further efficiencies that could be reached. Clearly, this review must be performed before the budget for an information system is set (Moore, 2005).

Such partnerships within the organization require working closely with upper-level managers and executives. Corporate culture needs to be at a point when those upper-level managers and executives often are as desirous to learn and get advice as records managers are anxious to speak to them to ensure a successful records management program. This takes a measurable amount of pressure off the records manager who is being sought out as an expert, not as an equal. In other words, records managers do not have to have all the trappings of the executive suite to have an audience. Corporate partners can include line-of-business managers, IT directors, or the CFO. Nonetheless, records managers need to understand their would-be partners' concerns. If their concerns are to protect the organization's information assets to a particular degree, and records managers cannot convince them to set that protection to a higher level, then records managers must work with their partners' goals. If partners' concerns are to create a tactical IT solution for a particular problem, records managers should advise them of the ramifications of managing a single problem. But records managers should not preach doom and gloom as an outcome of not creating an entire records program; rather, records managers must work with the goals of upper-level managers and executives (Brousseau et al., 2006).

One of the ways a records management department can become more effective is in being governed by a records management "council." This group, chartered by the board or CEO, includes the records manager, a representative from IT, the legal department, the CFO, and often someone from the compliance or quality office, and line-of-business managers. The council is responsible for creating or reviewing policies and procedures and approving training for employees, as well as for monitoring the records management audit system. This council must have authority to perform its duties, not just the responsibility to do so. The records manager must be a voting member of the council in order to ensure full and appropriate participation is given to the program. The records manager may be the director of the council, but must be able to bring and vote on issues to the council. The records manager's and council's efforts will not be effective, however, unless there is an "expert" in each department to help answer questions within the department and to translate those questions into action by the records management program. These people are usually called "records management coordinators." The coordinators have added training and duties within their department for being a liaison. Those duties must be registered within each coordinator's job description and performance evaluation or the assigned employee's activities will not include records management. Limiting this addition to the job description and performance evaluation only to the coordinator is also a recipe for failure. If employees who handle documents or manage databases are not held accountable in some way, the records management activities of filing and retention will not get done.

Another communication challenge is the problem of social and ethnic differences between the employees of the records department and the other employees within the company. This can be quite minimal in manufacturing where the ethnic and social diversity of the plant floor is greater than that of the records department. It can be quite pronounced in law firms where the ethnic and social diversity of the records department is so great as to create a caste system between the attorneys, secretaries, and paralegals and the records department. Yet records managers can become the bridge between the records department and other employees. Records managers must develop strategies for responding to other employees' derogatory comments about records program employees such as, "Those people can't even speak English." They will need strategies for responding to corporate trends like upwardly mobile managers making corporate "points" by denigrating the service of the records management department at corporate meetings. These strategies first require knowledge of how such attitudes and behaviors can be toxic to the entire work environment, not just to the records management department, and second, require working with the Human Resources Department to find the underlying causes for the inappropriate behavior. Such attitudes and behaviors must be addressed if the records management department is to have any ongoing efficacy. Quite often other employees of the corporation are unaware of how much education members of the records management department have or what special skills and training they deploy. This can be communicated through articles highlighting a particular records management employee in a newsletter or even a publicly announced award for special recognition (Hewlett et al., 2005).

Trust is key to ensuring a program reaches its objectives. The records manager must speak truthfully and directly to employees and to her or his organization. Trust, like a garden, is cultivated and can be killed. The trust that a records manager can encourage, however, is limited by how much the organization itself cultivates trust. Employees must trust the records manager to defend them outside the department, but to come to them with a clearly defined issue, like employee harassment, observed ethical breaches, or process and policy problems. Employees must trust that they can come to the records manager with issues and problems that will be addressed and the results communicated back to the employee. As noted earlier, that trust can be hard to sustain when the employees within the department are not defended against the assumptions and prejudices of the rest of the organization (Hurley, 2006).

STRATEGY

Understanding strategy is difficult for most people. My working definition of strategy is a plan of action created and executed to ensure
the continued existence or credibility of an organization. For a records
manager it is made more complex by the fact that what he or she manages has not been viewed as a strategic asset. It is also made more complex by the nature of records managers' personalities. Records
managers like 100 percent solutions and believe that an 80/20 (Pareto's
Law) solution is no solution. Yet it is humanly impossible to manage
100 percent of all organizational information 100 percent effectively.
Most programs grow incrementally as their effectiveness is proven. A
records manager must learn that strategy requires a different view of
the goals for which one ultimately strives. A good example of a strategic goal records managers use is a vital records program. Delivering a records management program that manages 100 percent of
corporate information might seem strategic, but it does not balance
cost and effort with value to the organization. Information is, in fact,
what is used to create strategy. Strategy requires researching the world,
including the organization in which records managers work, and looking at trends to understand what could damage our credibility, put us
out of business, or provide a remarkable opportunity if we are willing to take on definable challenges.

Records managers have witnessed such issues firsthand in prepa-
rations, reaction, and cleanup from Hurricane Katrina, the effects of
Sarbanes-Oxley on publicly traded companies, the demise of a great
accounting company, and the haphazard social use of e-mail providing fodder for the litigation mill. In each instance, their knowledge
and skills could have averted or ameliorated disaster, but they had not
been invited to the table to prepare for such disasters. After those
events—and during them in some instances—records managers were
frantically called to boardrooms and congressional offices to discuss a
subject they knew in depth in a new context: strategy. Unfortunately,
each of the examples provides reinforcement about the risk value of
information; any asset not managed properly creates risks. Assets managed properly, including information, create opportunities. Therefore,
records managers must work hard to communicate how properly managed information creates efficiencies within business processes, but only
so much efficiency can be wrung from a single business process.

One of the most important strategic concepts to be learned is effectiveness. Effectiveness is wielding an asset as a tool rather than as a step in a process. A step in a process can be made more efficient, but viewing how the information is used within the entire organization could lead to creating a new tool. This means stepping back from looking at how information is used in the particular step in the process to look at how information is used in the entire enterprise. Creating opportunities requires managing information at the enterprise level—at the level of the records manager who looks across business processes to see patterns of opportunities. Strategic opportunities include innovations in processes, services, and products. One of the tools at the enterprise level that can be used on a regular basis is the retention schedule. The retention schedule is architecture for the entire enterprise, an enterprise information architecture. This is in contrast to the way "information architecture" is used in library and information science to refer to the structure of a Web site, which is more like a departmental file system (Drucker, 2002).

Records management strategy is not an oxymoron. It is simply the opposite side of the coin from records disasters. Few organizations are ready to hear about the opportunities good records management can provide because their leaders are too busy dodging the proverbial bullets from the examples cited above or from litigation subpoenas. The successful records manager communicates that the activities required to ameliorate risks from poorly managed information are the same ones needed to create innovative opportunities, with the addition of a few metadata fields, for example, security/privacy, output management, or alternative sort orders. These can dramatically improve an electronic document management, records management or content management system implementation as well as improve business processes.

However, technology issues may undercut the strategic solution. Too often, organizations choose a tactical technology solution to a problem only to discover the solution has created more problems for corporate strategy. E-mail archiving is an excellent example of a technology solution that either creates greater problems or provides only a small tactical benefit. Because e-mail archiving technology actually solves only one problem—how broker/dealers can collect all communications in one place to be kept for six years—implementation of these products cannot help other types of organizations because no other organization has the same strictures on outgoing communication as broker/dealers. These products may be used to manage those e-mails with one or two retention periods that would not be used in litigation, but this is only a tiny subset of e-mails within any organization. A knowledgeable records manager can explain the problem, but will never appear more knowledgeable than an IT director bent on purchasing this tactical solution.

Here is one juncture where communication skills and relationships come into play. Whereas an IT department has the capital funds to purchase solutions, it may not have the authority to do so without approval of the records management department. This requirement exists in several very large corporations today and encourages consultation and cooperative approaches. Under those conditions, the value of both the IT department and the records management department are recognized. IT provides the pipes or the shelving, the department or workgroup provides the content, records management provides the organization, and the board or upper-level executives provide the organization's strategy.

Understood this way, records management has a large role to play within organizational strategy. That strategy has a vision, an outcome defining what success looks like, that everyone can see because it is well articulated for everyone in the organization. The strategy has goals, outputs that are qualitative or quantitative that can be reached within a few years. The strategy has objectives or measurable tasks. The records manager needs to take the time to review and understand the strategic plan and then place all of his or her resources—time, people, and budget—to achieve the organization's stated objectives.

If one of the corporate goals focuses on the response time for sales, the records manager should look at how all information within the organization that affects sales either helps or hinders what the sales department does. Information needed as an input, an output, or a decision tool for any business process may not be readily available, may not be in the right form, or may be mixed in with too many other things to be easily found. The records manager is uniquely situated to do this, because she or he is the only one in the organization who would understand how all the information the sales office needs is kept. IT will have oversight of some of the information, but not all of it. The input of records management into this particular goal is measurable.

Articulating records management's strategic role to the line-of-business manager, IT, and the executive in charge creates a powerful argument as to why the records manager's project and budget recommendations must be accepted.

RECORDS MANAGEMENT PROGRAM PLANNING

Vision

Because records management can serve the vision and goals of an organization so effectively, the records management department should have its own vision and goals. When the program is a complete success, what does that look like? This is the question that should be asked when the records management program first is visualized. The records management department's vision will not be the same as the organization's vision, because the program is a component of the organization's larger strategic program. The records manager's vision, worked out with staff however, must reflect the higher vision of the organization. The vision should be grand and possibly unreachable, but it is an ultimate target to show how the program is an essential element in strategic planning. The vision should describe a reality wherein everything has gone according to plan. Your program may not be the only component in attaining your vision. Part of your challenge may be to convince administrators outside the records management division to support and contribute to your vision in their programs' visions and goals. For example, a records management department may have as a vision to find more records, but this suggests there are a lot of lost records. This vision is measurable, so it could be an objective, but it is essentially an output. If the vision of records management is to be so effective that it helps organizations to innovate new products and services, this would be an outcome worthy of strategic planning.

Goals

Goals—the next level below the vision in the strategic plan—are achievable, but may be difficult to measure. Goals may be quantitative or qualitative. A quantitative goal, e.g., improving the speed of delivery, is measurable by definition. We can measure the present state and then measure the same variable at different points in time. Goals may not have a precise number to them because they are a guideline for what needs to change, not a dictation for how much change is needed. Year-after-year improvements may vary and targets for improvement may also change due to resources. Qualitative goals, such as improving employee trust and confidence in the department, are difficult to measure. A well-honed survey with questions such as "My concerns are taken seriously by the RM staff (never, sometimes, most of the time, always)" could give some indication, but this is not measurable in the same way as speedy delivery is measured.

Objectives

Objectives, such as "Improve the speed of delivery by 25 percent the first year," are specific targets for each goal. By giving a specific number, e.g., 25 percent, records managers can set a specific target to meet and perhaps even exceed. For qualitative goals, "Improve employee trust and confidence," objectives such as "Improve problem resolution time by 25 percent" would contribute directly to employee trust and confidence. Objectives should be measurable, hence they are outputs, as contrasted to outcomes as described above. Outputs are in sharp contrast to outcomes. Outcomes are the state of success whereas outputs are measurable tasks performed to get to that state. Success means something different to each employee, department, and organization, hence the need to define it at each level. When all of these agree, they are in alignment.

In order to achieve both outputs and outcomes successfully, a records manager's staff must be involved in creating the department's vision, goals, and objectives. People "buy in" to a vision if they are part of making it and can see themselves in it. They will be able to tell if the objectives are unobtainable or too ambitious and to work with the manager on goals that are realistic but ambitious. Their involvement provides buy-in, but also gives them training in setting goals, both ultimate and short-term—a very important part of staff development. A records manager may even want to encourage them to create their own vision and goals. When all of the visions and goals of the employees and the departments aim toward the main organizational vision and goals, it is called alignment. As the leader of his or her department, the records manager is responsible for the vision and goals of that department and for encouraging the employees to align theirs with the department and organization. A records manager may want to invite her or his supervisor and other managers responsible for similar goals to join the planning process so the records department creates a vision and goals that harmonize with those of other departments in sequence as well as in content. For example, if the IT department is working to decrease the use of storage space for personal information by 75 percent the first year, the records management department may not be able to improve response times for responding to questions. The records manager may, however, be able to encourage an increase in the use of departmental filing systems by 75 percent in the first year and leave response time improvement for the second year.

After creating the vision, goals, and objectives, each records manager should work with her or his staff to create an annual operating plan. The annual operating plan is the specific activities staff will take to execute the objectives in the long-term plan. This may include projects to improve an aspect of the department, like creating a metadata database for a specific set of information assets. Activities may include working with the off-site storage company holding boxes and tapes to ensure quicker and more accurate delivery or assigning a department records coordinator who will help identify and interpret problems so the records department can respond more effectively as well as efficiently.

The operating plan may require working with the department's staff and other parts of the organization to discern priorities for improvement. For example, several employees may be in great distress that retrieving archived boxes takes 24 hours, but a large number of other employees may be so overwhelmed with the number of folders in their Outlook personal folders that they inadvertently misfile e-mails. One aspect of a records manager's job is to find out what it will take to fix each of these problems, and to work with the various units involved in creating the solutions to prioritize them. He or she may find an incremental change in what the staff are doing will create a large improvement in efficiency. Each records manager's operating plan will be her or his contract with the organization for the actions to be taken during a particular year to bring greater value to the organization (Behn, 2006).

EMPLOYEE DEVELOPMENT AND LEADERSHIP

In the previous sections I described how a records manager must be a promoter of the records management program's services, a negotiator between the organization and his or her employees, and an assessor of risk against the organization's stated and unstated risk management plan. A challenging aspect of records management program excellence is developing employees to ensure the department can deliver the services that the organization will require. The challenge arises from records management employees' qualifications extending from entry-level and poorly educated to highly skilled and highly educated professionals. Personalities will range from the timid to the aggressive—and this may not be a reflection of the level of the employee's education. Finding training opportunities for the lowest level employees is always difficult and, until the past few years, finding training opportunities for the highest level of employee has also been difficult.

Training and motivating entry-level employees can often be difficult because records management is not viewed as part of the organization's career path. An entry-level records management employee with only a high school education might rise to the level of metadata supervisor, but without a college degree may not be able to rise further. Local Association of Records Managers and Administrators (ARMA) chapter programs may provide some training, but may not be sufficient to facilitate long-term career development. Sending these employees to the national ARMA conference may be too expensive or too time-consuming, even if the conference is held nearby. Working closely with those employees and discussing the challenges they are confronting can often be the first step in determining a "curriculum" that would be helpful. Sometimes going through a records management textbook such as *Information and Image Management* (Ricks and Gow, 1992) can be useful. Providing them with supervisory training and a few opportunities to lead teams in brief projects can also be valuable.

Mid-level employees are the easiest for whom to provide development opportunities. They benefit tremendously from ARMA chapter meetings because the training and information provided is in a collegial atmosphere where any question can be asked or followed up after the meeting. Larger cities often have monthly meetings for industry groups that can be even more informative. Legal records management groups, pharmaceutical groups, and manufacturing groups, among others, can be a great source of knowledge and information. These employees may be candidates for ARMA's national conference, but may need guidance in selecting appropriate sessions. College and graduate classes may also be helpful, though these are not plentiful. Locally held seminars on supervisory skills are necessary as well if the employees are to advance, but such courses should emphasize the supervisor as a manager, not just a personnel supervisor.

Upper-level employees, including records managers, who are performing as analysts or advisors should be encouraged to attend local seminars on legal discovery, information technology, and leadership skills. These employees should be attending the national ARMA conference every year as well as every local ARMA chapter meeting possible. Opportunities should be sought for these employees to learn management skills such as project management, risk management evaluation, employee development, communication and negotiation skills. This is the group of employees from which a successor or deputy program director should be sought. That means the development of this group should be at the same level as the records manager. It would not be unusual to encourage individuals in this group of employees to seek an advanced degree in business, law, information technology, or library and information science.

Each and every employee should be encouraged to think of himself or herself as a leader. This process can be fostered by providing training in basic management skills like time management, prioritization, and decision making. Every employee can and should be given this type of training if for no other reason than it brings a sense of pride to the department and the individual employee. Those skills are the same as the ones found in Peter Drucker's *The Effective Executive* (Drucker, 2002) and elaborated upon by Stephen Covey in *The 7 Habits of Highly Effective People* (Covey, 2004) and in *The 8th Habit: From Effectiveness to Greatness* (Covey, 2005). After having been given the skills training, the step from understanding what they do as employees and managers can be seen through the lens of leadership using Drucker's and Covey's books. Training seminars on these concepts are available live, online, or on DVD. This leadership development process is not a complicated one as long as it is neither forced nor required. Employees' understanding of their role as a leader can improve esprit de corps and self-esteem in addition to improving the bench depth of the department.

Employee development also requires celebration and recognition of small successes like an improvement in performance by both the employee and the department. Big improvements come through incremental change. Recognizing an employee for having conquered what might have seemed to him or her a barrier builds confidence, even if the issue may not seem like a great challenge to others in the program. Managers should work with employees on their development programs, including discussing possible projects, assignments, and development opportunities (Cohn et al., 2005).

PROJECT MANAGEMENT

Project management, a largely neglected management requirement, one vital to the success of any program, is actually a combination of day-to-day management skills with several specialty skills. Project managers spend 90 percent of their time communicating in one way or another. They communicate change and progress, they negotiate resources and conflicts, they measure risk and budget, and they ensure that the project moves through its phases from planning and initiation to completion. The most difficult of those communication challenges is communicating change. Every project is a change from the norm and will affect someone in the organization. Records managers organize, move, and convert information. Each stage will affect at least one employee's job and possibly his or her livelihood—improved processes can mean elimination of jobs. The records manager must ensure the benefits of the project are explained and realized. More than creating a Gantt chart, project scheduling requires defining tasks and estimating time and resources needed to complete the tasks within the defined project timeline, quality, and budget restraints. Progress in completion of tasks must be measured and marked. When problems arise, the effects of those problems on the end result of the project must be determined and, if adverse, worked out with the team and the sponsor.

The records manager must be able to create a team from disparate elements of the organization. This requires negotiating time for each team member to perform his or her role in the project; ensuring the team member is clear about duties; and then ensuring each person has the resources—time, budget, material, workspace, etc.—to perform the tasks. Regular meetings of the team must be scheduled to synchronize activity, identify problems, and celebrate progress. Creating a team requires team-building skills. A team cannot be built at a weekend retreat supporting one another on ropes and falling for others to catch. Team building first requires becoming acquainted with one another, working to define the project, and building a minimum level of trust. Time must be set aside at each meeting for members to give a small amount of information about who they are, what they do, how they got there, their personal goals, etc., because trust happens over time. Virtual team building may mean searching for technology that is easy to use, but that reflects each member's personal method of learning, including visual, aural, and reading. Multicultural team building may require understanding cultural issues such as different negotiation styles, social hierarchy, community relations, and communication styles. Differing cultural communication styles may include offering ideas right away, waiting to hear others' ideas and then contributing, waiting to be asked for an opinion, or speaking one-on-one (Brett et al., 2006).

Records managers as project managers will be expected to negotiate conflicts within the group, to hear disagreements and help the team to work them out without being the "referee" for every issue. She or he must bring issues to the team for resolution and ensure that team members' conflict resolution preferences are addressed and respected. Above all, the records manager must be honest. When a team member is not contributing, the project manager must address this directly, and truthfully tell the team whether the person should or should not, can or cannot, be removed from the team. All of these skills develop trust, which, like day-to-day management, is one of the most important tools for reaching goals (PMBOK, 2004).

In a supportive environment, a records manager can use projects to make inroads into repetitive problems. Small projects, such as tracking the number of documents not found within 24 hours (including where the documents were found), when undertaken with a strategy can permit the program to exceed objectives in organization and delivery of information. Minimal support is required to accomplish these projects, but executed properly, just training employees well can make a huge improvement to the entire organization. With maximum support including a budget to undertake a major project, the records manager can deliver an order-of-magnitude improvement in services. Large projects, however, must be researched and planned more thoroughly, and, once begun, must be followed through to the end.

ORGANIZATIONAL ENVIRONMENT

The organizational environment in which a records management program operates can help or hinder the program. A supportive environment is one where upper-level executives execute the goals and values of the strategic plan in a straightforward and transparent way and where the role of records management within the organization is articulated and supported both verbally and financially. A program that is viewed as a line-item in the budget through which a line can be drawn when the organization is tight on money is not likely to be highly appreciated even when money is plentiful. Because organizations often see records management as a cost rather than as an investment, initiatives to improve the program are often nearly impossible to fund. Where this is the case, the records manager must focus on ensuring good customer service, e.g., finding information quickly and delivering it to the end-user. When information cannot be found within a reasonable period of time, the records manager needs to get back to the end-user and let him or her know what the problem is and when further communication will occur, whether successful or not. The records manager may want to create guidelines for end-users, like a service-level agreement, about when they can expect a call if information cannot be found. This requires employees who are comfortable speaking to others, trained about how quickly to get back to end users, and know how to be truthful without blaming anyone.

CONCLUDING OBSERVATIONS

What I have described and analyzed in this chapter are skills that most records managers are obtaining only *now*. Professional meetings in the field, unfortunately, have not caught up with the needs of records managers in modern corporations. Although papers are being presented and discussions are being held at professional meetings, what are truly needed are presentations and discussions on specific leadership and management skills. A few abilities that records managers would do well to hone include communication, relationship management, strategy development, employee enhancement and leadership, project management, and negotiating organizational environments. If records managers address and acquire those aptitudes within the next few years, records management excellence will be enhanced greatly and records management programs will function successfully within the wide variety of organizations that are served by the profession.

Leaders of organizations should be attributing at least part of their success to records management programs. Improving the records management program will certainly help to make this happen, but an even more important element of the records management program is a records manager with leadership skills. I have not mentioned obtaining skills in information technology or the law because these are tools and guidelines for the programs we direct, and do not affect the core of records management. In addition, the skills and knowledge of IT and the law will vary from organization to organization even within the same industry, whereas the skills and knowledge of records management are very consistent. To enhance the necessary leadership skills, records managers need not get an MBA because many of the skills required, like project management, are not taught in most MBA programs. Professional associations, such as ARMA, can help define skills that are needed and provide opportunities to obtain those skills or guidance in where to get them. Local ARMA chapters can include leadership skills in monthly meetings and arrange for local training opportunities. Records managers should discuss their development plan with their managers and look at the type of training upper-level executives within the organization are pursuing.

REFERENCES

Behn, Robert D. 2006. "Performance Leadership: 11 Better Practices That Can Ratchet Up Performance," *Managing for Performance and Results Series.* Washington, DC: IBM Center for the Business of Government.

Brett, Jeanne, Kristen Behfar, and Mary C. Kern. 2006. "Managing Multicultural Teams." *Harvard Business Review* 84, no. 11 (November): 84–91.

Brousseau, Kenneth R., Michael J. Driver, Gary Hourihan, and Rikard Larsson. 2006. "The Seasoned Executive's Decision-Making Style," *Harvard Business Review* 84, no. 7/8 (July/August): 110–121.

Choksy, Carol E. B. 2006. *Domesticating Information: Managing Documents Inside the Organization.* Lanham, MD: Scarecrow Press.

Cohn, Jeffrey M., Rakesh Khurana, and Laura Reeves. 2005. "Growing Talent as If Your Business Depended on It." *Harvard Business Review* 84, no. 4 (October): 62–70.

Covey, Stephen. 2004. *The 7 Habits of Highly Effective People.* New York: Free Press.

Covey, Stephen. 2005. *The 8th Habit: From Effectiveness to Greatness.* New York: Free Press.

Drucker, Peter. 2002. *The Effective Executive.* New York: HarperBusiness Essentials.

Gottfreson Mark and Keith Aspinall. 2005. "Innovation vs. Complexity: What Is Too Much of a Good Thing?" *Harvard Business Review* 83, no. 10 (November): 62–71.

Hamm, John. 2006. "The Five Messages Leaders Must Manage." *Harvard Business Review* 84, no. 5 (May): 114–123.

Hewlett, Sylvia Ann, Carolyn Buck Luce, and Cornel West 2005. "Leadership in Your Midst: Tapping the Hidden Strengths of Minority Executives." *Harvard Business Review* 83, no. 1 (November): 74–82.

Hurley, Robert F. 2006. "The Decision to Trust." *Harvard Business Review* 84, no. 9 (September): 55–62.

Lev, Baruch. 2004. "Sharpening the Intangibles Edge." *Harvard Business Review* 82, no. 6 (June): 109–116.

Moore, Geoffrey A.. 2005. *Dealing with Darwin: How Great Companies Innovate at Every Phase of Their Evolution.* New York: Portfolio.

Peterson, Elaine 2006. "Beneath the Metadata: Some Philosophical Problems with Folksonomy." *D-Lib Magazine* 12, no. 11 (November). Available: www.dlib.org/dlib/november06/peterson/11peterson.html.

PMBOK. 2004. *A Guide to the Project Management Body of Knowledge: PMBOK Guide.* 3rd ed. Newtown Square, PA: Project Management Institute.

Ricks, Betty R., Ann J. Swafford, and Kay F. Gow. 1992. *Information and Image Management: A Records Systems Approach.* 3rd ed. Cincinnati: South-Western Publishing.

Chapter 5

From Cultural Luxury to "The Way We Do Things . . . ?" The Influence of Leadership in Archives and Records Management

Peter Emmerson

INTRODUCTION

Archives and records management programs are seldom seen as vital components of corporate life or essential for corporate success. Even when they do reach "core" status, the core continually changes as corporate strategic objectives and imperatives, and the senior managers responsible for them, change. New technologies and techniques appear to offer new solutions. Software replaces "gray-ware" and expertise that was once thought critical to the organization's success is seen as redundant. Many record-keeping programs have not been sufficiently responsive to, and aligned with, these strategic objectives. This inevitably makes them vulnerable to changes in fashion and the blandishments of technological "snake oil salesmen" offering senior decision makers simplistic solutions. Effective leadership and strategies seek to minimize these risks by ensuring that the record-keeping program stays aligned to changing business needs and circumstances while continuing to deliver excellent services (as defined by customers), and effective, business-centered solutions meet professional best practice and professional standards. Based on the author's experience as head of Barclays Bank's Records Services operation (1987–1999) (and as a consultant), this chapter will look at what this means in practice and attempt to draw out the key strategic and leadership points.

One of many definitions of a leader is "someone with followers." This suggests that leadership can only be provided to subordinates or peers. In setting up a new program, the "followers" will also include superiors and leaders in other areas of the business. A clear understanding of the business and what drives it and the operational concerns of managers at all levels and the resistance in the business line to corporate initiatives is essential. The records professional must also demonstrate the wider business benefits that can be delivered by a more dynamic, and professionally led, approach to the task. Only in this way can they combat the inertia and resistance to change in corporate functions whose turf includes some record-keeping responsibilities. The key is in being able to demonstrate the unique expertise and experience that you bring to the table, a clear vision of what is needed to move the organization onto a higher record-keeping plane, an understanding of cost and an ability to articulate benefits in terms of cost savings, the strategic objectives of the business, and the risks inherent in its business activities. This needs to be combined with an understanding of what constitutes success and how it should be measured by the business.

IN THE BEGINNING . . .

In the case of Barclays Bank, I was recruited in 1987, initially on a two-year fixed contract, to advise the company on the development of a best practice approach to the management of its "historical records" and a program for centralizing and managing them in a single, corporate facility, which did not yet exist. The upcoming tercentenary, then thought to be in 1992, was the primary driver of renewed interest in history and archives. Barclays Bank is one of the "big four" banking groups in the United Kingdom, offering a full range of retail and investment banking services nationally and internationally. Tracing its history back to the formation of a Quaker goldsmiths' partnership in 1690, it was incorporated in 1896, bringing together 20 family-linked private banking partnerships. It developed its international business through Barclays Dominion, Colonial and Overseas (DCO), which later became Barclays Bank International (BBI). The domestic and international arms of the bank were finally brought together into "One Bank" in 1987. In the same year, deregulation of the U.K. banking industry allowed the bank to move into investment banking and market making. The archives and records management program applied specifically to the retail banking side of the business during the author's time with the company. A senior bank executive proposed a "magisterial" history of the bank but doubted that the very modest existing archival program could support it.

It emerged later that the board and executive of the company were less than unanimously committed to the project, preferred a "coffee table" company history, and felt that focusing on the company's past would prevent it from becoming the forward-looking organization that they thought it should be. Despite these negative influences, the project presented an opportunity to develop a "best of breed" corporate archive operation in a high-profile and highly profitable business. The company had no strategy or policy for the management of its records, which highlighted the potential to extend the project beyond the original narrow "historical records" scope into a wider record-keeping development.

A number of issues became clear as part of the initial data collection and consultation process. The existing holdings, systems, equipment, location, and people were totally inadequate for the task. Many of the records, which were recorded as being held in the regions, had already been transferred to the bank's head office but were not captured in any of the control documentation. Some regional directors were unhappy about the centralization process. They saw it as part of a much wider, imminent reorganization, which would establish a series of (fewer) regional offices, based on geography rather than on the historical location of the principal offices of the original private banks. There was not enough time before the tercentenary to do everything that needed to be done to prepare the sources, let alone write the history. Not only were the archives poorly managed but most of the bank's operating records were virtually uncontrolled. Perhaps most important, the project's sponsor was about to move to a new position; his successor would need to be encouraged to share his enthusiasm for the project.

These potential threats made it important to accelerate the work. The expected survey work had turned out to be largely redundant, although it did provide an excellent opportunity to talk to senior managers in the regions about their wider record-keeping concerns. The project quickly produced a simple but comprehensive database as both accession register and primary finding aid in addition to the material already centralized. We encouraged the existing company archivist to support the vision of a more professional, comprehensive service, ensuring that he remained committed to the emerging vision and strategy.

The work on identifying and describing the archive holdings and building the database was carried out by university graduates, who were recruited through the postgraduate archive schools for precourse experience. We subsequently used the graduate recruitment approach as a precedent to establish a training post filled competitively each year by a graduate referred to us by one of the major university archive schools, a trendsetting action. To demonstrate our leading-edge approach, we engaged with the bank's newly established microcomputer support team to build a descriptive database using the bank's preferred software product. We developed the bank's first PC network to hold the database. In so doing we provided the "microshop" with a successful, and much publicized, reference site to demonstrate the potential benefits of PC networks. It had the effect of raising our profile and standing with the IT community as a whole, which proved very useful as we moved into the management of line-of-business records in later years.

THE CHALLENGE OF CONSTANT CHANGE

Records professionals are not isolated from the change that is going on around them. In the Barclays case, the changing management relationship and the separation of the archives project from its principal sponsor created an almost immediate challenge. The commitment to the original vision needed to be underpinned by underlining the potential benefits that could accrue from a more comprehensive approach. The restructuring of the bank in the late 1980s opened up an opportunity to address its full record-keeping needs, support the changes taking place in the bank's business, and tap into the more professional management culture that was being established. The newly appointed chairman and chief executive of the company was the first who *was not* a member of one of the founding families. The first group of fast-track graduate management trainees was beginning to emerge into the most senior management posts. Increased market competition, a widening customer base, and a demand for faster and more responsive personal and corporate banking services made the company more conscious of its costs and administrative processes. Accelerating the delivery of the expected report on the company's archives created an opportunity to catch this wave.

The report, delivered in February 1988 as the reorganization was finalized (six months into the project rather than after two years), identified best practice, recommended steps to get there, and advocated the planned survival of records of current business to form the archives of the future. This seemed to be an alien concept. Most managers assumed that only pre-twentieth-century records should be seen as archives. They were surprised and, in some cases, alarmed to discover that all records might, ultimately, be archives, including those that were on their desks at the time. The report also highlighted operational and financial benefits that would accrue from managing records holistically, a topic beyond its original scope. This recommendation enabled the program to be uncoupled from the "old records" syndrome and to emphasize the potential of assisting the company to manage its records more effectively.

The report removed the perception that the archives project was one person's obsession. It was necessary to establish a relationship with a new potential champion for whom a more direct business benefit would clearly be of more value. It also provided the opportunity to develop and lead a record-keeping program that was intellectually coherent and more in line with my own view of the need to integrate the management of all corporate records throughout their lives. Instead of being viewed as a cultural luxury, the report showed that managing the organization's records, including the selection and appraisal and control of archival material, could deliver effective practical, commercial benefits.

This approach was much more in line with the thinking of the senior executive to whom our parent division now reported. It also fitted with the business philosophy of the new senior managers who were promoted under the reorganization. They were prepared to give us a hearing and to allow us to demonstrate the possibilities. Following the delivery and acceptance of the report, I moved onto the bank's permanent staff, initially as its chief archivist and ultimately as head of Barclays Records Services, with responsibility for implementing the report's recommendations. At the same time, the projected developments for the historical records went ahead as planned. We were allowed to recruit additional staff for the nascent Group Archives Unit (GAU) and subsequently for the in-house consulting team that was to become the Records Management Projects Unit. Resources were promised for developing a suitable building to house the archives and to equip it with the necessary systems and facilities in line with the then British standard (BS 5454:1989) on the storage and exhibition of archival documents.

TRIMMING TO NEW BUSINESS REALITIES

It was at this point that we were forced, not for the last time, to adjust our programs to the changing business realities within the bank. The original proposal was to develop the planned archival facility on the outskirts of London, within easy reach of the city but in lower-cost facilities than would have been available there. Although the bank's property specialists had begun to search for suitable premises based on the specification we had provided, they were under pressure to use an existing building if one could be found within the bank's extensive real estate holdings. As it turned out, such a building existed but on the outskirts of Manchester, 200 miles to the north, rather than on the outskirts of London. Part of this building had been acquired to provide an overspill storage area for the bank's central record store (CRS), which was then part of the stationery services operation. Accommodating to the building department's needs, we agreed to establish the operation in Manchester, on the rationale that we intended the archives operation to focus primarily on supporting the bank's business needs rather than external research needs or those of the general public. At the same time we recognized that the bank had a wider societal obligation to make its archives available for research. We persuaded the project sponsor that even-handedness was important to avoid accusations of opening up the archives only to those whose research we approved. We were the first of the major banks in the United Kingdom to develop a formal policy on access.

Our aim was to establish an effective archives operation that did more than provide pretty pieces to support public marketing campaigns. It was also important to ensure a natural flow of material from the management and administration of the company through into the archives to avoid repetition of the gap that existed in the records between 1900 and 1980. Archivists in the other major banks had been heavily dependent on being able to track down accidental survivals and on the memories of staff members. Our aim was to create a more managed process which would, in turn, provide the benchmark for other organizations. It was important to ensure that we were able to control the process of ultimate survival of the records.

We put forward a strategy for developing comprehensive classification schemes and records retention schedules covering the whole of the bank's business, and, in particular, the records of key core business functions. The selling points for this proposal were a combination of space saved in expensive city accommodation and more certain retrieval of information needed to support the bank's compliance, risk management, and reputational needs. As part of this process we would undertake business analysis of the bank's primary functions and develop comprehensive function-based classification schemes for most of the business units. This was the first time that such an approach had been attempted in a major U.K. bank. We demonstrated a willingness to put forward something new and progressive in a conservative and risk-averse business culture and the professional expertise to ensure its delivery.

We needed to be able to cope with opposition from others who had turf to protect. The bank's organization and methods team held the brief for records retention in the branch network and saw what we were doing as cutting across their traditional turf. They were a classic internal control function: Everyone should do the same thing and at the lowest possible direct cost. They had designed the central records store and its processes. We worked around their opposition by focusing, for the time being, on nonbranch operations. We used our own senior management structure to escalate our proposals to their executive peer group in the Banking Division, in which O&M reported, as a way of ensuring that our message reached them unfiltered by turf-protecting concerns and stressing our specialist expertise against their generalist knowledge.

There was also some opposition in the major business units nominated by the head of the retail bank as the pilot areas for the records management development program. They instinctively reacted against anything imposed from above and it became important to promote the immediate local benefits that the work could deliver, playing down the corporate dimension. This approach worked well and had the added benefit of helping us to develop convincing arguments for change and to focus on business outcomes rather than on the processes, procedures, and tools that we were designing. Building a constituency of satisfied customers provided a sound support structure when we transferred to the operational services division of the bank in 1994.

LEARNING FROM EXPERIENCE

We were determined to avoid the challenges experienced by other organizations' records programs that overemphasized storage and retrieval and disposal of records at the end of their working life and operation of large records centers. When the original space was fully occupied, records program managers had to appeal for capital to extend the storage facility, undercutting the savings and benefits case. Similarly, it was difficult to justify competing for resources against what appeared to be more central business needs. Our aim was to avoid the concentration of resources and management time involved in managing large buildings full of relatively inactive hard-copy records. An initial goal was to establish intellectual control over the records to reduce the volume and improve their use to support current business. Additionally, we wanted to ensure that records of archival quality would be identified as early as possible in the development process and earmarked for ultimate transfer to the Group Archives Unit. The fundamental basis for this work lay in developing function based systems at a time when such systems were only just beginning to emerge as leading-edge practice in other parts of the world and in other businesses.

ENGAGING WITH REALITY

As noted earlier, we decided to accept the offer of the Manchester building on the understanding that we would still be able to develop and implement, over time, the high-quality archive facilities and systems included in the original brief. Co-location with Central Records Store (CRS) beginning in 1989 meant, inevitably, that we came under pressure, as the now resident records "experts," to take on responsibility for what was then a very basic inactive records storage and retrieval operation. I could see the potential in an operation that could be enhanced to make a more effective contribution to the bank's business and support streamlined record-keeping. We had already demonstrated our expertise by advising the managers of the CRS on increasing the storage density of the facility and improving the systems used to manage the contents. Stationery Services were determined to unload responsibility onto the archives and records management service despite our best efforts not to become involved.

In the end, despite misgivings on the loss of management and professional focus, we agreed to take on the storage operation in 1990. New legislation, which was to be introduced over the next few years, would impose an enormous burden on the bank by creating a need to store a great quantity of high-bulk transactional documentation. We recognized that using our experience and expertise to help the bank to deal with this problem would demonstrate the contribution that experienced professional records people could make. The downside of this decision was that the records center operation, which grew to be the largest of its kind in the United Kingdom, became the primary focus of the section and diverted management attention away from the more important task of establishing intellectual control over the bank's records. Its increasing budget, and its relatively large industrial and clerical workforce, raised its profile and senior management's interest in the section as a whole.

When the Records Services Section budget rose to be more than 50 percent of that of its original parent department, it was transferred in 1994 out of a generally supportive headquarters (HQ) function into a much more challenging and less sympathetic operating division that was home to all the bank's large-scale central branch support operations—check clearing, cash management, loan security perfection, regular payments processing, stationery services—and was not a comfortable environment for either records management or archives. We resisted attempts either to close these units down or to relocate them elsewhere in the bank, which would destroy the strategic vision and integrated record-keeping structure that we had worked so hard to promote.

Ultimately, however, the uncomfortable administrative setting worked to our advantage. The budget for our program was tiny compared with those of the other, much larger, units in the division. As a result the savings achievable in breaking it up or closing it down were not seen as being worth the management effort and reorganization cost. We also compared well to our colleagues operationally. Our dedication to customer service and customer needs also meant that we had a much higher satisfaction rating from our customers than any of the other services. We had a reputation for accurate budgeting; good financial control; effective people management; and, successful integration of our directly employed staff with those provided by employment agencies. We used our expertise to develop and deliver innovative services to other business units within the division, which helped them to meet their mission. This in turn led to members of the team being in demand for major business change projects affecting the delivery of retail banking services.

The Group Archives Unit was also able to benefit from its location in the operating division. The Manchester facility turned out to be far from ideal, with environmental, security, and space limitation issues. An opportunity arose to improve the situation radically in 1995 when senior executives decided to relocate the bank's bulk post operation, housed in a building adjacent to the records center, to a new, enhanced site. The building was a relatively modern, brick-built, standalone warehouse with office and workspace and a dedicated loading bay. It was also available on a very long lease which meant that, although there was more storage space than would be needed immediately, the economic impact of carrying the additional space would be small. Converting it to house the GAU seemed to be an obvious solution. At the same time we were negotiating to take on an additional task—providing high-activity storage and retrieval services for a newly established back-office business unit serving the branch network—for which we would need additional staff. Plans to move the central mailing unit had stalled over the issue of the future of the part-time employees who worked there. We put together a proposal to take on the displaced workforce to staff our new operation in exchange for acquiring and converting the redundant building for use by the GAU. It would be a challenge to integrate them into the newly developed customer service culture but it seemed to be a risk worth taking on behalf of the long-term preservation of the company's historical records. The building was not entirely suitable but we provided a copy of the relevant standard to our colleagues in the property company and asked for what would be, in effect, a state-of-the-art facility, including air-conditioning and double insulation, inert gas extinguishing, and very early smoke detection alarms (VESDAs). To our surprise, the whole project was signed off without question by the divisional director. "Amounts this small," he subsequently told me, "don't even get onto my radar."

Taking on the CRS had a degree of risk because it was probably the least valued operation in the bank. Because it provided services to all areas of the bank, the CRS's ability to deliver effectively could be seen as a key element in establishing the reputation for excellence of the whole of the service. By replacing an ineffective, static records store with a best-of-breed records center supporting a "can do" customer service culture, we could meet an immediate need and deliver enormous front line benefits to the bank. Although we did not plan it that way, it also developed a level of management goodwill, particularly in the property services operation, which led them to cooperate willingly with the necessary extension to the records center operation during the next decade and to look for creative solutions, which minimized the development costs. We consolidated the change by renaming the operation (following a staff competition) Barclays National Records Centre (BNRC).

The availability of an effective records storage and retrieval service also enabled the bank to replace Victorian and Edwardian branch buildings with "shop front" facilities with minimal records storage space. The records program was aligned to the bank's developing customer service proposition and its increasingly centralized approach to delivering back office functions. Similarly, the new office buildings developed or acquired to facilitate the reorganization of the bank, its move to a new business model, and the relocation of many of its support services out of central London could be built without the extensive records storage space that had been the norm since Victorian times.

SEIZING THE OPPORTUNITIES

The rebuilding of the bank's central London headquarters in 1990 provided a similar opportunity. We had already proven our effectiveness to the Property Services Office by negotiating the location of the Group Archives Unit; taking on the Central Records Store; and by the Records Management Projects Unit (RMPU) completing a major project to rationalize, reorganize and restructure Property Services' records which led to a 60 percent reduction in storage requirements and a measurable improvement in speed and certainty of access to information. This success led BPS to incorporate the approach into all future development planning and execution.

The RMPU, as a result, became an integral part of the HQ redevelopment project and played a major role in not only minimizing the office-based records storage requirements in the new building but also in improving the quality of the records and information available to the business functions which moved back there. At our suggestion, all functions relocating to the new HQ building started with a zero-sum allocation of storage space and equipment until the RMPU had completed an operational retention review and assessment.[1] Most important, the costs of this records assessment process and the associated disposal and transfer activities were borne by the re-development project.

The impact was staggering. The project team had set the records volume reduction target at 40 percent but the final reduction averaged 65 percent with some functions able to achieve 80 percent. The new systems installed allowed them to achieve better control of their records and to retrieve records and information more effectively, both in-house and from the records center. Departments began to manage their records as a matter of regular maintenance rather than occasional panic. The RMPU was able to demonstrate its value and the success of our approach. It became directly involved from that point onward in all major development and relocation projects and in the planning of new record-keeping processes arising from changes in the bank's business model. Displaying knowledge and their consummate professionalism paid healthy dividends.

SERVING THE "DOERS"

We also wanted to develop and deliver services that support the large number of people who work on the front line. In the case of a retail bank, these are the people who make the money on which the rest of the business feeds. They are frequently the most ignored, most controlled, and most in need of assistance and relief from bureaucratic burdens. Identifying their felt needs and working to deliver services that meet those needs is a major factor in embedding any internal service into "the way we do things around here." They are also more numerous and, ultimately, more influential than their functional colleagues. As a result, improving support to them delivers more immediate value than work in headquarters. Identifying those needs and then servicing them efficiently, effectively, and promptly, creates a well-spring of support and goodwill that can be called on for support when, inevitably, the value of the records operation is called into question.

Many HQ offices regarded the branch network with open suspicion and issued instructions that largely ignored the difficulties under which they operated and some of the business risks inherent in the way they worked. Many of the systems and approaches were outmoded, dating from an era when many employees were paid in cash rather than by check or direct credit transfer. Branch records systems concentrated on storage space rather than the ability of staff to retrieve individual records and to return them to the container from which they had been removed. The storage pressure on most branches was becoming intolerable. In one branch boxes of cancelled checks were stored on the floor of the men's restroom. The impending introduction of new regulations to combat money laundering would extend the retention period on cleared checks, kept in branch storage, to six years from three, doubling the problem.

This created two opportunities: (1) building a new relationship with the branches, and (2) modernizing the records storage program. The first step in a new approach to the branches was to break with the Barclays tradition by asking regional directors and their branch managers what they needed, rather than second guessing their requirements and telling them what was best for them. I conducted a series of visits with regional operations directors, who requested that we remove check storage from branches and allow the transfer of the envelopes containing the "days work" vouchers and control sheets to the records center after one year in branch storage rather than three. They had, it turned out, been pleading unsuccessfully for a change in the rules for some years. They had been given the business equivalent of a "pull your socks up and get on with it" message.

We now faced something of a dilemma, which we turned into the second opportunity: We needed more space and a more effective operation and approach to managing inactive records. The space part was dealt with by putting forward a proposal to extend the records center, using the numbers that we had gathered from our survey of regional operations and from our calculations of the impact of extending the retention period on the key operational documents which were already stored. The threat of prosecution under money-laundering regulations acted as a valuable lever in persuading management. After making every effort to find an existing building that would meet our requirements, the property department decided it would be simpler to build something to our specifications. This involved the acquisition of a greenfield site and the agreement of a major property development company to build the new center as a commercial proposition, reducing the bank's capital commitment to the project and making the development more attractive. In order to take the project forward, the property company needed the agreement of our senior management. We persuaded them that that support would be forthcoming, even though it was far from fully agreed, and promised that we would refund any losses that they incurred if the project did not go ahead. The risk was worth taking; approval was received just in time to make a local authority planning approval deadline.

The existing service and facilities had been structured around storage rather than retrieval and would not have been able to cope with an exponential increase in volume and retrieval activity. There were no statistics and no performance metrics. Planning was nonexistent and there was nothing on which to base the necessary expansion of the business. Documentary control was basic, depending on a simple "card for every customer" to which location numbers were added once the material had been shelved. We needed to develop systems and processes that would turn the CRS into a fully functioning records center and to convert its management and staff from passive custodians into proactive customer service providers.

The first step involved introducing fairly straightforward and standard records center processes—listing contents, randomized storage, and telephone rather than internal mail-retrieval requests. We worked to persuade managers and supervisory staff that this would make their job more fulfilling. The unit was undermanaged, overtime was excessive, and everything was geared to the way in which the warehouse staff chose to work rather than to effective operation, driven by customer demand. They did not see the owners of the records as customers of the service and treated them in an off-hand and casual way. Retrieval turnaround time was about two weeks. Attitudes needed to be changed by a combination of persuasion and compulsion, as well as the use of technology to broker change.

Persuasion started with a message about treating the internal customer in the same way as an outside bank customer would be treated. How would they, as customers of banking services, feel if branch cashiers and customer service operatives treated them differently from other customers? Wouldn't they feel better if they recognized the contribution they were making to the service the bank could provide to its customers? More basically, if they had to spend the time between breakfast and their evening meal at work they might as well enjoy it. We tried to engage their interest by seeking their input to the process changes needed to cope with major activity growth and the development of training programs and opportunities that had not been available before. Most important, we put effective power back in the hands of management by introducing a work planning system to smooth out the peaks and troughs in the work and eliminating automatic overtime unless the system suggested it was necessary.

As a way of sugaring this pill, we undertook to create new job descriptions for all the jobs to ensure that the changes in role were recognized by the remuneration system. The harder edge was provided by reminding the warehouse operatives in particular that working for the bank put them way ahead of the local market for the kind of work that they were doing. This meant that any potential outsourcing contractor would find it easy to undercut the in-house operation. By responding and subscribing to the vision they could reduce the likelihood of retrenchment. They could also contribute to the development of a best-of-breed operation which, if successful, could be held up as a model for others and in which they could take pride of ownership. A "can do" organization would also develop a group of satisfied customers and make it easier to obtain continuing investment in the operation, helping to make their jobs more secure. Despite some skepticism, a majority of the employees accepted the challenge.

Technology helped reinforce the change. The bank's systems development team, with an external software house, developed a records center management system based on an existing warehouse management system, but tailored to meet our specific needs. The development had two principal benefits in promoting change. First, we selected an insider to work with the development team to advise on the existing working practices, to act as a conduit between the team and the operational people, and most importantly, to learn the system and act as an advocate for it. This decision demonstrated that we were prepared to give credit to the views and expertise of the workforce and to encourage the development of talented but untrained people. Second, computerization facilitated changes in working practices and ensured that everyone had to be trained to be able to use the new system. This allowed staff to feel confident in using computer equipment and systems. In turn it became easier to introduce more sophisticated systems in future years involving real time, radio data control systems, and high-speed, conveyor-fed processes supporting special operations. Because the computer now planned space allocation in the warehouse and generated reports that showed how much work was being done and who was doing it, the warehouse foreman's "expertise" had been made redundant and the need for routine overtime working was all but eliminated. Most important of all, the quality of the service to our "customers" rose to unprecedented levels leading to consistently "excellent" responses to regular customer surveys. The fact that our customers rated us highly in all areas of our business was a major plus in pursuing additional resources and resisting the inevitable pressure to close down or outsource our operations. It also gave the operational workforce a real sense of pride in the service they now provided.

ENTREPRENEURIAL APPROACHES

A service activity is always threatened by changing attitudes and priorities. Changes in senior management can lead to change in attitudes to the record-keeping function and technology acts as a continual spur to look for new opportunities to refresh and sustain the business. The success of the records center operation meant that any records or information storage requirement was brought to our door. At the same time, people had become aware, through the work of the RMPU and the development of records management standards, that there was specialist expertise in the bank for developing new and innovative ways of managing records and information. Our strategy was always to say "we can do that" and then to look for ways of solving the problem.

This took us into strange and unexpected territory. We worked with a project team developing an approach to the high-speed imaging of checks and vouchers as they passed through the sorting machines in the Clearing Centre, demonstrating to them the retrieval curve which needed to be managed by the system and developing a cost model for the various alternatives. We supported a pilot project for a new semiautomated, self-service branch where the customer paper would be transferred to the records center at the end of each day from the Clearing Centre without returning to the issuing branch. We helped colleagues assess the value of proposals for specialized storage management operations, which they wanted to outsource. Our records management standards were adopted by the bank's computer auditors to provide the "archiving" section of the risk management rules that they were developing for managing the bank's core business systems. Being in demand was the best way to survive and prosper.

The most impressive development was taking on the storage and retrieval of the documentation from the newly centralized regular payments centers in 1995. Traditionally, regular payments—standing orders, direct debit mandates—had been handled in the branch where the customer's account was held. Centralized processing allowed the development of more effective management systems, economies of scale, and improved turnaround times, and made it easier to deal with those major consumer businesses that handled large volumes of instructions. But the operation collapsed under the weight of the records volume and the inefficiencies of the storage and retrieval system. We were asked to advise on improving the situation. The RMPU devised a better way of sorting and organizing the materials while they were in the Regular Payments Centre (RPC). They were then transferred three days after processing to the records center Working with a team of logistics experts, we converted part of the original records center building to provide a confined space within which to house the material, operated by dedicated warehouse staff, and linked by conveyor to an area of previously unused office space equipped as a specialist retrieval area. A dedicated computer link allowed RPC staff to place requests directly into the records center system. Copies of the requested documents could then be faxed back to the RPC or directly to the customer's branch. We had rescued a flagship change management operation from disaster by simply applying our expertise.

THE HUMAN FACTOR

Getting people to buy into change is a major management challenge in any environment. In the case of the original central records store, we were dealing with an embedded workforce suspicious of management and likely to assume that change would be transient if they resisted it long enough. Each new management broom had tried to change things and then, in the normal modern corporate way, had moved on before the change had fully matured. Consequently, some employees worked against the change process where they could and subverted the system rather than using it willingly. This problem remained until the major expansion of the operation in 1992 allowed us to recruit new people who were more inclined to buy into the new philosophy. At the same time we tried to break down the barriers which had been built up between the warehouse side of the operation and the customer service section. All staff were trained to do all the work.

We encouraged people to help redesign processes, on the basis that they knew the real task better than their supervisors, and to devise and agree on their own team-performance targets. As the new operations came on line, we moved high-performing people from the old to the new to set the pace for their new colleagues. Initially, these teams worked without direct supervision. However, the volume of business grew to a point where a level of intermediate management was necessary because the Records Centre Operations Manager found it impossible to spend enough time on each of the three sites to resolve the inevitable minor conflicts between the operating teams. People rose to the challenge, accepted individual responsibility for what they did, and grew in the job. When the third site came on line in a totally different part of the country, we took the opportunity to test new ideas with a workforce completely unfamiliar with the "customs and practices" of the older sites and then fed those ideas that worked back into the older operations. Healthy competition between the sites was used to boost overall performance still further.

The bank was still reluctant to allow the records services operation to recruit new permanent employees. The RMPU, almost throughout its existence, had only one permanent employee—its head. In the GAU, both the senior archivist and her assistant were initially recruited on short-term contracts "with a possibility" of continuing, which was realized. Some staff members were successfully rethreaded from other parts of the business. We became adept at using "short-term" agency staff, trained to the same level as their full-time colleagues and fully integrated into the operation. They were often reluctant to leave even when better, permanent jobs came along and many were eventually offered permanent terms when the bank recognized that there was a continuing job for them to do.

Employing agency staff and encouraging them to contribute fully brought talented people into the business that might otherwise have been missed. For example, the head of customer services had returned to work half-time as a camera operator in the microfilm unit when her children went to school but was clearly capable of more challenging work. The warehouse team leader on one of the new sites was a fine arts graduate who crackled with ideas. The computer systems supervisor had originally come on board to drive a forklift. Over time, all these people became key contributors to the development of strategic and business plans and to ensuring the continuing success of the minibusiness.

SETTING PEOPLE FREE

It is important to have confidence in your subordinate managers. One of the downsides of the impact of the records centre business on management time was that the records professionals running the RMPU and the GAU were forced to work on their own initiative. It was important that they felt both able and competent to do so. They responded well to working to agreed plans, results and outcomes. They were given the opportunity to discuss and agree what needed to be done without being told how to do it. They were encouraged to use their own initiative and best judgment and to look for help and guidance only if they felt that a challenge was totally beyond them.

They were also encouraged to recruit the best and the brightest people they could find to support them in their work. For the RMPU there was a shortage of qualified records professionals in the marketplace at the time the work started. We decided that it was more important to use intelligent, trainable people, rather than insist on having fully qualified professionals. In addition, the bank was reluctant to allow the recruitment of permanent staff to carry out what they saw as an interim operation. The solution was to recruit other information professionals through a specialized agency and then train them in the techniques that we expected them to use. It was clear that the development of academic professional training for record-keeping people was geared more towards the public sector and mainstream archival work. Despite their best efforts to widen the take up of their courses, the universities providing academic education could only select from the candidates who applied. The majority of those continued to be attracted to the profession because they wanted to work with "old documents". Younger archivists were also reluctant, initially, to take on fixed term contract work of the kind that we were offering.

MANAGING THE FUTURE

Most corporate record-keeping operations suffer from the difficulties of continuity and succession planning. Small units, flat management structures and an absence of promotion and personal development opportunities make retention of talent and a natural transition almost impossible to achieve. Although we worked hard at building loyalty and expertise amongst our professional staff, it was not always possible to keep the brightest and best of them. It was essential to maintain a flat management structure across the record services operation because the company had become very sensitive to the "management creep" which had occurred in other areas of the business. Consequently, the unit managers were all at a similar level, and there was no effective deputy. In the case of junior staff, there were few promotion opportunities within the bank, which meant that, having recruited highly qualified, able and ambitious young professionals, we were unable to keep them for longer than two or three years. The relatively high remuneration packages provided by a major commercial bank also meant that the second-tier managers became effectively tied to the bank, unless they were able to find a promotion post in a similar organization. There was very little mobility.

The older professionals had a challenging and financially worthwhile position. Their subordinates were therefore waiting for dead men's shoes if they wished to maintain their career within the bank. The alternative was that they could retrain to do something else, while remaining inside the organization, or they could leave in pursuit of something more challenging and suited to their experience and expertise. We were effectively training and developing young professionals for the benefit of other organizations. This is a not uncommon situation amongst records professionals in the United Kingdom. Succession planning, using existing staff, was difficult, and it was almost inevitable that succession would involve external recruitment.

The inherent risk was that, when the time came, the bank would choose to do what many other organizations had done and split up the record services business and destroy the integrated approach which had been the basis of everything we had done. Flat management structures mean that subordinate managers are recruited for the skills they bring to the specific task rather than for their potential to lead the organization. There is little room or opportunity to develop any one of them as a deputy to ultimately inherit the leadership seat even though they were provided with every possible opportunity to enhance their skills. If for any reason the external recruitment process was delayed or postponed, the organization would be without professional leadership, a management vacuum would be created and the coherent co-ordinating vision would be lost. The individual units would continue to function but on different terms and within a less committed environment.

At Barclays, the integrated records services operation was broken up in 2001, though the individual component parts continue to work in different parts of the business and still maintain a close functional relationship. This mirrors, at least in the United Kingdom, the fate of many corporate archives and records management programs, which have failed to survive the departure of the relatively strong individual who established the pioneering program. At Barclays only the size of the records centre operation gave real impact and weight to the integrated business. The centre has remained strong and, despite attempts to contract it out, remains within the bank. Even though the amount of paper in the banking system has reduced substantially, the tipping point has yet to be reached and large quantities of paper records are still generated and need to be managed. The Group Archives Unit has been able to embed itself in the corporate culture because we deliberately aimed at making it serve the corporate body, but the aim of a managed flow has not been fully realized.

Breaking up the integrated whole meant that the initial strategy proved unsustainable. The RMPU, despite doing excellent work at a local level, never really achieved a complete breakthrough in developing record-keeping systems. Its time and effort were constantly being re-focused into supporting shorter term programs, effecting changes in the way the bank delivered its customer services. We were contributing to the bank's strategic operating needs but unable to achieve our wider strategic record-keeping objectives which would have benefited the organization in the long run. Relocating the records services business to an operating division reduced our ability to directly influence management at the highest level on the wider need for improved record-keeping practices. Our revised record-keeping strategy, designed to help the bank manage in the electronic world, was recognized as providing a strong case for action and for identifying real and realizable benefits. However, our divisional director was reluctant to take it forward to the next level because he felt, probably quite rightly, that, given the other initiatives which were occupying his colleagues at the time, there would be little appetite for it. The projected savings of £35 million per annum in year 3 were simply not sufficient to catch the eye in a change program expected to deliver savings of £5 billion. What was more important was the initial cost of the project itself. Spending £3 million on a "filing" project would never get off the ground at a time when they were preparing to spend £15 million on a high speed cheque image archive system which ultimately failed to deliver.

Significantly, real progress has only recently been made as a result of an influx of powerful executives from the United States into Barclays' investment banking and capital markets operations. Concerned about the potential impact of the Sarbanes-Oxley Act (2002), which tightened record-keeping and accountability requirements in the United States, they set up a project in the Group Risk Division to develop effective records retention programs across the Group. Finally there were executives in the business who at last recognized good record-keeping as a priority in managing risk and were prepared to invest some of their money and their influence in making it happen. Our strategic wheel had been totally reinvented by non-records professionals with real executive clout.

CONCLUSION

Most large records programs in the U.K. corporate sector have ended in relative failure. Very few survive intact in the absence of strong leadership because they appear to be solving yesterday's problem when management is trying to find a solution to tomorrow's challenge. This is particularly true when outcomes are neither tangible nor visible. Senior managers like to see tangible returns on their investment. We were able to obtain investment in large storage facilities and the equipment to run them, both because the warehouses were assets which could be sold in the future and because the operating space released was immediately realizable. Managers are prepared, often under pressure from the substantial marketing budgets of technology vendors, to invest in equipment and software for managing record-keeping but not the essential professional expertise to ensure the investment is fully realized. Record-keeping risks are not fully understood or are dismissed as being too difficult to quantify. Change management issues are not appreciated or allowed for in development programs. Similarly, the strategic aspects of the records program are easily overlooked once the "big things" have been achieved. Momentum is difficult to sustain once these become part of "the way we do things" and so lose their immediate edge. All the component parts of the Barclays' record-keeping operation remain in place but they have become routine rather than strategic and leading edge. The "way we do things" changes and appears to need new solutions from new people with new ideas, rather than the continued application of sound professional principles in new circumstances. The records professional needs the flexibility and knowledge to ensure that the record-keeping strategy remains aligned with the wider business. The inevitable breaks in the leadership chain in most corporate programs, combined with the difficulty of maintaining continuity of executive commitment, make this difficult, if not impossible, to achieve.

NOTE

1. Operational retention reviews were a "quick and dirty" approach to reducing the volume of hard-copy records in office areas aimed at providing immediate benefits to the sharp-end of the business. The method involved identifying the principal functions and activities of the business unit concerned and the series of records generated by those activities and then deciding with the people involved what it was that they needed, day to day, to do their job. The resultant schedules did not define the ultimate retention period for the records concerned but acted as a trigger for immediate action. Those that were not so designated were either destroyed if they if they were ephemeral or boxed, listed and shipped by the project team. Final retention periods were added subsequently, following more analysis and research, to create a formal retention schedule for the business unit. We have used this practice with some success in our consulting practice as a pragmatic way of meeting challenging relocation and accommodation requirements.

Chapter 6

Competing for Relevance: Archives in a Multiprogram Organization

James E. Fogerty

Achieving relevance is the key to successful management of archives within a multiprogram organization. This relevance has two dimensions: (1) the internal relevance achieved when an archives identifies and serves the parent organization's objectives, and (2) a relevance of equal importance that is achieved when the archives' management correctly identifies external constituencies whose support contributes to both programmatic and financial success.

"OPPORTUNITY AND ADAPTATION"—THE ARCHIVIST'S MANTRA

Archives have not often been seen as places of leading-edge innovation, and archivists have seldom been held up as paragons of adaptability. Even now one is often pained to hear the recriminations of one's colleagues against the ravages that time and forward movement have had on archival practice. Archivists have always had to contend with change, but seldom has that change been visited upon them with such velocity as in the past 20 years. The advent of electronic communication and information has altered archivists' relationships with both their clients and their chief products as surely as it has brought the *wares*—software, hardware, groupware, etc.—into their shared lexicon. It is fashionable to view an apparently endless cycle of adaptation as exciting. For once fashion may be accurate, for in the current world of information creation and delivery both the opportunities and the adaptation they demand offer archivists unparalleled chances to control the information that is their most important product. These chances will be realized to the extent that archivists seize them and realize what they provide and whom they serve.

Most animals gravitate to the familiar and distrust the unfamiliar and the different; the human animal is no different than any other in this respect. Archivists have been characterized (when they have been characterized at all) as among the more reluctant human animals to accept—much less to court—change and the choices it brings. Part of this undoubtedly has to do with the lack of resources archivists have had to work with; it is hard to deal with change when one has barely assembled the resources to deal with the way things are. But we live and work in an era in which few things are more certain than change itself. It is imperative that archival managers understand and even embrace this reality and create a working climate that encourages their staff to do the same. If archives are viewed as past-oriented and resistant to change they will suffer accordingly in resource allocation.

INSTITUTIONAL CONTEXT

All writers bring their own experiences to bear on the topics they address. In order to lend some context to my own observations, let me provide this note on my own experience in directing archives and oral history programs.

The Minnesota Historical Society (MHS) is a multiprogram institution that is one of the largest historical organizations in the country. It is a private organization that receives the majority of its funding from the state—though the percentage of the budget that is state funded has declined dramatically in recent years. The archival operations form an important component of the society's work, but they are only one aspect of it. The MHS employs more than 300 people, operates a network of 20 historic sites across the state, maintains an education office and museum, and in 1992 moved into a new $80-million headquarters in St. Paul. We deal with more than 100,000 elementary and secondary school students each year, and with teachers in schools throughout the state.

Although our programs are large, as is the funding that supports them, we are only too well aware of the very real bottom line. Like any business or cultural institution, we must deal with demands for service that often exceed our capabilities. And we are strongly aware that our success in acquiring funds for our programs is directly related to the success of our operations. We cannot afford mediocrity; neither can we afford the dubious luxury of hand-wringing over the need to match work and resources.

In the field of archives, the MHS holds one of the two largest collections of business records in the United States. The other is at Hagley Museum and Library in Delaware. Among the scores of companies whose archival records are held by the society are those of 3M, Northwest Airlines, International Multifoods, Honeywell, American Crystal Sugar, and the Great Northern, Northern Pacific, and Soo Line railroads. The railroad archives alone include more than 10,000 cubic feet of records that document the settlement and industrial development of the entire northwestern third of the United States. Business history is thus central to the Society's work.

IDENTIFYING INTERNAL NEEDS AND OBJECTIVES

The success of any unit—including archives—in any organization will hinge on the ability of its managers to correctly identify and serve the needs and objectives of the parent entity. It is most helpful, of course, when top management has embraced change and understands—and supports—programs that emphasize service as an important component of the archives' mission. Clearly, the organization's top management unit is the most critical client of all—but it is seldom the only important client. There will usually be other units with needs that are seen as highly important to institutional success, and the ability to identify and serve those needs is critical. Inherent in this work is the archival manager's ability to discern which of the other units are, or should be, key clients of the archives.

The concept of *intraprise*—the internal marketing of products and services by one corporate unit to another—has gained considerable momentum, and can be applied to archival units as well as any others. "Free intraprise empowers ordinary employees to start a 'business' (or intraprise) within the organization if they can find the customers and capital to do so" (Pinchot and Pinchot, 1993: 114). The archives of the Royal Bank of Canada has chosen this approach with great success (Rabchuk, 1997: 34), and even in nonprofit organizations like MHS this concept works very well. We aggressively pursue opportunities to provide products and services to our Development Office, Education and Exhibits departments, and to senior administration. We employ our holdings as assets and use them to earn a real return for our work.

The key to building such support is knowledge of the work and the needs of other institutional programs. Talking with other unit managers, learning their operational goals and the audiences they serve—and wish to serve—will help identify those areas in which the archives can provide support. Education programs need content and support to develop compelling programs for a variety of audiences, from schoolchildren to families and seniors. Publication offices also need content, and can benefit from connection to researchers whose use of the archives may produce potential publications. A Public Relations Department is always in need of information, and of staff who can articulate information about institutional resources and serve as informative and interesting commentators for local news outlets.

No archives manager can afford to neglect the institutional Development Office, which is often the conduit to funding and to visibility at the highest levels of institutional management. Archives staff can provide critical links to existing donors and important service in the work of dealing with new and potential donors. Donors of family and business materials to an archive, for instance, can become important donors of financial support to the institution, thus establishing the archives as a key player in this vital activity.

The identification of internal objectives is key, but it does not ensure the level of staff buy-in needed to initiate a successful program based on service rather than on the production of traditional archival output. Staff must be relentlessly reminded that the world has changed, and that their relevance is directly tied to the value placed on their work by a wide variety of constituencies for which they must provide service.

At MHS this work has been greatly facilitated by administrative support for initiatives that have channeled archives material and staff expertise into a large number of institutional programs. It also helps that archives staff have been actively engaged in rethinking and refining everything from appraisal to processing with an eye to reducing labor while increasing service. The widely known (if somewhat controversial) "Minnesota Method" (Greene and Daniels-Howell, 1997) and the recent work of Mark Greene and Dennis Meissner (Greene and Meissner, 2005) are testament to that thinking and its results.

IDENTIFYING EXTERNAL NEEDS AND OBJECTIVES

Perhaps the most important step in identifying the needs and objectives of external constituencies is an understanding of the institution's own goals and objectives. Who are key constituents currently important to the institution, and who are those the institution wishes to become important consumers and supporters of its resources and programs? The answers to those questions will help identify the external constituents of greatest importance to the parent institution.

Think creatively—and beyond the confines of regular archival management. We live in a service economy—and archives can provide an array of services to a variety of clients. Be entrepreneurial when seeking opportunities. As with business records—you do not have to *take* the records in order to accomplish a task. Indeed, the work of managing records for others may well mean far more in terms of meeting both internal and external needs and objectives than any attempt to take on ownership of the materials in question. Strategies for developing such projects will be addressed in the following section.

Peter Drucker, the late management guru whose appreciation for history provided critical support for much of what archivists do, made many comments over the years of value to archival managers. Noting that we live in unsettled times, and that the future structure of business is far from certain, he gives explicit advice that archivists can hardly afford to ignore. "A time of turbulence is a dangerous time," he writes, "but its greatest danger is a temptation to resist reality." Turbulence is not necessarily a negative in Drucker's view, but rather a time "of great opportunity for those who can understand, accept, and exploit the new realities. It is above all a time of opportunity for leadership." Drucker points out the absolute need for "the decision maker in the individual enterprise to face up to reality and to resist the temptation of the certainties of yesterday, which are about to become the deleterious superstitions of tomorrow" (Drucker, 1980: 4–5). Archivists are such decision makers, with clear opportunities to influence the future of documentation and its uses. But to do this they must be players in the game—not spectators and not victims of change. Archivists are players when they heed Drucker's advice, embracing reality for what it is and taking an active role in dealing with it.

An example of this opportunistic approach to archives management is given by Laura Linard and Brent Sverdloff of the Harvard Business School Archives, who recognize what archivists at the Hagley Museum and Library and the MHS have known for some time: Business history is, if not yet a sideline, at least no longer primary. Nontraditional users are primary and the ability to recognize these emerging constituencies and their needs is critical. Linard and Sverdloff (1997: 97) state that "we are in an age of interdisciplinary studies. Scholars across the board are crossing conventional boundaries . . . ," and they note among their users those "examining the evolution of shopping arcades from the Turkish bazaar forward, to a Jane Austen scholar seeking more information on people and events alluded to in her novels." Thus, an academic archives with a fairly well-defined clientele can embrace service to new and varied groups of users, enhancing its utility and its relevance.

WHY BUSINESS?

Many of my comments focus on building relations with business—corporate America. The reasons for this are few and simple. My own experience in building archives and associated programs such as oral history has most often focused on corporations as likely partners. Corporations have many needs that can be addressed by the sort of information organizing and generating talents that resourceful archivists have in abundance. There are a multitude of businesses in a plethora of industries—with both common and quite individual needs.

Beyond that reality is the fact that any large, multiprogram, nonprofit organization is constantly in need of funds—and business has money. The timely intersection of program expertise, service needs, and available funding is evident.

We live in a corporate age. The heroes of the day are people like Bill Gates and Warren Buffet, Donna Karan, and Ralph Lauren. These people may not have started out to be corporate leaders, but corporate leaders they became and are. Business is at the center of American life, and increasingly it is at the center of life throughout the planet. The Soviet Union has collapsed and entered—however tentatively—the market age, and China—a centuries-old citadel of capitalist ardor despite the years of Maoist rhetoric—is now the home of countless new companies and no fewer than four stock exchanges.

At the same time governments have undergone a sea change in popular sentiment concerning their size and the ways in which they spend their money. In the United States this trend is pronounced, as federal, state, and local governments come under pressure to reduce their size and expenditures. Nowhere has this change in attitude produced more angst—and, belatedly, change—than in the world of the nonprofit, cultural institution.

Most archival programs belong to the world of nonprofit, largely cultural organizations that live and die by the strength of their funding channels. Without much earned income, and with legal restraints on many avenues of entrepreneurial development, they depend upon the interested generosity of individuals and corporations. While many continue to feed at the public trough, few can afford to indulge in the illusion that complete reliance on public funding is possible, much less probable—or, I might add, even desirable. They must rely increasingly on funding from nongovernment sources, and in particular from business.

I mentioned earlier that cultural institutions depend on the generosity of individuals and corporations. That sounds quite accurate and yet it is not quite true. They rely, in fact, only on individuals. Corporations are, after all, aggregations of individuals who make decisions based upon their individual and collective sense of what is useful in a given situation. Just as family giving may change with the generations, so corporate giving changes with the philosophy and interests of those in power within the corporation. Those interests may not be the only determining factors, but they are never unimportant. Corporate giving also changes—as does personal philanthropy—with changes in fashion, and the successful curators and development officers are those who are able to sense those trends and relate their work and needs appropriately.

The reality of corporate partnering is often fraught with difficulty for the staff of a cultural institution seeking partners. A good part of this difficulty may be in the minds of the staff members themselves, often reared and even trained, unfortunately, to distrust corporate affiliation and to feel, or at least to affect, disdain for the affairs of the marketplace. It is never easy to raise money from people whose work you do not understand, and whose motives you distrust.

Raising money in one way or another is, never doubt it, at the root of all desire on the part of cultural institutions for corporate relationships. Whether the support comes in the form of an outright grant to an endowment fund, direct support for an exhibit or special project, or a corporate partnership that creates advertising opportunities that the institution could never afford on its own, the bottom line is money.

Making such a partnership work requires, if not a leap, then at least a giant step of faith on the part of both parties because individuals in both are subject to preconceptions about the others. Staff of the cultural institution are likely to view their corporate counterparts as experts in last-minute decisions and unreasonable demands that argue poor planning and a misunderstanding of what it takes to stage exhibits, events, and other programs within the institution. They view them as superficial, arrogant, and in high-handed search of something for nothing.

The corporate staff view of the cultural institution is not much different. Their view is likely to be that staff of the nonprofit are slow, unresponsive, and far too academic to make suitable partners. They may view them also as demanding and unschooled in the realities of corporate life. And they certainly may reciprocate the view that the nonprofit's staff is in earnest search of something for nothing.

How, then, can such relationships be made to work to serve the objectives of both potential partners? The first step can be taken by the nonprofit staff when they accept the fact that gifts—especially substantial gifts—very seldom come without expectations. Individuals expect recognition—witness the often bewildering array of named galleries, courtyards, fountains, libraries, and less-exalted spaces in any successful museum, and the private briefings, behind-the-scenes tours, and special displays churned out like clockwork by the staff of any institution involved in fund-raising. Expectations will always be there—on both sides—and need to be clearly delineated so that everyone understands exactly what they are.

For the cultural organization, this process entails understanding what its objectives are in seeking corporate partnerships, and in articulating what it is—and is not—willing to do to make such an alliance work. All too often such attempted partnerships flounder because staff of the nonprofit have one of two attitudes toward them: (1) "Give us the money and we'll tell you what we can do for you," or (2) "Give us the money and we'll do anything for you." Neither will work, of course, but that does not appear to stop any number of institutions from trying them.

I'll illustrate one form of successful partnership from my own experience at the MHS. The corporate records, oral history, and sound and visual collections have proven especially useful in building corporate partnerships.

I have noted that the MHS holds one of the largest archives of corporate records in the United States. The holdings have always been strong in the area of business, but that strength has deepened and broadened greatly in the past 20 years, as have the services we've developed to offer corporations. Simply getting in the door to discuss a corporation's historical records can be a challenge, and I learned early on that history and the social value of business records were not particularly effective marketing tools in and of themselves. That's part of another lesson: If you're going to market what you do, you'd better learn the consumer's language. Telling corporate managers—as one archivist confided to me he had done—that the corporate records they controlled should be given to an archives because the company owed it to society and to history, is an argument that still (nearly) deprives me of speech. It is, unfortunately, not an isolated argument. But it is seldom going to prove successful.

At MHS, our success in working with corporations is built upon a solid foundation of understanding—of our own goals, and those of the companies with which we work. Those goals include a clearly articulated desire to enhance the value of our business collections to users from inside and outside the companies themselves. We have developed archives and oral history projects that add value to our holdings while creating value for the companies that become our partners. Although the management of corporate archives by an agency outside the corporation may strike some as unusual, the MHS (and the Hagley Museum and Library in Delaware) have been involved in such programs for more than 50 years. The corporate archives are governed by contracts negotiated between the MHS and the donor corporations, and the MHS employees involved in managing those records sign confidentiality agreements that mirror those signed by corporate employees.

Constructing partnerships that actually mean something to corporate staff and management is challenging, but it can be done if one takes time to learn about their work and needs. That acquired knowledge can lead the archival manager to devise successful strategies to address specific needs. The work we do with our corporate clients tends to fall into one or more of the following areas.

Records Management and Archives Development

Most companies have far more records lying around than they need to do business. While throwing out records is a not uncommon corporate pastime, there is a far more widely felt disinclination to part with records without some guidance on what to keep and what to throw out. That is where the records management comes in. Archives development comes in play in managing the retained records—which need organization, storage, and easy access in order to retain value. For example, MHS has helped organize corporate archives for General Mills, Pillsbury, H. B. Fuller, and Medtronic. Recently the Society took on the task of organizing and processing the archives of Andersen Corporation. Such work can provide a revenue stream (thus proving to institutional management the value placed on archives work and skills in the business world), and also invaluable partnerships. Major funding for the nonprofit's institutional programs is much more likely to come from corporations that have benefited from skills provided by the nonprofit. Please note, once again, in such cases the archives doesn't have to *take* additional records at all, but rather to provide service and expertise as a product for pay.

Oral History

As inventor and company founder Earl Bakken once told our director and me, "The records are all very fine. But if you don't know how a product was really developed—who worked with whom, how refinements were produced, which ideas worked and which didn't and why—you are missing the core of the story. None of those pieces of information are written down," he said. "They are all in people's memories."

   The creator of the implantable heart pacemaker—and of corporate giant Medtronic, the largest company in the world in that field—was right. Our corporate oral history program is based on that home truth—that in people's minds lies far more information than is ever written down, and that the telling of it in their own words adds immeasurable color and interest and value to the historical record (Fogerty, 1997). In addition to oral histories with individual companies, we managed an industry project called "Pioneers of the Medical Device Industry." Funded by industry leaders, it collected vital information from the people who made the history. Anyone who has seen the video interview with Earl Bakken and Dr. C. Walton Lillehei—the surgeon who worked with Bakken to develop and perfect the pacemaker—knows the power of oral history. Even before the medical device project was completed the interviews were already in demand. Commercial and scholarly writers, a television producer, and two national medical associations were working with the material before we finished the final work. An excerpt of the Bakken-Lillehei interview was shown to several thousand people at a national medical convention and brought the Society additional attention and credibility with both donors and users.

Corporate Product Enhancement

By corporate product enhancement I mean just that—the work of ensuring that certain defined products developed by or for the corporation are enhanced by partnership with a non-profit institution. Examples include the production of corporate histories, advertising campaigns, exhibits, corporate events, and employee training.

Here are some recent—and some continuing—examples of actual work in corporate product enhancement. American Crystal Sugar Company, one of the largest beet sugar processors in the nation, recently completed a centennial history. We helped select the firm hired to write it, provided extensive special assistance in accessing the records and in particular the spectacular photographic archives of the Company held at MHS, and even worked to ensure that digital images of all the photographs used were created on site at the Society, with staff assistance.

For 3M Company we provide access to records needed for immediate uses such as a corporate review of executive compensation, an executive biography file needed for a news release on the death of a former executive, advertising copy needed for the reintroduction of a product line, and the production of a corporate history and video for the Company's centennial celebration.

For Northwest Airlines we worked with marketing teams preparing an international celebration of the company's 50 years of trans-Pacific service, produced an exhibit on that milestone event, and encouraged the selection of the Minnesota History Center as the site of the huge international party Northwest threw to launch the anniversary year. The success of all these endeavors—and especially of the exhibit produced under the gun of a deadly timeline—has stood us in good stead with this corporation.

For Graco, Inc., we have undertaken two oral history projects. The first documented the growth of this major Minnesota corporation and included an interview with one of the Company's founders only a year before his death. That vibrant, table-thumping, cigar-chomping narrator provided an invaluable (and colorful) look at the Company's early years that has been widely used since. That project was followed by acquisition of the company's archives, and now by a second oral history project to document the Company's transition from family management to management by outsiders. As a note, the longtime CEO of this corporation later joined the Society's Board of Trustees and served as president and a tremendously influential fundraiser.

Within the past year, a major bank expressed a desire to partner with the Society in the production of several events for its wealth management units and their clients. The archives became the major vehicle used in the production of these events with their emphasis on legacy and the value of family and corporate history. The work involved was considerable, involving dozens of staff in the production of elaborate exhibits and programs that, in each case, were available only to this elite audience for the duration of the event.

The benefits of this work were also considerable, as clients of great interest to the Development office were gathered to celebrate their own legacies and to experience the Society's role in legacy preservation. The events reinforced ties to existing supporters of the Society, while bringing in others who had not previously interacted with the institution.

I hope you have noted the common thread linking these selected real-world examples: each of them involved projects of business interest to our corporate partners and clients. Each involved definable contributions to the company's own plan of work—and yet served the Society's aims and goals as well. None of them involved the marketing of history for history's sake alone. There must be tangible, mutual benefit, or the partnership will not work.

Above all, I'd like to banish the notion that "history just doesn't sell in corporate America" and that business is uninterested in it. History—properly packaged and presented with an eye to the mutual benefit of corporations and the holders and purveyors of history—has a very definite place in world of American business.

CREATING THE MIND-SET

Linking service provided to an understanding of a company's culture is critical to archives, whether they exist within or outside a profit-making corporate structure. Part and parcel of this understanding is recognizing that many organizations—including businesses—have been transformed into what Peter Drucker has called the "information-based organization." He predicted that the business of the future—already in development—will resemble in some ways such entities as universities and hospitals—"knowledge-based [and] composed largely of specialists who direct and discipline their own performance through organized feedback from colleagues, customers, and headquarters" (Drucker, 1991: 46). Archives retail knowledge and information, and as our colleagues in records management have already noted, "it is indeed time for those of us in the alleged information business to determine if we are in the paper schlepping business or true participants in the management of information" (Constantini, 1994: 27).

In realizing this goal—of managing and retailing information—archivists must be creators as well as managers, a role that has not come easily to many. Archivists have been slow, for instance, to adopt the use of oral history to expand their reach and resources—not only because of the added expense, but because it forces them to create new documents rather than waiting passively to receive them. If archives and the information they contain are to receive tangible value in an increasingly value conscious world, then the real, bottom line value of documentation must be made clear. This does not mean that every corporation will subscribe to investment in archives or history, but merely that the opportunity to sell such an investment to management is considerably greater when such links can be made. The links, of course, must be supported by more than words and promises; the documentation itself must support such uses. It can, if an archives is managed with imagination and attention to the real needs of both corporate personnel and a wider audience than that provided by the traditional users of history.

Concern with the bottom line is not restricted to archives in the

United States, nor is it exclusive to business archives. Michael Moss and Lesley Richmond of the Scottish Business Archives Centre, writing in *The Records of American Business* (1997: 385), note that "archivists in European countries where there has been a more corporatist tradition are no more insulated from financial pressures than their counterparts in North America. There have, for some time," they state, "been severe constraints on the finances of government, both national and local, which provides the bulk of archives services either directly or indirectly. This has forced many archives to look for ways of exploiting the revenue-earning potential of their collections." Such pressures seem likely to increase in the future.

SEIZING OPPORTUNITY—EXAMPLES FROM THE REAL WORLD

Media Partnerships. The term is quite current, and holds the promise of everything the media offers in a land where access to public consciousness seems the key to relevance and survival. Media equals publicity, access to thousands with a single message, and the glamour of being where the action is. It is television—the American invention, with its ability to thrust its audience into the center of any story. It is newspapers, with their headlines scrutinized daily even by those who read little. It is radio, with its access to another great American icon—the automobile—and those who occupy it for hours each day.

To be in partnership with any facet of the media is the dream and the work of at least a few people in nearly every enterprise that needs to spread a message quickly and effectively. Advertising—buying time in the media to spread a message—is open to those with fat wallets, aided by a phalanx of professionals whose work is the use of media to the end of whatever message they are paid to manufacture. The media are reviled at the same time they are courted, and regardless of the often brazenly commercial world in which they operate, play key roles in determining the image—and thus the success—of virtually every endeavor that wants attention and a favorable place in the public mind.

Cultural and educational organizations do not often excel in finding and exploiting new avenues to popularize their work. In recent years, however, most major—and even some minor—cultural institutions have employed at least one person (and sometimes many more) to publicize their work, their holdings, their exhibits, their benefactors, and their goals. Seeking this publicity can be a daunting task, especially from a beachhead in an institution with staff that have only reluctantly accepted the need to court media attention—even in the cause of winning public favor. An investment in working with the media may be seen as effort diverted from the core work of the institution—even as that core work suffers from a lack of resources. It is this decline in resources that has led some institutions to reject the decision to suffer passively in silence and anonymity.

Archivists and librarians have come late to the decision to court the media, and many have not made the decision at all. Witness the failure to date of several attempts to market a public relations workshop within the Society of American Archivists. Can the same people who complain endlessly of a lack of adequate funding not make the connection with the need to market their resources and their relevance to a wider public? There have been exceptions, of course—Elsie Freeman Finch, David Gracy, Karen Benedict, Bruce Bruemmer, and Elizabeth Adkins come to mind. Freeman's landmark work in "advocating archives" remains a standard (Finch, 1994).

One of many examples of media partnerships at the Society is that negotiated with KSTP Television, a major Minnesota station owned by Hubbard Broadcasting. Hubbard is one of the largest independent television and radio companies in the nation, with a large presence in satellite broadcasting as well.

A producer at the station came to the Society with a proposal for a prime-time documentary entitled "Family Portraits." It was to be based on the multigenerational histories of three Minnesota family groups, and would demand considerable staff input and use of items from the collections. Working with producer Teri McCormick from the beginning gave us a chance to influence both the selection of the families, and to some extent influence the way in which the stories would be told.

A major factor in the process of developing the documentary was the Society's role both in choosing the families and in persuading them to consent to the project. There was an obvious and necessary stipulation, given the nature of television, that at least one and hopefully more present-day members of each family would consent to appear on camera to be interviewed about family history and its influence on the current generation. KSTP personnel were clear in their expectations that the Society would undertake this work, thus leveraging the institution's credibility as a repository and guardian of the historical record. In one case the leading member of a prominent family consented to the use of her family in the story, but refused to appear on camera. That effectively ended the possibility of including her family— all my powers of persuasion could not move her to consent. In all other instances, happily, family members did consent, as did people like former governor Elmer Andersen, who appeared to comment on a prominent political member of one of the families. In all cases, it was the Society's participation in the project that led family members to agree to appear on camera. They were delighted and honored, a fact that did not hurt the Society at all.

Research for the documentary was excruciating at times, for, as McCormick once phrased it, "television is greedy." She meant that in a visual medium the need for constantly changing images to maintain interest and to illustrate both people and stories is never ending. We were always pushed to uncover yet more photographs, more film footage, more letters, diaries, civil war uniforms, wedding dresses, and the like. And each family segment demanded some on-site shooting, in addition to the taped interviews with family members. Much of the research was either done by or with the aid of our staff. We viewed the effort as an investment, and it paid off in a high profile product that was extremely successful.

What did we learn from this process? A great deal—and all of it valuable. Our media partners learned, too, and found the experience satisfying. The principal lessons we learned were these:

- BE FLEXIBLE: Television is a world of deadlines, most of them yesterday. Television producers will want you to allow a use of your collections that you may not allow to every user. Give way when you can, and strive to learn what they really need so that you can determine what is a genuine need, and what would simply be nice if it were possible. If you are genuinely flexible they will be, too. I well remember the moment at which the producer asked for the oil portrait of grain industry titan Frank Peavey to be brought from art storage for taping. We do not usually allow that, preferring to supply transparencies and slides. When I stated that I would produce the slides, one look at McCormick's face let me know her reaction to that suggestion. She carefully explained why she preferred to film the actual portrait, and I made the decision to have it brought up immediately for filming. It was a compromise in a good cause.

- BE HELPFUL: View the experience as a valuable chance to present something of what your institution is and does to an audience you will not reach through any other means. Suggest items from your collections that will add to the interest and attraction of the product. If your ideas don't make sense to the producer, you will find that out. But often you will find that person pleased that you are part of the team, trying to ensure success.

- BE INVENTIVE: Inventory your holdings in your mind, at least, and think of them (and your programs) in light of the stories they represent that may tie in with current events, anniversaries, or personalities. Think of your institution as a storehouse of material for stories—whether they lend themselves to newspaper, television, radio, or other media use. Remember that the media are always in search of fresh perspectives, contrast between historical and current events, and anything at all that is unusual, provocative, or likely to be of interest to a wide public.

- LEARN: Use the experience to build knowledge of what this rarefied group of clients wants and needs. Watching a television crew work—whether in producing a newscast or a documentary—and participating in the development of a story and its presentation, is a terrific opportunity to learn about the requirements of an exacting medium. Watching Emmy-winning videographer Tim Jones of KSTP-TV turn photographs, portraits, and documents into living images was magic. Teri McCormick proved to be an outstanding professional with whom to work—articulate, demanding, challenging, but always willing to consider suggestions and to compromise as we compromised. Tim Jones was a consummate artist with his camera—weaving our collections, on-site photography and video interviews into a remarkable tapestry, and always able to work with us to ensure the safety of the materials while showcasing them beautifully in the production.

What do the media learn? Well, at best they learn that an archives is a source of information—both visual and textual—that can contribute to their work. They learn that preservation and use are not enemies. I had a goal of working to ensure that KSTP—and subsequently our other television and newspaper partners—emerged from their work with the Minnesota Historical Society with an appreciation of the variety of opportunities the institution offers them, and with satisfaction at the relative ease of working with our staff. I wanted it to be an experience that led them to say, "Hey, let's do this again!"

They have worked with us. The careful cultivation of local media, and cooperation with their objectives and timelines, has made the archives and oral history program regular contributors to the news. When Pillsbury was sold to General Mills, when International Multifoods was bought by Smuckers, when recording family history is featured, our staff become the on-air providers of information, perspective, and authority. We have become a valued source of data and commentary, and the very public credit the Society receives for this work is priceless. The institution is presented to a wide public as a major source of trustworthy information and impartial content, and earns air time we could never afford to purchase.

In the end it is service that provides the best evidence of commitment and the most memorable testaments as well. With one of the largest television newsfilm archives in the country, I need hardly add that timely delivery is everything. The need is immediate and the product must be located and delivered with absolute accuracy. The rapid movement of events and the utter uselessness of film delivered even one hour too late for use on the evening news dictates a level of commitment that the archives must demonstrate time and time again. I have on my desk a very heartening letter from the news director for that broadcaster—and news directors are not noted for either generosity or patience. His lavish praise for our staff's ability to repeatedly deliver film segments within an hour of request is appreciated, as is the fact that he copied his letter to the president of the television company and the chairman of its parent corporation.

It is that level of trust and expectation that can reap tangible benefits for the archives. In this instance we not only hold a resource of enduring and increasing value, but also received nearly a million dollars for equipment and preservation as a gift from the donor corporation.

So it goes. The presence of a Public Relations and Marketing Office, strong support from administration and board, and the enthusiastic participation of many staff have made our media partnerships work. Let there be no pretense—*it is more work*, on top of work that never seems to end. But it is worth it! We live in visual, media-influenced times, and we must use the media—work with the media—to fully realize the potential archives have to figure as major resources in this fast changing world. In the pursuit of resources one must increasingly demonstrate relevance to the world in which we live, and to a wide spectrum of interests. The media can help us do that, and we, in turn, can help the media supply their insatiable demands for material.

Stanley S. Hubbard, the media mogul whose vision has helped so very much to pave the Society's way in the competitive and fast-changing world of television, sees far greater opportunities in the future—and the not-so-distant future at that. Knowing the increasing segmentation of the television market brought about by the advent of cable, the profitability of offering information to people with specialized interests, and the desperate need for ever more programming, he has predicted far greater use of archival resources in the creation of program vehicles and the provision of data and visual material for them. THIS is relevance and utility on a scale that helps balance the traditional archives reliance on genealogists and scholars. It is the packaging of our materials into products that reach far beyond the walls of our institutions, bringing both visibility and a sense of perceived value in ways not possible before. It is the future, and it is now!

CONCLUSION

If the goal of the multiprogram institution is relevance in the world around it, then a judiciously managed archives program is a critical component of that effort.

Relevance—real and perceived—is critical to *every* program, whether in a non-profit or for-profit setting. The test of relevance may seem more rigorous in a corporate environment, but in this day of funding challenges, no program can assume a free ride. And while the reality of relevance is highly important, the perception of relevance is hardly less so. Image may not be everything, but it counts for much in the rough and tumble world of resource allocation and fund raising. Archival management must be adept in creating relevance through use of the archives' holdings and its staff expertise, and equally adept in advancing the perception of relevance to both internal and external clients.

The perception must be supported by reality, of course. Efforts to create and enhance the relevance of archives can only succeed when they become "programmatic, not casual; regular, not occasional; integral institutional components, not add-ons" (Mooney, 1994: 63).

Success can be measured through a variety of means—from money raised, to institutional programs benefiting from archives support, to public relations initiatives that rely at least in part on the use of archival materials and the cooperation of the archives' staff. Satisfied constituents are also measurable—remembering that numbers do not always tell the tale. Key constituencies may be measured in hundreds and thousands when education and other public programs are considered, but key constituents may also be audiences of very few. A corporation or a prominent family may as easily be a key constituent as any other, and their satisfaction just as important in measuring overall institutional success.

It is helpful, of course, when the institution's administration is receptive to change, and actively supports efforts to incorporate it into the institutional ethos. Staff may be more reluctant to change traditional work patterns, but will usually respond to leadership and a clear indication that changes bring rewards in terms of increased appreciation for their skills and work—and thus their relevance to the organization.

Balancing investment with return is not always easy, especially when traditional activities are in part displaced by a new emphasis on service and competition. The cries of "sell out" will surely resound, at least for a while until the rewards of relevance become clear. While many programs will occasionally be subject to the crosswinds of pressure from various constituencies, I would argue strongly that the greater good is best served from a solid platform based on real, tangible support. One must place the greatest emphasis on those who deliver that support, both within and outside of the parent institution.

REFERENCES

Constantini, Jo Ann M. 1994. "Survival Skills for Information Professionals in the Decade of Turbulence." *Records Management Quarterly* (January): 26–31.

Drucker, Peter F. 1980. *Managing in Turbulent Times*. New York: Harper & Row.

Drucker, Peter F. 1991. "The Coming of the New Organization." *Harvard Business Review* 66 (January/February): 45–53.

Finch, Elsie Freeman, ed. 1994. *Advocating Archives: An Introduction to*

Public Relations for Archivists. Chicago: Society of American Archivists.

Fogerty, James E. 1997. "Facing Reality: Oral History, Corporate Culture, and the Documentation of Business." In *The Records of American Business*, 369–390. Edited by James M. O'Toole. Chicago: Society of American Archivists.

Greene, Mark A. and Todd J. Daniels-Howell. 1997. "Documentation with an Attitude: A Pragmatist's Guide to the Selection and Acquisition of Modern Business Records." In *The Records of American Business*, 161–229. Edited by James M. O'Toole. Chicago: Society of American Archivists.

Greene, Mark A. and Dennis Meissner. 2005. "More Product, Less Process: Revamping Traditional Archival Processing." *American Archivist* 68 (Fall–Winter): 208–263.

Linard, Laura and Brent M. Sverdloff. 1997. "Not Just Business as Usual: Evolving Trends in Historical Research at Baker Library." *American Archivist* 60 (Winter): 88–98.

Mooney, Philip F. 1994. "Modest Proposals: Marketing Ideas for the Expansionist Archives." In *Advocating Archives: An Introduction to Public Relations for Archivists*, 55–63. Edited by Elsie Freeman Finch. Chicago: Society of American Archivists.

Moss, Michael M. and Lesley M. Richmond. 1997. "Business Records: The Prospect from the Global Village." In *The Records of American Business*, 251–273. Edited by James M. O'Toole. Chicago: Society of American Archivists.

Pinchot, Giffort and Elizabeth Pinchot. 1993. *The End of Bureaucracy and the Rise of the Intelligent Organization.* San Francisco: Berret-Koehler.

Rabchuk, Gordon. 1997. "Life After the 'Big Bang': Business Archives in an Era of Disorder." *American Archivist* 60 (Winter): 34–43.

Chapter 7

Trying to Lead from Good to Great and Some Reflections on Leadership at All Levels

Mark A. Greene

INTRODUCTION

This chapter describes and reflects on my attempts to play a leadership role—envisioning needed changes, developing the rationale for those changes, making the necessary decisions, and putting the changes into effect—in several settings. My leadership work includes experience as a "lone arranger" in a private college archives (Carleton College); a low-level manager in a huge public/private historical society (Minnesota Historical Society); a mid-level manager at a private museum and research center (Henry Ford Museum and Greenfield Village); and as an upper-level manager at a small public university (director, American History Center [AHC], University of Wyoming, 2002+, where I report to the vice president of academic affairs/provost). I played leadership roles in each of these positions and in professional associations, particularly the Midwest Archives Conference and the Society of American Archivists. Most of my chapter focuses on my AHC role directing a large repository. But *leadership can and should exist at all levels of an organization.* Leaders "are ordinary people who decide to exercise leadership. They see relationships between their jobs and the larger environment. They see opportunities to be involved, to be innovative and to make a difference both personally and profession-

ally. Leaders facilitate change and movement into unfamiliar areas . . ."
(Mech, 1996: 345). The basic characteristics of leadership in an archives or manuscript repository are similar to those in a business or
library setting. "Leadership is not just for people at the top. Everyone can learn to lead by discovering the power that lies within each
one of us to make a difference, and by being prepared when the call
to lead comes" (Williams, 2006: 5). The chapter focuses on three key
leadership characteristics: (1) defining, disseminating, and implementing a vision; (2) defining and managing change; and (3) making decisions.

THE LEADERSHIP CHALLENGE AT AHC

Begun as the personal collection of distinguished University of Wyoming (UW) professor and trustee Grace Raymond Hebard, the nucleus
of UW's manuscripts and special collections were donated to the school
prior to Hebard's death in 1936. Twenty years later, the Department
of Western History and University Archives, created in 1945 and
housed within the University Library, welcomed a new director who
stayed for nearly 40 years (Shelstad, 2003).[1] The department grew and
was renamed the American Heritage Center; the director earned
praise for his vision and broad collecting but critics felt the collecting
lacked focus and that AHC had become "the vacuum cleaner of the
Plains." Hundreds of collections consisted of single publications, a
folder of newsclippings, or even copies of materials in other repositories. Several of AHC's largest and best-known collections, such as en-
tertainment (radio, TV, and movies), had little relationship to the
university's geographical region, which bothered some faculty and the
president hired in 1997. Virtually all of the department's resources
were devoted to collecting; little to cataloging, reference, or even
proper storage. By 1983, there was a 30,000-cubic-foot processing
backlog. Formal external reviews in 1980 by leaders of the Society of
American Archivists confirmed that the lack of collecting guidelines
and the "disproportionate amount of resources . . . concentrated on
soliciting for and acquiring archival collections at the expense of making them available for research" were professionally unacceptable
(Joyce, 1980: 5).

   A new director was appointed in 1988, professional staff were hired,
and concerted efforts were made to retrospectively acquire deeds of

gifts for undocumented collections previously acquired, end the most egregious collecting practices, and process the backlog. Staff worked with teaching faculty to bring undergraduates in for research in the collections. The professional archivists were granted faculty status, bringing them both increased stature and pay increases. But most of the archives program faculty were not confident enough to participate professionally outside of Wyoming and Colorado. A new building constructed in 1993 at huge expense to house the AHC and the University Art Museum was a frustrating failure in many important functional respects. The second director was let go in 2000, much to the consternation of some of the faculty and staff.

That same year, the vice president for academic affairs (provost), probably at the behest of the president, created a review board to determine whether the AHC should retain its administrative independence or be merged under the University Libraries. The administration was concerned about unfocused collecting, unprocessed backlogs, insufficient curricular engagement, and an antagonistic relationship between the director and the dean of the Libraries. Faculty and staff interpreted this as an attack on themselves and the AHC. Morale was low; employees were very defensive. The well-liked interim director was not hired for the permanent position. Instead, when I was appointed in 2002, after a national search, many people assumed my charge would be to gut the collections in line with the president's opinion that everything not related to Wyoming should be jettisoned. In fact, the university's expectations were much more supportive and comprehensive than that. The vice president for academic affairs who hired me asked me to critically assess the collections; improve intellectual access; expand AHC support for the undergraduate curriculum; make the AHC a regional leader in digitization; solve the stack space crisis; repair strained relationships with one of the university's most important friends who was also a collection donor; raise the stature and visibility of both the faculty and the AHC within the archival profession and the research community; and establish strong collaboration with the University Library and the University Art Museum.

I accepted the position for several reasons. The job brought me back West, where I spent my teen years, and closer to my father and sister. But more importantly, it was clear to me that the AHC was on the cusp of becoming a great institution, based on progress made since 1989: a core of exceptional collections; skilled, dedicated staff and faculty; successful commitment to broad access; dedication to outreach;

relatively new but aggressive digitization efforts; and a shift of emphasis from collecting to processing. I believed my experience and skills could help it achieve greatness: experience in collection development and definition; success in archival scholarship and professional service; the ability to promote a program in terms that resource allocators cared about; a willingness to take chances to achieve results; the capacity for setting visions and goals, identifying and managing change, and making the decisions and taking responsibility necessary to implement change. I had credibility with the university administration because of my record of publications and professional leadership and the vice president was very supportive.

The AHC in 2000 included an 85,000-cubic-foot manuscript collection, the university's archives, and a 45,000-item rare book library and served 9,000 researchers that year. The budget was approximately $1.2 million—45 percent from public funds (part of the university's block grant from the state) and 55 percent from endowment income, annual funds, and user fees. The AHC had no formal collecting policy or collection management policy. The one grant in place was for a digitization project called Western Trails. Depending on whether the number of collections or the volume of collections is considered, the AHC had 16 or 34 percent of its collections unprocessed, respectively. Only 20 percent of its collections were cataloged online. The center had a robust speaker's bureau and an active, mostly in-state traveling exhibit program and it administered the state's "History Day" program. There were 12 faculty members and as many nonfaculty employees (professional, paraprofessional, and administrative support), plus student workers. Only a few archivists, however, were active in the profession.

But I soon found that the program had strengths and potential. AHC reference faculty were working with more classes and more students than their counterparts at renowned repositories at world-class universities, and more than realized or appreciated by UW administration (Panitch, 2001). The state of its collecting policy, collection analysis, and processing work was really not much different from many other large repositories. AHC had developed a Web site that was among the most popular at the university and was cooperating in a collaborative digitization project. Part of my job would be communicating more clearly with the university's administration about the center's substantial accomplishments, as well as managing expectations about how much more we could do in certain areas with existing resources. By the same token, I had to work to communicate to the AHC faculty and staff that they should be proud and confident about their accomplishments, while at the same time starting to identify areas where change and improvement were needed.

CREATING A VISION FOR THE PROGRAM

Some important coincidences helped address a number of areas of concern. New directors were hired for the library and the art museum at the same time I was appointed. We quickly established solid personal and working relationships and collaboratively solved some long-standing problems: a new merged OPAC for AHC and library collections, a new protocol governing the acquisition of art materials. The unhappy vice president was appeased by assigning existing staff to process his large collection, reversing a previous decision to wait until he raised funds to pay for the work. I quickly provided ample evidence that it was common for major university special collections to acquire holdings outside the school's geographic area, so long as those regional and national collecting areas were well-defined and within the repository's resources. Addressing the remainder of the provost's concerns became my goal. I also added: raise employee morale and faculty confidence and scholarship expectations; bring in more grant money and monetary donations; convert paraprofessional processing positions to faculty level; improve the infrastructure; and establish my personal credibility and reliability. My goal was to accomplish most of this in five years.

As it happened, my arrival coincided with the beginning of university strategic planning for 2004–2009, a perfect opportunity for a strategic planning process involving AHC staff and faculty. I started the process by providing my own vision and guidance by placing some ideas on the table, insisting on a combination of realism and hope, and mediating the process of developing the vision and its change points. "The leader who can take the role of a facilitator blends his or her role of visionary decisive leader with that of listening and empowering leader" (Moore, 2004: 231). My vision was of a repository that would be a model to the profession in: collection management policy; collection analysis and policy, including deaccessioning as a tool for bringing existing collections into line with our new collecting goals; donor relations, acquisition, and appraisal, particularly in the areas of politics and business; intellectual access to collections, including reduction or elimination of our backlog and implementation of new processing approaches; reference (including bibliographic instruction and guest lectures) and outreach to undergraduates, K–12 students (including our administration of Wyoming History Day), and international researchers; security and holdings maintenance; general outreach to the public; broad participation and visibility of our faculty in national professional organizations; fund-raising; digitization efforts that are not solely dependent on grant funding but instead proceed as inherent institutional priority; and strong faculty and staff morale.

Our new plan, worked out through discussions over the next several months, was designed to address those issues. Our collection analysis and processing reengineering has meant understanding our holdings as a whole rather than as thousands of distinct accessions; our integration of building maintenance, holdings maintenance, and security systems has meant viewing our physical environment as a whole. Our conscious connection and interrelating of acquisition, accessioning, processing, and reference unified what are too often, in practice, disjointed functions. Vision was the key. "Leadership, in its essence, is the ability to articulate a vision or a desired path of progress and to motivate others to strive for that vision" (American Library Association, n.d.). I favor a simple definition of vision: "a vivid idea of what the future should be." This brief statement can be complemented by the following:

1. It should be tough, but achievable given sufficient effort.
2. It must be possible to tell when it has been achieved.
3. To maintain an impetus, it might also have a time limit so that people can pace their activity rather than getting winded in the initial push. (Blair, 1996)

The process of creating a new vision and mission statement relied on several full-day and part-day meetings with the entire center faculty and staff. The mission and vision statements went through several iterations, each time being presented for broad comment. While wordsmithing became difficult, the basic components of the statements achieved consensus relatively easily (Greene, 2003). My personal vision was not fully reflected in the formal statement that emerged, but that was to be expected from a collaborative process that commenced less than a year after I arrived at the AHC and relied on honest inclusion of multiple voices. I later concluded that the document would have been strengthened by including more coverage of the integrated approach to our work, broadening access, effective collection development, support for K–12 education, our desire to bring distinction on the university, and a statement about how we make our collections accessible to users—not just through cataloging but also through superior reference work, award-winning Web sites, etc.[2]

The next five-year planning process has already begun, and like the first round, will be informed by input from all AHC employees. But the mission and vision will not be the result of waiting or searching for consensus to emerge. As Herbert White, a dean at Indiana University, put it, "Many managers *seek* consensus, which is a determination of what the group wants. . . . Leaders, by contrast, do not *seek* consensus. They *build* it by persuading others to share their goals and their dreams" (Sheldon, 1991: 39).

In addition to articulating a vision, it is equally necessary to ensure that the vision—and its link to changes in the organization—is consistently and frequently made clear and visible. I was not sufficiently aware of the importance of consistent and constant repetition and reinforcement of the vision and goals. This affected faculty and staff perception of the meaning and purpose of the change, and hence to some extent undermined morale, but it did not handicap our success in achieving the plan's priorities. Even a process of defining vision that brings employees at all levels into the discussion and has strong initial buy-in quickly loses immediacy and fades from consciousness unless it is continually reinforced. While the boss may quickly internalize the vision and encourage the same in his or her department heads, the rest of the staff may quickly return to focusing on daily tasks. As time goes by, the relevance of those daily tasks to any larger purpose or goal becomes less and less clear, even if the vision has not changed since inception. As Ed Holly, a library administrator at the University of North Carolina, noted, some leaders "think they are great communicators, and they understand where they believe they are leading their organizations—but the people who are trying to do what the leader wants done, either don't understand it or are frustrated because they feel that they don't know what the two or three major things are" (cited in Sheldon, 1991: 11). Fortunately, if the vision exists, the opportunity remains to alleviate confusion and alienation by refocusing and re-emphasizing that vision. We have begun to do that at the AHC, albeit three plus years after the first creation and enunciation of the vision and mission.

IDENTIFYING AND MANAGING CHANGE AT AHC

Implementing a vision means bringing about change. "To realize a new vision, people usually can't keep doing the same things they've been doing. They need to conceive, design, and put into practice new ways of interacting and organizing" (Ancona et al., 2007: 98). It is essential to create action that fulfills the vision, to operationalize the change encompassed by the vision, and to reinforce the connection between changes in process and the new vision. It is not easy to envision change in the first place, since we are all products of and thus to some extent captive to the goals and processes we already know. This is true not only for chief officers, but also for every employee. They are not simply used to the old operating procedures and purposes, but their evaluations have been based on them. Then, along comes someone with a vision that inherently destabilizes the old way. "Any vision is a dream, but it will remain an impossible one without reinventing the context from which action takes place to fulfill it. It is the breaking of old habits, questioning previous assumptions, challenging the status quo, asking 'what if . . . ?' questions, and engaging in open dialogue that allows for discovery and new meaning at work" (Lloyd and Maguire, 2002: 154–155). At the AHC there was by no means a complete absence of vision and creativity (though there was some aversion to risk) as we began implementation of the new plan in 2003. But in the most immediate past, leadership had been hampered by uncertainty over the status of the program and the permanence of the top administration. Outdated processes from the past needed to be changed.

> Many organisations seem to be defined by their processes, rather than using them as a means to an end. So they end up using totally inappropriate vehicles and fail to move forward. Processes are vital, but in constantly changing competitive landscapes, they must be as agile and flexible as the people they serve. People can only be expected to react flexibly if they are helped to understand the purpose behind what they are being asked to do. (Lloyd and Maguire, 2002: 153)

My responsibility to change processes depended on my establishing credibility as someone who knew enough about archival administration to make changes that were workable, particularly in collection development and processing, and that would be respected by the profession. I had to convince the faculty and staff that such changes would clearly and quickly benefit the center, and raise its status within the profession and the university. I had to convince the individual employees that they had the potential of becoming nationally and even internationally prominent as professionals. I gave priority attention to three areas, discussed in turn in the following sections: *processing*, *faculty guidelines*, and *collection policy*.

Change in Processing Policies and Procedures

Luckily, I was already engaged in a fellowship (funded by the National Historical Publications and Records Commission) that would result in a major article redefining processing norms (Greene and Meissner, 2005). A successful grant proposal to NHPRC in 2004, for a project to implement new processing approaches and support collection development through massive deaccessioning, provided additional credibility as well as specific impetus for change. I asked our processing manager to ramp up the changes over three years, 2002–2005. The first year we eliminated removal of metal fasteners and organizing material within folders, and achieved a doubling of cubic feet processed. The next year we eliminated most refoldering, reboxing from record center cartons to flip-top boxes, photocopying newspaper clippings, and l-sleeving torn items, and achieved another doubling of cubic feet processed. The third year, beginning to use NHPRC grant funds, we shifted most processor time to cataloging unprocessed collections, with the goal of providing basic intellectual access to all of the collections that our collection analysis (being carried out in tandem with the processing work) indicated would be retained. In two years (2005–2007) we accomplished that feat, making all of our collections visible to researchers; in coming years we will return to minimal processing of now-cataloged collections. Simultaneously, to help prevent future uncataloged, unprocessed backlogs, we overhauled accessioning procedures to include creation of skeletal MARC records and box-level description.

Problems began to arise when long-distance researchers began requesting detailed information about collections that we had cataloged but not processed. We adopted three responses: wording for our Web site that explained the various states of arrangement and description of our collections; allocation of student work hours to create quick-and-dirty folder lists for collections being requested by researchers; and automatically moving such collections to the front of the queue for processing.

There was resistance to these changes, some resulting from a simple disinclination to learn new procedures, and some from a concern that I was asking the processors to do more rather than to do differently. Resistance was mitigated by moderately successful efforts to raise the job grades and salaries of the paraprofessionals (who made up more than half of our processing staff) and by making raises largely contingent on successful implementation of the new procedures. I also heralded the achievements of our processing team in reports to UW administration and in our external newsletter, as a way of identifying "short-term wins."

> Creating short-term wins as a way to motivate employees is critical during a long change effort. . . . One must plan for and create visible performance improvements. Employees involved in those improvements should be recognised. Without specific important and visible short-term wins, people may give up and default to change resister status. (Lloyd and Maguire, 2002: 154)

This change has had definite positive ramifications. The university administration is excited and grateful that we have eliminated in four years a backlog that took almost five decades to build. Although we have not seen tangible rewards for this achievement, no one would underestimate the importance of the provost's and president's thinking that the center has worked a professional miracle. Three of our faculty won slots on sessions at regional, national, and international conferences to discuss our backlog strategies, thus enhancing their professional stature.

Change in Faculty Guidelines

One other significant change was the revisioning of our guidelines for extended-term and promotion for AHC faculty. The professional archivists at the AHC received faculty status in the mid-1990s. Along with UW librarians, archivists became eligible after six years for extended-term contracts (in lieu of true tenure) of five years, along with promotion steps from assistant to associate to full archivist. The university regulations and guidelines that defined the qualifications and expectations emphasized state and regional professional service, scholarship, and professional development. The scholarship expectations could be fulfilled by publishing book reviews in journals and articles in our own newsletter. There was little incentive, and little support, for more ambitious undertakings. Yet it was clear to me that the university administration and academic units put great emphasis on the national and international distinction of faculty and that the archivists at the AHC had the education, skill, experience, and ability to more than meet the administration's benchmarks. I assembled a task force of assistant and associate archivists to review and revise the regulations and guidelines; the revision, including approval by the vice president for academic affairs, took over a year.

The revised expectations focused on state and regional distinction for assistant archivists, regional and national distinction for associate archivists, and national or international distinction for full archivists. Scholarship guidelines were raised to expect presentations at regional, national, and international conferences, article publications in peer-reviewed regional, national, and international journals, and other substantial and far-reaching research and synthesis such as curating major exhibits. Book reviews were shifted from evidence of scholarship to evidence of service. Higher expectations were developed for professional service and continuing professional development. Peer review of each faculty member by every other faculty member was no longer to be an uncritical praise fest; instead, well-supported critiques (even if constructive) were expected. The professional and academic visibility of the center's faculty began to rise almost immediately. As with the change in processing approach, this was not accomplished solely by changing expectations, but also by providing direct support, in this case a doubling of funds available to faculty for travel to professional meetings and creation of a mini-sabbatical program that permitted individuals to apply for a four-week research leave to work on presentations and publications for national audiences.

As these changes went into effect, the productivity and visibility of AHC faculty continually rose as more of our staff gave papers and workshops at professional conferences, served on professional association committees, and assumed other leadership roles. The distinction the center's faculty have brought to the repository and the university has been substantial. In particular faculty presentations and publications have placed the AHC in the forefront of archival and rare book library's efforts to connect to undergraduate and K–12 researchers, care for and curate photo collections, reduce processing backlogs, administer fee-based collections and nitrate image material—not to mention prominence in a handful of academic pursuits (e.g., prostitution in "end of track" Western towns; Hollywood high society in the 1940s–1960s; Western photography). Despite the obvious success, this change, too, has encountered resistance, not surprisingly because it has increased the demands placed on faculty for their time outside their nine-to-five jobs. Choosing faculty status always meant a certain level of extracurricular demands, but the expectations are higher now. While support has also increased, limited university raise pools have mitigated efforts to fully reward increased performance.

Change in Collecting Policy

In many respects, the most significant and visible change I have initiated at AHC is analyzing and redefining our collections and collecting goals. The collecting efforts in certain areas were successful enough to create true critical masses of research, but in many other areas we wound up with one or a small handful of collections that would hardly justify any researcher's trip to Wyoming. Many of the collections were marginal to say the least; others represented split collections. Archivists and scholars had long been concerned about unfocused collecting, and storage space was a pressing issue. The importance of assessing our collections and defining our collecting policy was codified as the first priority action item in our strategic plan. I launched a series of internal task forces, composed of faculty and archival staff, in late 2002 to analyze all of our major collecting areas. Each task force was charged to (1) analyze the quantity and quality of AHC holdings in its assigned topical areas and where necessary break down the analysis into more workable subcategories; (2) determine the location and holdings of other repositories in the United States with collections directly related to AHC holdings; (3) analyze use records for the major subcategories and prioritize likely user groups for current and future collections, including use by UW faculty; (4) recommend a specific collecting policy for each of the subcategories; (5) recommend, based on that collecting policy, extant collections at AHC for deaccessioning or significant reduction; and (6) recommend, based on that collecting policy, appraisal guidelines for retained and yet-to-be acquired collections. The task force reports were discussed and revised by the AHC's department heads. Final review will soon be under way by UW administration and, after their approval, the new policy will be released to the public.

The reevaluation of our collections and collecting policies led to a massive deaccessioning effort. This activity was also supported by the 2004 NHPRC grant, because it linked directly with our effort to eliminate the cataloging backlog—if we are not going to retain a collection we do not have to catalog or process it. The new approach is a complete change from the unrestrained and undefined collecting activities of the center during the 1950s–1980s. It further cemented a change in the perception of the AHC within the archival profession, and perhaps more importantly among members of the university administration. Instead of requesting more storage space, as the center had done all through the 1990s, we could now declare an end to the storage crisis. While there is no direct evidence of a connection, as the backlog disappeared and deaccessioning advanced to full swing, the university administration decided to support several key facility needs of the center, to the tune of $2.5 million dollars: upgrade of our electronic security system; replacement of a failing dry-pipe sprinkler system; and major exterior renovation to address water leaks that had plagued the building from its construction in 1993.

MAKING DECISIONS AND TAKING RESPONSIBILITY

One of the arts of leadership is the willingness and ability to make decisions, accept responsibility, and move on, even in the (inevitable) face of incomplete information for decision making. As one corporate librarian put it, what sets leaders apart is:

. . . having the courage to act, because often we get paralyzed by the circumstances and the situation. Most of us tend to wait until all the conditions are in our favor, paralyzed by a case of the "if onlys." We keep waiting for this last piece of the puzzle to come. A leader, however, finds the wherewithal to act in spite of the circumstance to implement a stratagem. Too often we make a poor decision, or the wrong decision, by failing to make one at all. Leaders make things happen. (St. Lifer, 1976: 38)

Part of the ability to make decisions in the face of incomplete information is the willingness to use "intuition" or judgment. "Your judgment is your experience and knowledge combined. It's what you get paid for in cases like this." Applying judgment—experience and knowledge—to data, advice, trends, and reports "is just another way of saying that you're making an educated guess . . . this lack of precision is what makes decisionmaking so difficult for some people" (Fagiano, 1992). On the other hand, "A leader lives the thinking, always rethinking, always ready to think again and make a new decision, yet never quite knowing if the decision is right" (Smythe and Norton, 2007: 80). This is not to say that a leader can vacillate; only that she or he must understand that most decisions are not carved in stone, and may need to be rethought depending on circumstances.

Decision making may be the most important facet of leadership because it is the one most frequently called upon. Whether the answer is *yes* or *no*, leadership is partly about making hard, sometimes agonizing decisions, often on the fly, that nobody else is willing or able to make. I believe that the single trait most responsible for my having advanced in my profession and administratively is my ability and willingness to develop ideas and take initiatives rather than waiting for someone to define my priorities and activities for me. My best bosses encouraged this trait, in part because it made their jobs easier (most of the time) not to have to be thinking through my job as well as their own.

These decisions may be large or small. All too often they can concern minutiae, at least from the decision maker's perspective. Leaders "do things, sometimes big things, but mostly a lot of little things" (Carucci, 2006: 36). On a daily basis, leaders often earn their pay with these small decisions, taking the burden of decision off others, and shouldering responsibility. Leaders cultivate leadership in others, and encourage others in their repository to take responsibility and make decisions, but this is often a slow and sometimes frustrating experience. In most situations I have encountered there are a range of decision makers, including those who operate independently for long stretches without coming to their supervisor; those who seem to vacillate between taking charge and needing decisions made or verified by a supervisor; and those who hardly make a move without direction or decision by their supervisor. Knowing when to insist that others make decisions is difficult because those uneasy with the responsibility cannot always be counted on to think through the situation rationally and calmly in the first place. If there is time, walking them through the decision-making process is ideal, so they can verify step by step that they can do so competently.

"More importantly, 'real leaders do difficult things.' Moving a library forward means making hard choices among competing priorities" (Mech, 1996: 346). Notwithstanding the myriad small decisions, leaders are best known and probably most highly prized for making more profound decisions: "In business, courageous action is really a special kind of calculated risk taking. People who become good leaders have a greater than average willingness to make bold moves, but they strengthen their chances of success—and avoid career suicide—through careful deliberation and preparation" (Reardon, 2007: 60). This is a learned process, based on trial and error. Learning over decades is an enforced progression, most often, since the majority of us begin in positions where our decisions, while they may be bold in context, are relatively small in the grand scheme of our repositories; with luck we refine our ability and success rate before we wind up leading an archives and having the fate of an entire program and its employees in our hands.

Although leaders must make decisions, they can and usually should share the decision-making process. "Although the old-fashioned 'command and control' model of leadership will continue to be important, especially in situations where clarity and speed are requirements, most organizations will find that a facilitation model of leadership works better. In the high-performing organization of the future, decisions will increasingly be made by bringing people together, pooling ideas and information, and moving toward some form of consensus" (Russell and Stephens, 2004: 4).[3] Consensus is not unanimity, but rather acceptance of the final choice even without full agreement. It is more important there be "a high level of commitment to the chosen course of action and a strong, shared understanding of the rationale for the decision" (Roberto, 2005: 1). Determining who to bring into the process and how much authority and responsibility to give them in shaping the decision is sometimes as difficult as reaching the final decision itself.

Defining a vision and implementing major changes entailed both major and minor decisions. The development of the vision, the content of the faculty guideline revisions, and the specifics of the collection analysis and policy were decisions made with considerable consultation with many employees. On the other hand, the decisions to revamp processing, to undertake a change in faculty guidelines, and to embark on a comprehensive analysis of our collections were essentially mine alone. My decision-making approach is a blend of collaboration and command/control, particularly for big decisions. In certain instances, stages of the same decision call for distinct approaches. The first meeting I had with the university's development director to discuss AHC priorities for a mini fund-raising campaign for our Alan K. Simpson Institute for Western Politics and Leadership I attended without the Simpson curator, because my experience with the development vice president had taught me to ensure that there was one clear voice in the conversation. However, after establishing major goals and broad categories, I consulted with the curator to make decisions on refinements and define further focus.

Smaller decisions are more apt to require quick answers. Recently, a question came up about how to accommodate an unusual reproduction request that did not fit our normal guidelines. The patron was in the reading room waiting for a decision, and the reference manager wanted to be certain that she would have my support if the patron balked at the answer. This is an example of a situation where the reference manager could in fact have made the decision, because she should have known, based on past experience, that even if I disagreed with the decision I would have—within broad limits—sustained her in front of the patron. Or, a situation may call for quick answers—long deliberation and consultation may be possible but often are not worth everyone's time and effort given the small stakes. For example, when I determined early in my tenure that the AHC's brochures needed a uniform look, I asked my administrative assistant, who is a talented graphic artist, to do a mock-up of her suggestion. I could have circulated that design and asked for input from our department heads, but instead simply approved the template.

On the other hand, there are times when broad input is well worth pursuing, because participation can promote support of a decision and whatever program the decision relates to. When an employee satisfaction survey highlighted problems with employees feeling disconnected from center activities beyond their departments, and feeling that recognition of individual efforts was uneven, I consulted not only with our department heads but with the entire staff to gather suggestions for improvement. While it was important that decisions be made fairly quickly, in order to demonstrate recognition of the problems, it was equally important that employees felt they had a say in redressing their own grievances. Defining a process that allows time for input but draws a firm closure to the consultation process to ensure timely implementation is difficult. Too often, individuals who are consulted but whose views do not prevail, feel embittered, that they were not listened to.

It is also difficult to walk the line between consultation and abdication where decision making is concerned; requiring consensus before taking a decision is a form of abdication that is all too easy to make.

Eventually, one person will decide. The decision maker is the single point of accountability who must bring the decision to closure and commit the organization to act on it. To be strong and effective, the person with the D [decision making responsibility] needs good business judgment, a grasp of the relevant trade-offs, a bias for action, and a keen awareness of the organization that will execute the decision. (Rogers amd Blenko, 2006)

After gathering input on redressing the employee morale issues, I had to decide. In the end, this is what leaders do—"sit around all day making (or avoiding) decisions" (Stewart, 2006).

LEADERSHIP AT OTHER LEVELS IN THE HIERARCHY

This section deals briefly with making decisions when you're not "the boss"—the top program director. My experiences over the years have provided opportunities to try various approaches. In 1991, I was the still relatively new (and relatively young) curator of manuscripts acquisition at the Minnesota Historical Society, in charge of a unit that consisted of one other professional, in an organization of over 300 employees. One of my unit's responsibilities was documenting the state's congressional delegation. We aggressively contacted and pursued the congressmen to donate their papers, but we asked for and accepted *everything* among their papers, including fairly bulky series of requests from constituents for flags flown over the Capitol, for various government publications, and for passes to the congressional galleries.

As a result we had amassed a huge, unprocessed volume of congressional papers. I made a proposal to develop a new appraisal approach for congressional papers that would be much tougher than previously, and briefly outlined my reasons. The department head, James E. Fogerty, accepted my basic premise but cautioned that the most effective approach to developing new appraisal guidelines for congressional papers would be to bring other interested parties into the process. This went completely against my grain at the time—I protested that forming a committee would not only delay but inevitably water down the recommendations—but his approach prevailed. We assembled an interdivisional committee to review our past collecting and issue appraisal guidelines. The committee represented the Acquisitions and Curatorial, Reference, Research, Processing, and State Archives Departments. In the end, the committee approach worked. It forced me to continuously and clearly justify my arguments. We succeeded in fashioning strict appraisal guidelines that met with the acceptance of the committee. This meant that we could forward the guidelines to the director for approval, with a strong committee imprimatur. It further meant that actually implementing the guidelines, both prospectively and retrospectively, went smoothly, without significant internal resistance.[4]

This vignette illustrates leadership traits at two levels of an organization. As a department head Jim Fogerty exhibited the important trait of mentoring, welcoming and shepherding a raw idea (from a still pretty raw individual) to fruition, and letting his subordinate gain the individual accolades for a project that Jim himself had a strong hand in seeing through to success. He demonstrated three key components of what one author identifies as "Level 5 Leadership." He attended to people (me) first, and to strategy second. He ushered "the right people to the right seats," letting them play to their strengths. He looked "out the window, not in the mirror, to apportion credit for success," that is, he let credit fall to me, knowing, I suppose, that my success would also redound to his benefit as a leader as well as encourage me to undertake other initiatives (Collins, 2005: 141, 142).[5]

Another way of looking at Jim's leadership approach in this instance is as facilitator. "The leader who can take the role of a facilitator blends his or her role of visionary decisive leader with that of listening and empowering leader. As a facilitative leader he or she involves followers as much as possible in creating the group's vision and purpose, carrying out the vision and purpose, and building a productive and cohesive team. Facilitation can be seen as a leadership *approach*" (Moore, 2004: 231).[6] Though unarticulated, my vision at the time was to make the MHS the leading institution nationally in curation of congressional collections. The development of appraisal guidelines and their subsequent implementation, along with visibility and leadership positions in the SAA Congressional Papers Roundtable, were the concrete change initiatives toward achieving the vision. The congressional repository vision was not mine alone, but shaped and shared with Jim

Fogerty and with associate curator Todd Daniels-Howell, as well as with the committee.

Like vision, change can come from any level of an organization, when supervisors allow it. As the lone arranger in the Carleton College Archives at the very beginning of my career, my (never formally articulated, but frequently enunciated informally) vision for embedding the archives in both the college's academic curriculum and administrative functions (such as college fund-raising) was shared and shaped by faculty members and administrators. I inaugurated many changes in the archival program in which my bosses were completely disinterested, but which made a significant difference to the visibility and usability (and use) of the archives. These changes included establishing an exhibit program, processing collections and creating finding aids, offering the Archives' services to the development office and alumni office for historical content and photos in brochures and other publications, and contacting faculty members whose courses suggested they might find some of our holdings pertinent for their students. I also began to write a column for the student paper, highlighting the college's history, which brought positive attention to the archives.

It is important to emphasize again that decision making is not something only bosses do. Indeed, ideally, change should occur incrementally in every organization without the top leader being aware of it—if all change has to pass approval by the boss, there is little likelihood of it occurring at all. Anyone at any level can and should strive to make decisions, first within their clear parameters of authority and later by seeking to expand those parameters based on previous successful decision making. But to make tough decisions, emerging leaders must learn about competing priorities. As a younger archivist I sometimes could not (or would not) see those priorities that might be competing with my opinion, idea, or initiative. If I did see those priorities I often dismissed them disdainfully as "politics." But as I rose in administrative hierarchy, I came to agree that "politics involves knowing who to work with and how to work with them," and is essential for a leader to achieve success for his or her organization (Bellman, 1992: 75–76). But sometimes the priorities established above me in the hierarchy were also simply issues of resource allocations or required choices between two "goods." "How does one choose between two valued objectives? Sometimes we overcome doubt with faith, sometimes we privilege one set of values over another. And sometimes we just live with the burden of making choices when there are no easy answers"

(Nohria and Stewart, 2006). Now that I am a higher-level supervisor, I am constantly aware of how often others in my repository do not appreciate what I see as competing priorities.

DEALING WITH CHALLENGES

Humility is a key component of leadership, one often overlooked in writings that emphasize a more heroic and authoritarian leadership style with no room for modesty or self-analysis. I admit to being far from a completely successful leader. A recent employee survey at the AHC, for instance, showed room for improvement in the areas of employee acknowledgment and morale and clarity of mission. The experience confirms that "great leadership raises personal and organisational self-esteem to the point where people are confident enough in themselves to question, admit mistakes, give feedback, be honest and learn from each other" (Lloyd and Maguire, 2002:. 151). Leadership is a growing experience. I can take comfort in having been willing to conduct the assessment in the first place and I plan to address some of the significant trouble spots.

I also endorse the view that "many executives who attempt to foster trust, optimism, and consensus often reap anger, cynicism, and conflict instead," and that "no single person can possibly live up to the expectation that a leader do all things equally well" (Ancona, et al., 2007: 96, 92). It is important to understand that (1) complacency is the first enemy of good leadership—in this case, conducting the employee survey earlier would have been useful; (2) leadership can be undermined by conditions that may be beyond the boss's control (e.g., certain legacy problems in an organization that simply cannot be fixed immediately, particularly given the constraints of personnel systems and of budgets); and (3) leadership success can never be complete—it is not possible to please all of the people all of the time, and some necessary conditions of leadership (decisive decision making, for example) in and of themselves alienate some people (indeed are apt to alienate anyone not consulted in formulating the decision no matter how many people *were* consulted).

Any evaluation of leadership should be taken seriously and the response positive. "The CEO may publicly ask for feedback on her/his leadership style, whilst being positively grumpy when receiving it from a subordinate" (Lloyd and Maguire, 2002:.155). On the other hand, openness to feedback can result largely in complaining rather than constructive dialogue and learning. How many unhappy employees does it take to invalidate a leader's work? How should the balance be struck between internal assessments and external assessments? Generally speaking, what measures, particularly in an archival program, should be used to measure the quality of leadership? It is not enough to simply count the number of collections accessioned or processed, the number of grants or donations brought in, or even the external reputation or comparative benchmarks. The quality of the experience of employees does matter, just as much as the quality of service to patrons. Awareness of weaknesses and willingness to improve are traits of a good leader but success, rather than "trying hard," is what marks a good leader from a mediocre one. Still, while leadership calls for facing mistakes frankly and learning from them, it is important that they not paralyze further activity or result in extended navel gazing. Ultimately—and the quicker the better—the leader has to move past the errors and move forward.

CONCLUSION

In my experience, many archivists seem to be reluctant to assume leadership roles. There is a certain lure to retreating into just doing traditional archival work, not looking up or around, and keeping quiet. Such a proclivity may be the result of personality to some extent. One study indicated that the archival profession includes many individuals who are more comfortable with facts than with possibilities, for example. "As professionals, archivists are down-to-earth people who are comfortable with factual evidence and who subscribe, or, perhaps more accurately, understand its values. The intuitives . . . are more focused on larger possibilities and see patterns and combinations which are possible rather than actual" (Craig, 2000: 87). But archival training emphasizes method almost to the exclusion of management and, furthermore, offers little about leadership, which is different than management. Managing is "more analytical and logical, more planful and conservative, whereas leading is more intuitive and organic, more visionary and emergent" (Bellman, 1992: 15). Archival education (at least until recently) and training has focused on analysis, logic, planning, not intuition and vision, which are essential leadership traits. We need more attention to the latter, in education, in internships and first jobs, and in our professional associations. Being a leader takes conscious attention; it does not happen (or at least it does not happen well) if we pretend it evolves naturally with our rise in rank.

This chapter has given me the opportunity to study and reflect further on the complex and sometimes counterintuitive demands and characteristics of a successful leader. Setting vision, managing change, and having a clear, confident decision-making style are seemingly the three most important traits of a leader, at least in my case. Leadership can be learned, just as it can be practiced throughout one's career no matter where in a hierarchy one may be situated. Leaders must learn from shortcomings and failures as well as from strengths and successes (and not be too impressed with themselves by the latter, because the former will certainly arise to shatter smugness). I think I have a better grasp of the challenges of leadership for others as well, if not yet a clearer conception of how the archival profession can successfully work to expand and improve leadership within its ranks. Some steps have already been taken—SAA holds a forum for leaders within the organization every year at its annual meeting, to support effectiveness by elucidating how to get things done within the society. To date, however, this forum has not concentrated so much on encouraging vision, change, and decision making within SAA's sections, roundtables, committees, and task forces. Our major programs in graduate archival education offer many courses in management but few in leadership.

Changing this situation is important for our profession. We acknowledge the need to be better recognized by our resource allocators and by society at large, given more resources and better compensation, have more influence in everything from IT systems designs to public records legislation. How can we hope to do any of this without more, stronger leaders with vision, willingness to see how things might change for the better and how to change them, and decisiveness married to the ability to bring others along with the decisions? We need such people in our professional organizations, and in our institutions. To get them we must be more conscious about educating and cultivating them. Perhaps we need to conceive of leadership institutes; to define expectations for leadership training in our definitions of adequate graduate archival education; to develop a second mentorship program within SAA that is specifically geared to leadership, not broadly to archives administration. Each of us as individuals needs to spend some conscious energy on examining his or her own leadership potential and style, and taking steps—wherever in the hierarchy we might be—to exercise leadership. The first step might be to start defining a vision, and the steps necessary to get there. We need to stop focusing on what we *do not* have and start envisioning and leading toward what we *can* have—for our collections, our institutions, and our profession.

NOTES

1. Unless cited separately, this paragraph and the next is based on Mark Shelstad, "Collecting and Mediation at the University of Wyoming," Paper presented to the Fall 2003 Midwest Archives Conference Meeting (October 24, 2003). Used with permission.
2. The Vision and Mission statement are available at: http://ahc. uwyo.edu/documents/about/administration/mission2003-07-20.doc. The 2004–2009 Plan can be found at: http://ahc.uwyo.edu/documents/about/administration/academicplan/PlanFinal.doc.
3. Quoting Stringer, *Leadership and Organizational Climate: The Cloud Chamber Effect.* Upper Saddle River, NJ: Prentice-Hall, 2002, p. 220.
4. For the full story of the development of the appraisal guidelines, see Greene, 1994; for the aftermath, see Daniels-Howell, 1998.
5. The five levels of leadership Collins identifies are highly capable individual, contributing team member, competent manager, effective leader, and executive. I would like to think that in 1991, I was somewhere between levels two and three.
6. Quoting Fran Rees, *The Facilitator Excellence Handbook: Helping People Work Creatively and Productively Together.* San Francisco: Pfeiffer, 1998, pp. 17–18.

REFERENCES

American Library Association (ALA) "Ladders to Leadership: Leadership and Vision," Available: www.ala.org/ala/nmrtbucket/leadvision/leadvision.htm#1 (accessed July 11, 2007).
Ancona, Deborah, Thomas W. Malone, Wanda J. Orlikowski, and Peter M. Senge. 2007. "In Praise of the Incomplete Leader." *Harvard Business Review* 85 (February): 92–100.
Bellman, Geoffrey M. 1992. *Getting Things Done When You Are Not in Charge: How to Succeed from a Support Position.* San Francisco: Berrett-Koehler.

Blair, Gerard M. "That Vision Thing" (Thu, 23 May 1996 16:08:48). In *Standards for Vision Statements: A Discussion Thread*. Edited by Ken Kuskey Available: www.albany.edu/cpr/gf/resources/Vision.html (accessed July 11, 2007).

Carucci, Ron. 2006. "What Emerging Leaders Need and What You Might Be Missing." *Harvard Business Review* 84 (November): 36.

Collins, Jim. 2005. "Level 5 Leadership: The Triumph of Humility and Fierce Resolve." *Harvard Business Review* 83 (July/August): 136–146.

Craig, Barbara L. 2000 "Canadian Archivists: What Types of People Are They?" *Archivaria* 50 (Fall): 79–92.

Daniels-Howell, Todd. 1998. "Reappraisal of Congressional Papers at the Minnesota Historical Society: A Case Study." *Archival Issues* 23: 35–40.

Fagiano, David. 1992. "The Art of Decisionmaking." *Supervision* 53 (n.p.).

Greene, Mark A. 1994. "Appraisal of Congressional Papers at the Minnesota Historical Society: A Case Study." *Archival Issues* 19: 31–34.

[Greene, Mark A.] 2003. "American Heritage Center: Academic Plan, 2004–09," Available: http://ahc.uwyo.edu/documents/about/administration/academicplan/PlanFinal.doc (accessed July 11, 2007).

Greene, Mark A. and Dennis Meissner. 2005. "More Product, Less Process: Revamping Traditional Archival Processing." *American Archivist*, 68 (Fall/Winter): 12–15.

Joyce, William. 1980. Report to the American Heritage Center Review Committee, the University of Wyoming. June 23.

Lloyd, Margaret, and Sheridan Maguire. 2002. "The Possibility Horizon." *Journal of Change Management* 3: 149–158.

Mech, Terrence F. 1996. "Leadership and the Evolution of Academic Librarianship." *The Journal of Academic Librarianship* 22 (September): 345–364.

Moore, Thomas L. 2004. "Facilitative Leadership: One Approach to Empowering Staff and Other Stakeholders." *Library Trends* 53 (Summer): 230–237.

Nohria, Nitin, and Thomas A. Stewart. 2006. "Risk, Uncertainty, and Doubt." *Harvard Business Review* 84 (February): 39–40.

Panitch, Judith M. 2001. *Special Collections in ARL Libraries: Results of the 1998 Survey.* Washington: Association of Research Libraries.

Reardon, Kathleen K. 2007. "Courage as a Skill." *Harvard Business Review* 85 (January): 58–64.

Roberto, Michael A. 2005. "Why Making the Decisions the Right Way Is More Important Than Making the Right Decisions." *Ivey Business Journal* 70 (September/October): 1–7.

Rogers, Paul, and Marcia Blenko. 2006. "Who Has the D?" *Harvard Business Review* 84 (January): 53–61.
Russell, Keith and Denise Stephens. 2004. "Introduction." *Library Trends* 53 (Summer): 1–5.
Sheldon, Brooke E. 1991. *Leaders in Libraries: Styles and Strategies for Success*. Chicago: American Library Association.
Shelstad, Mark. 2003. "Collecting and Mediation at the University of Wyoming." Paper presented at Fall 2003 Midwest Archives Conference Meeting. October 24. (Used with permission.)
Smythe, Elizabeth and Andrew Norton. 2007. "Thinking as Leadership/Leadership as Thinking." *Leadership* 3: 65–90.
St. Lifer, Evan. 1976. "Prime Leadership [an Interview with Eugenie E. Prime, Manager of Hewlett Packard's Corporate Library]." *Library Journal* 123: 36–38.
Stewart, Thomas A. 2006. "Did You Ever Have to Make Up Your Mind?" *Harvard Business Review* 84 (January): 12.
Williams, J. Linda. 2006. "Leadership: Shaping the Future of the Profession." *Knowledge Quest* 34 (May/June): 4–6.

Chapter 8

Meeting Leadership Challenges: Lessons from Experience

Edie Hedlin

Thirty-five years of experience in the archival profession, much of it engaged in some level of management, carries with it many lessons. Whether the archival program is part of a business, a cultural organization, or a governmental unit, I have learned that certain methods can be highly successful while other approaches invite failure. The goal of this chapter, then, is to help other archivists achieve more success and experience less frustration, by sharing insights and lessons from my varied archival career. Some of the maxims articulated below reflect the application of sound leadership and management practices. Others, however, are the result of learning through mistakes, unintended outcomes, and inevitable failures. These lessons and insights may be summarized as follows:

- Support the goals of the parent organization
- Define and constantly articulate your mission
- Seek and work with allies to advance your program
- Develop careful plans and set priorities
- Focus on staff productivity
- Evaluate your leadership or management style

SUPPORT THE GOALS OF THE PARENT ORGANIZATION

We begin with a focus on context. Certain activities may characterize virtually all archival programs but all archival programs are most decidedly not alike. Corporate archives differ from the methods and intent of government archives, which differ from university archives or religious archives. Even within the governmental context there are multiple placement possibilities that translate into differing organizational imperatives. These placements have meaning beyond the relative status or visibility of the archives; indeed they have major implications.

Given that most archives are a subunit of a larger entity, the successful archival program leader will quickly absorb lesson number one: *work with, rather than against, the goals of the parent organization.* Learn the values, language, and culture of the larger entity and describe your program accordingly. Frame your arguments, tailor your activities, and account for resources in ways that are understood by the larger entity. Pursue the archival mission faithfully, but always with the understanding that to flourish, the archival program must be viewed as contributor to the larger enterprise.

I have had the good fortune to work in multiple settings, including national archives, state archives, corporate archives, multiple institutional archives, and records programs in international organizations. Core professional work took place within each setting, but the differences were many. They included the archivist's authority, the scope of the collecting effort, the size and source of funding, and the program's constituency. They included the larger organization's mission, and in particular its dominant culture.

What constitutes "the dominant culture"? Cultural values are determined somewhat by the goals and work assumptions created by senior management but in today's fluid workplace there is frequent senior management turnover. The prevailing culture, therefore, tends to come from an organization's dominant professional group, the one that carries out its core business. This group often sets the tone, creates the assumptions, and represents the values of the institution. This is the group that a savvy archival leader will serve well.

Let me provide two examples. The World Bank's culture is set primarily by economists while the Smithsonian Institution's culture has gradually moved from the dominance of scientists to museum curators. Economists and curators (or scientists) constitute very different professions but within their respective organizations they will assert their prerogatives and will see themselves as the embodiment of the organization's values. They will speak on behalf of those values when addressing senior management. Because their influence is pervasive, they influence workplace methods and prevailing attitudes. Thus, they affect the collecting strategy and internal constituency of the organization's archives and are a key internal audience for archival products and projects. Finally, these groups strongly influence general institutional opinion about the archival program.

In looking back, I wish I had more assertively adopted as a goal the cultivation of these key workers while employed by the above institutions. Instead of complaining about how poorly these groups understood or supported the archives, or resenting their sense of entitlement, or focusing on the internal demands of the archival program, I would have more fully advanced the archival mission in each institution if I had aggressively cultivated these core constituents, enlisted their continuing feedback and support, and sought ways to respond in particular to their archival needs.

Context is crucial in other ways as well. Wells Fargo Bank and the Smithsonian Institution (SI) both have institutional archives but their programs have been defined by very different imperatives. These differences are multiple. Wells Fargo's archives was created solely to serve the interests of the parent organization while SI always assumed public access to its archives. Although both hold historical records, Smithsonian Institution Archives (SIA) also deals with temporary records and therefore requires a large allocation of staff in support of a records management function. SIA is one of several archives at the Smithsonian while the Wells Fargo program is without internal competition.

With regard to leadership, SIA is organizationally separate from the other archival programs and, although it traditionally has been viewed as the leader of the Smithsonian archival community, this role is muted internally by the quite natural tendency of its fellow repositories to respond primarily to the wishes of their respective hierarchies. On the other hand, SIA reports to the senior management so has a shorter, more direct line of communication with top management than the other Smithsonian archives or the Wells Fargo archives. On occasion, this allows SIA to represent its needs or those of the larger Smithsonian archival community to the highest levels.

Each of these differences has an impact on the influence and visibility of the program. It is fair to ask, however, whether these differences translate into a stronger foundation for one archives than the other. This question, like others, is complex. SIA may have fewer archival staff relative to the volume of records, but it has a larger program overall. SIA can seek grants or cultivate donors to help compensate for funding shortages while Wells Fargo's archives is within a for-profit entity and would be ineligible or noncompetitive for grants or donors. On the other hand, the head of the Wells Fargo's archives need only convince a few senior managers of the program's worth to increase internal funding while SIA's funding requests are vetted through a longer and more complex process.

Each of these differences affect both daily operations and, for the wise program leader, longer-term strategy. They each can be seen as either an advantage or a disadvantage, but in every case these factors influence the scope, impact, and opportunities afforded the archives. In short, leaders of these archival programs must analyze the characteristics of their contextual placement and find ways to minimize the weaknesses and maximize the strengths inherent in their organizational setting.

Differences may abound but there are some aspects of archival leadership that are constant. Indeed, there are skills that all managers should develop regardless of contextual conditions. I believe these skills characterize good leaders of any program, not just archival programs, and in my view they make the difference between muddling through and leading confidently. These skills may seem obvious and their execution simple, but experience has taught this archivist that the steps listed below are challenging and are the shoals upon which many managers fail.

DEFINE AND CONSTANTLY ARTICULATE YOUR MISSION

We archivists know what we do and why we do it. We understand the logic of our ways, and the reasons for our methods and approaches. We understand the intended outcomes of our labor. We know the value of the records we preserve, and the products we create. What we often seem *not* to know is how unclear this all is to nonarchivists.

It is unclear for many reasons, not the least of which is the small number of individuals engaged in archival work compared to, for instance, libraries. Additionally, archives, although more uniform in practice today than ever before, are still idiosyncratic and, as has been noted above, will differ from one organization to another. It is unclear because the users of archival records within any organization are typically small in number. It is unclear because archivists are content to let it be that way.

Leading your program often means explaining, defending, and advocating for your program. To do that effectively, you must be able to articulate in a simple and consistent manner the archives' mission. As has been noted, you need to use language that is understandable to the staff of the larger organization, and if there are key constituencies beyond the parent organization, you need to construct statements that are meaningful to them as well. Most importantly, your statement of mission and goals needs to be clear, concrete, and concise.

You do not need to be entirely consistent. The use of different language when addressing different audiences, for instance, is desirable, as is the slight movement of focus from one key program activity to another, again depending upon the audience. It is therefore not necessarily good, from this archivist's perspective, to have a formal "mission statement" that is used as an all-purpose explanation for the archival program. These statements can be wordy and awkward, especially if they are the product of a staff exercise and reflect the compromises needed to obtain group support. Mission statements should not be designed to please staff but to demystify for nonarchivists the goals and purpose of the archival program.

Ideally, however, staff will embrace the need to frequently articulate the program's mission and seek ways to convey it in outside presentations, discussions, and reports. Enthusiastic explanations of one's purpose and goals will serve the archives well over time, and there is probably no such thing as too frequent articulation of the program's mission. Everyone, including the archives' head, should assume that unless there is evidence to the contrary audiences large and small need an explanation of the goals and purpose of the archives. This archivist, in hindsight, recognizes that more assertive promotion of her program on a regular basis would have increased the archives' visibility and conveyed enthusiasm that might have spread to others. Serene assumptions that the program's worth is self-evident may instead be self-defeating.

SEEK AND WORK WITH ALLIES TO ADVANCE YOUR PROGRAM

An important corollary to articulating your mission is to *develop allies*. This requires the archives head to simultaneously promote the archival program while understanding the value of responding to the needs of others. Charity and humanitarian instincts aside, it is politically astute for the archives to be viewed as supportive of the goals of others rather than esoterically involved in its own internal operations. Indeed, this corollary links to but is broader than the first lesson—work with the goals of the parent organization.

Developing allies, however, is a formidable challenge. This archivist found that opportunities for alliances often appeared to be much greater than they actually were, or the cost of performing a service to others was problematic. On several occasions, and in several organizational settings, I received requests from the parent organization for services that were labor and time-intensive. Meeting those requests would have greatly pleased the requesting unit and likely would have created a strong supporter of the archival enterprise. Doing so, however, often would have required the archives staff to set aside its planned work and instead focus on the new request. This balancing act is the most challenging part of developing allies and broadening the influence and impact of the archival program. Look for alliances that support the needs of others without undermining the basic work of the archives. Therefore, at minimum, the archives head should explore with other units the possibilities for joint projects that would benefit them both.

An example of such a project was one undertaken by Smithsonian Institution Archives in conjunction with the Office of the Secretary and the Office of General Counsel (OGC). SIA was approached by these units with a request to build upon an existing compilation of all federal legislation that included mention of the Smithsonian Institution (SI). The existing list covered SI from its inception in 1846 until the turn of the century. The request, then, would require SIA to expand beyond the Smithsonian's first 50 years to cover another 100 years of legislation. Clearly, this task was substantial. At the same time the resulting compilation would be an extremely valuable tool for scholarship broadly, for SIA's own reference and research activity, and for the requesting units. Therefore SIA's history office agreed to undertake this project even though it meant a multiyear commitment of time and effort. By assuming responsibility for a major undertaking desired by two key offices, SIA placed its program directly in service to those units and provided ongoing evidence of the practical value of internal historical expertise. At the same time, SIA's new ability to quickly answer questions related to the Institution's legal history has increased research requests of this nature and enhanced the program's visibility.

Another example involves the larger Smithsonian archival community. When it became obvious that SIA's lack of access to conservation services was a problem commonly shared with most Smithsonian archives, I sought to address this broadly felt need. First SIA converted a vacant archival position to that of paper conservator. Then we approached a donor (the Smithsonian's first paper conservator) to provide funding for a second conservation position. The donor's funds would support this position for two years, thereby making it possible to offer conservation services to other Smithsonian archives as well. With two full-time conservators on staff, SIA established the Smithsonian Center for Archives Conservation (SCAC), a service that conducted free assessments of the other repositories' conservation needs and engaged in hands-on work at greatly reduced rates. The two-year trial period established the value of SCAC to the entire archival community, and when the donor funds were expended Smithsonian management agreed to sustain the second position with institutional funding. By addressing common problems in a unified way, SIA improved its own access to conservation services, created a center that resides within SIA but is supported in part by the larger archival community, and offered other Smithsonian repositories quality services at reduced rates. The result has been improved collections care for all of the Institution's archives and heightened visibility for SIA.

Internal allies, then, can offer support for specific functions or for the broad, ongoing work of an archival program. Before leaving this topic, however, it is important to note that external allies are also important and should be actively sought. SIA's alliance with Rockefeller Archive Center (RAC) is a case in point. These two programs were different in many ways but with regard to electronic records issues they had similar problems and complementary assets. Recognizing the value of an alliance, I approached RAC with the suggestion of a joint grant proposal to develop electronic records projects in each archives. The grant would emphasize the importance of using common methods and approaches for these different programs, thereby creating tools that had promise for other archival programs as well. SIA's asset was a dedicated electronic records staff and project management experience. RAC's asset was a strong program overall and access to funding sources. Our joint proposal received a grant of $400,000 from the Rockefeller Foundation, permitting the hiring of project staff in both Smithsonian Institution Archives and Rockefeller Archive Center. The project is still underway and, although progress is impressive, it is premature to evaluate results. Nonetheless, its very existence is testimony to the value of partnership. Almost certainly neither program would have been able to accomplish alone what this joint effort has made possible.

DEVELOP CAREFUL PLANS AND SET PRIORITIES

Balancing the outreach and service efforts of the archives against the need for stable processes and a viable work schedule is a manager's constant challenge. The balance can be achieved only through *setting priorities* and remaining attentive to them. This, in turn, requires program planning. Of all the lessons learned slowly, this archivist found responsible program planning to be perhaps the most difficult. Nonetheless, a good program requires good planning, and here in particular the reader should take advantage of my lessons. Whether it is an annual exercise that identifies what products the staff will produce in the following year or a vision of the program's future direction, planning is a tool that the wise manager will handle with skill. Let me offer a negative example, one that shows how not to engage in the planning process.

Early in my tenure with one organization, I held an all-day retreat with the staff to discuss the future of the program. The response was enthusiastic. Many ideas emerged, with representatives of the various subunits suggesting ways that their respective function could be enhanced. As a follow-up I required each functional unit to create a more refined long-term plan for the execution of that unit's ideas. When the plans were completed and submitted to me, I realized that my approach had been a mistake. In retrospect, it was clear that I had failed to articulate the advisory nature of the staff input or my own vision of the program's future direction.

The staff had developed elaborate plans for an extension of all existing activities. In combination, their plans would require major funding increases that were virtually impossible. Even if the funds to support these plans were potentially available, from my perspective implementation of the staff's combined plans was not desirable. My colleagues had provided a vision of the program's future that was a greatly enlarged version of the program's present.

This was not my view of the future, and although I had noted desired program changes during the retreat, my decision to request more refined plans from the staff inevitably resulted in a strong focus on current program components. I was now faced with several unpleasant truths—there was no way to expand all program parts as the staff wished; even if there were such a way I would not be in favor it; and having assigned everyone this exercise I would appear cynical if not heartless to openly choose some plans and reject others. In short, my process for setting goals had created an awkward situation. To avoid further discomfort I decided to set aside all the plans and not mention them again to the staff.

Alas, this decision only compounded the difficulty. After investing considerable effort in preparing plans, the staff heard nothing whatsoever from me regarding their efforts. They eventually realized that I was not going to make use of their work, or even allude to it again, and when that reality dawned the disillusionment of all who had participated in creating the plans was considerable. They lost their vision of the program's future, they lost the time invested in preparing it, and they lost any understanding of why I had requested the effort in the first place. Thenceforward the staff was reluctant to engage in planning exercises.

Lessons to be learned from this unsuccessful process are multiple. First, a good manager invites input on the program's future but sets ground rules that articulate expectations—all ideas are welcome; no current practice or activity is sacred; initial discussion should be "blue sky," but the ultimate plan must factor in resources. Second, a good manager may require written exercises from the staff, but does not require major allocations of time for their creation and does not raise expectations that the exercises are other than advisory. Third, a good manager provides feedback even if the substance of the communication will disappoint. And finally, a good manager regularly reminds staff and resource allocators of the plan's components, encouraging both the work effort and the resources needed to meet goals and objectives.

The last lesson—the importance of creating and articulating priorities—is of great importance. All programs can be improved and, funds permitting, expanded. Staff and resource allocators should be clear as to which program aspects will receive heightened attention over time, what new directions the program head wishes to pursue, and therefore what activities will likely receive new funds. Additionally, staff needs to know the areas or activities that their manager deems most important and therefore must accomplish regardless of other demands and expectations. Finally, the staff and their program head should work together to establish targets for performance that give both clear measurements of productivity and a basis for rewarding excellence. Whether it is short-term or long-range, planning should be viewed as critical to program development.

A word of caution is in order, though, about productivity measurements. Several of the organizations with which I worked required one- to three-year plans that included concrete measurements for productivity. I discovered that although it is essential to involve staff in developing targets, one could not simply accept the staff's assessment of what, in the future, they could accomplish. Often they would overestimate how much they could undertake or complete in a given time, tending to forget the inevitable interruptions and unknown tasks that accompany daily work, and also perhaps anxious to impress the manager with their anticipated productivity. It sometimes happened, therefore, that staff performance when measured against staff-created targets appeared to be weak.

This experience taught me the need to set modest goals in planning exercises in order to ensure that the goals have meaning and are to be met. Additionally, it is better for staff—and for those above the archives head—to see targets exceeded rather than missed. Modest goals taken seriously are far better than ambitious ones set aside. Furthermore, one needs to have the flexibility to react positively to opportunities that were not envisioned when work plans were written. The project requested by two Smithsonian offices, for instance, was not initially on the work plan and was clearly labor intensive. Had the opportunity costs of accepting the assignment been excessive, the answer to this request would have been no. Always there is a tension and a balance between performing the ongoing work of a unit and reacting favorably to new requests or challenges.

It sometimes happens that plans fail because the larger institution withdraws needed resources or changes its own goals. Discouragement inevitably sets in, and one can easily feel frustration as senior management invalidates substantial efforts to achieve defined goals in set timeframes. Although it may be difficult, one should resist succumbing to the temptation to treat future planning activity with cynicism. The same flexibility that permits one to seize opportunities not planned for must be drawn upon to regroup, reprioritize, and create new plans that address the new reality. This archivist's experience over a range of institutions confirms assertions that the act of planning in itself is highly useful even if outside forces undermine actual execution. As long as the time invested in planning is not excessive there can only be benefits to thinking, and sometimes rethinking, one's direction.

FOCUS ON STAFF PRODUCTIVITY

Planning and flexibility are important but they are among many internal processes that require attention. Beyond identifying what to accomplish, managers need to review the methods used to achieve performance targets. This archivist found that frequently one needed to look at *staff productivity*. This may be necessary for multiple reasons but is a common phenomenon for programs that grow in size (e.g., to accommodate increased volume) without commensurate changes in program. Such conditions existed at the beginning of my tenure with both the National Archives and Records Administration's Machine Readable Branch (now Center for Electronic Records), and Smithsonian Institution Archives.

Although these units were very different in their focus and methods, they nonetheless had some characteristics in common. Both archival programs were established by forward-thinking leaders who developed strong initial programs that were carried forward in subsequent years by solid professionals. Both used innovative methods for the processing and control of materials and both units initially had high morale and a strong sense of esprit de corps. Unfortunately, time adversely affected these programs. Changing institutional priorities reduced the status and staffing base of one while space shortages combined with volume increases revealed process weaknesses in the other. The result in both programs was a large backlog and the belief among some staff that program improvement was not possible without substantial additional resources.

The need for more staff was indeed apparent, but so also was the need for changes in the existing staff's approach to work. Happily, changes did occur and both programs gained efficiencies that permitted increased levels of productivity. Among the catalysts for change that contributed to program improvements were the following. I urge archivists to consider using them.

1. *Encourage group discussion.* The best way to understand the problem is to hear it described from multiple points of view. Steps that might facilitate the work of one person may have negative consequences for the work of another. On the other hand, giving a group that has never before worked through an issue the opportunity to discuss processes can sometimes be liberating. Hearing a convincing case for change from a colleague might be all that is needed to move staff toward new methods and procedures.

2. *Value the input of new staff.* All of us become accustomed to performing tasks a certain way and the longer we function in a given pattern the less able we are to imagine other approaches. I have found that the views of a new staff member are invaluable windows into existing processes and convenient avenues for rethinking them. New staff is also likely to embrace change, having little investment in the "old" way of doing things.

3. *Push decision making to lower levels.* Sometimes layers of management above the individual archivist become multiple, thereby reducing the worker's sense of control and responsibility. Programs prosper when staff is sufficiently vested in outcomes to make the extra effort needed to assure quality products or meet quotas. I have witnessed a transformation among staff that is given increased authority for making decisions. In some cases they not only accepted this new level of responsibility but relished it. Control over one's work is often the most important "reward" that a manager can provide to capable employees.

4. *Review workflows.* There are often simple solutions to seemingly intractable problems if one looks at the work being performed and the method for achieving it. In one of the archives, for instance, the unit's productivity rate was severely affected by a long-time employee who was thorough but slow. Acting as a bottleneck, this person kept his colleagues from increasing the unit's overall production. The problem was resolved when staff decided to create a system that allowed for some of his work to go elsewhere. This left only complex jobs as the domain of the skilled but slow worker. Happily, this solution reduced frustration for all and led to substantial increases in unit productivity.

Another organization had the opposite problem. Unit managers placed value on a system that encouraged archival staff to undertake work in all functional areas. Giving heavy priority to their mentoring responsibility, the senior archival staff assigned a mixture of processing, conservation, reference, and records management work to all junior staff. As might be expected, work in one area was neglected in order to meet deadlines in another area. For instance there was limited progress in processing and preservation, areas that were less time-sensitive than reference work. The solution to this dilemma was obvious, and when implemented it was successful. Each staff member was assigned to a specific functional area and was held accountable for performance in that area.

5. *Consider creating teams.* The functional arrangement described above provided a basis for establishing a team structure within the archival program. The professional staff, then, was divided into four teams—reference, records management, arrangement and description, and preservation. Each team had the authority to choose its leader, define goals and objectives, create priorities and work plans, and establish team rules. If problems arose between teams, it was the responsibility of the teams themselves to resolve difficulties. This approach made a dramatic difference in staff productivity and carried the added advantage of reducing the hours that managers spent in oversight. This in turn allowed managers to assume special projects for which they had previously been unavailable.

EVALUATE YOUR LEADERSHIP OR MANAGEMENT STYLE

All these skills or approaches serve to improve the performance of staff and are therefore important to a successful archival program. One's own performance, however, may be of greatest importance. Indeed it may be the key ingredient for success or failure. As the program head, your behavior sets the tone and conveys messages whether you intend them or not. When carrying a group forward, your attitude is as significant as your actions, and may have more impact on those you are responsible for managing. On the basis of many experiences, I urge those heading archival programs at any level to recognize and respond positively to the following patterns of behavior.

1. *Do not overpromise.* Just as staff optimistically cite performance targets they cannot in actuality meet, you may promise a benefit or outcome that you cannot deliver. We all want to respond positively to worthy requests, and the head of a program is no less immune to this instinct than others. Promising what you then do not provide, however, will erode credibility. For instance, resist the temptation to tell an outstanding employee you will promote him or her soon unless you are certain you can make this happen. If his or her salary increase is dependent upon a future unknown budget allocation, the best you can offer is your intention to promote should resources permit. Do not assure staff that you will raise funds from prospective donors unless the donors have assured you they will contribute to the specific activity for which you need funds. Do not refer to a situation that you hope will go away as "temporary" if the situation is beyond your control. In short, promise only what you can deliver, not what you would like to deliver. Make this mistake only occasionally and the office staff will assume as a matter of course that you are unreliable and do not keep your word.

2. *Keep complaints and criticism to yourself.* While it is your responsibility to listen to, absorb, and resolve the complaints of others, do not assume that others want to hear you complain. In particular, a manager should be careful not to express to staff his/her frustration with superiors or colleagues. Complaints that others are failing to provide support as needed or promised may seem to the manager like openness with staff but an unfortunate outcome could be the perception that the manager is moving blame to others. The boss is supposed to successfully negotiate for needed support, or ensure the delivery of promised goods. Moreover, bosses who complain to staff about others will cause staff to assume that for a different audience *they* are the target of the boss' complaints. Finally, it is all too easy to cross the line between honest criticism and finger pointing, between discussing problems and whining, between acknowledging others' weaknesses and blaming others for your own failure. Too often, you may believe you're engaging in the former but are actually projecting the latter.

3. *Review your staff's work promptly.* Do not let the work of others sit for long in your in-basket. It is a mistake to assume that because you are engaged in a project that is time-sensitive or has a greater

priority for you than the staff product, you can put off reviewing the product and providing feedback. The consequences of inattention are multiple and negative. You will send a message that you do not value the staff's work and deny yourself the information awaiting your attention. Self-inflicted ignorance may cause you to react slowly to issues that, left unattended, create or exacerbate problems. Program heads who fail to manage their time well are particularly susceptible to this predicament and generally are less effective than more disciplined, organized individuals. Do not hesitate to seek time-management training if you struggle with this problem.

4. *Consult but lead.* Somewhere there is a line between being collaborative and being weak. Those reporting to you may wish for you to consult with them, and they may complain about past superiors who were not interested in their opinions, but in the end they want the boss to decide major issues and assume responsibility for those decisions. To do otherwise can be problematic for you and for your staff. Let me give you an example. I once attempted to resolve a space issue by asking a committee that represented each of the subunits reporting to me how to allocate the space. We were facing a move into greatly reduced headquarters that would require some staff to work at an offsite location. After many meetings the committee reported a heavy allocation of headquarters space to the staff of two subunits, while the staff of other units (including the core archival operation) were to be located elsewhere. This outcome was the result of committee give and take and it represented a consensus view, but I was unhappy with the result. Feeling that the presence at headquarters of all the staff of some program units while relegating others to an offsite location would project an unbalanced view of the program, I and some staff not on the committee regretted this outcome. In the end, the program received enough space to permit all subunits to be located at headquarters but in the interim I was left advocating for an arrangement I did not like. Here again, I should have assumed the responsibility for making hard decisions and then lived with the consequences rather than hand off decision making to the staff and regret the outcome.

5. *Say "Thank You."* These are the two most important words that a program head can use, and it is nigh impossible to overuse them. Financial rewards may be unavailable and promotions out of the

question, but expressions of appreciation go a long way toward making your staff feel that you value them. I was raised to believe that one did one's job without expectations of praise, but years of managing people have taught me that there is much to gain and nothing to lose in telling a colleague that you appreciate his efforts. The cleaning lady, the technician, the archivist, the manager, and the senior executive are equally desirous of being thought well of, and you may assure their cooperation at a key moment in the future simply by expressing your thanks for their efforts today.

By now an image should emerge of the successful archives manager. In large part the characteristics I have described are those of successful people everywhere. Plan well but be flexible; make decisions but seek input; praise but don't overpromise; look for ways to be of service to others while helping your staff improve its performance. Be positive. Communicate but keep complaints to yourself.

However, we do not all possess all of these traits, and each of us has some areas of strength and some areas of weakness. Archival program heads are expected to have sufficient ability to succeed, but the nature of success and the impact we have is dependent upon many factors. Success itself can be measured in different ways. Indeed, in my view, a good archives *leader* may differ substantially from a successful archives *manager*.

Archival leaders assess their programs constantly, looking at current needs but also future trends. They make difficult decisions that are intended to provide a better foundation for the archival enterprise in the future. They change the direction of programs that need new approaches, altering job responsibilities and relationships. They set goals and measure progress in areas where previously none existed. They listen to both the staff and the program's multiple constituencies, but in the end take decisive action even if it is unpopular. They look to the archival profession for the latest research and findings, whenever possible applying those findings to their own program. They seek nontraditional partners and find ways to make the archival program applicable to nontraditional users. In short, they welcome change, encourage innovation, and embrace new ideas.

Archival managers, on the other hand, possess a different set of virtues. Good managers are as devoted to stability as leaders are to change. Good managers make sure that staff is comfortable with work assignments, have the appropriate tools and knowledge, and establish clear expectations and reporting requirements. Good managers develop defined performance measures and hold staff accountable for meeting them. They create strong lines of communication, maintain consistent oversight, and seek continuing staff input. If intermediate supervisors report to them, good managers support rather than interfere with the line manager's authority. They remove obstacles to the performance of staff work and are advocates for the staff when addressing senior management. They are even-tempered and even-handed. They inspire loyalty.

Both of these skill sets are needed and to some degree every program head has at least some components of a good manager and a good leader. However, there are times when leadership and management come into conflict, and one's predilection at those times may indicate the degree to which one is more of a manager than a leader. Leaders tend to move toward the new, leaving less time for careful management. Leaders may stretch staff with their demands for expansion. Leaders may find that existing staff may be suited to the current work but are not appropriate for new tasks accompanying a change in direction. Leaders may create programs that carry the archives into the future, but at the expense of tension today. In short, good managers reduce risks and ensure stability while good leaders may well introduce risks and therefore invite instability.

As necessary as both skills may be, it is rare indeed to find both talents fully developed in the same individual. As has been noted, we are all better at some things than others and it is likely that each of us will be more inclined toward a managerial style or a leadership style. I have learned the value of thinking about one's own inclination, and in particular, about how to maximize the value of one's strengths while reducing the impact of one's weaknesses. The bustle of daily existence can blur self-awareness, but it is nonetheless very helpful to understand how one's own preferences, manner of expression, and style of interaction affect one's colleagues and the workplace.

It is also helpful to recognize the personal implications of leadership versus management. My own assessment is that either category brings rewards and disadvantages. Leaders may be viewed as empire builders, they may anger staff because of the stresses their initiatives create, and they risk eliminating a valued traditional activity for one that is new and questionable. Managers are protected from these criticisms but they may be viewed as unresponsive to changing needs, overly protective of staff, or lacking in flexibility and imagination. In general, it appears that leaders are more likely to receive praise from superiors while managers are more likely to be praised by their staff.

The ideal program head, of course, holds the respect of both. The best leaders should have sufficient management skills to reduce the impact of program expansion and change on staff, and the best managers should have enough leadership ability to respond to changing conditions. Either way, those heading archival programs face daily, continuing challenges. Repositories are typically underfunded and understaffed, a condition that only worsens with each new accession. The nature of those accessions today present immense technological challenges, greatly exceeding traditional media issues. Today's archivists must confront e-mail, digital photography, Web sites, and interactive databases along with paper, microfilm, photographs, and sound recordings. They must provide increasingly sophisticated reference services and increasingly complex records management services. They must control and preserve large volumes of material while digitizing (and therefore duplicating) substantial portions of their holdings. They must capture records that are technologically dependent in an era of constant technological change, and hold those records safe for the future.

To do this well, they must bring every talent to the workplace and push daily against the tide of organizational and professional issues facing them. Archival leaders today must confront our complex society and the records it generates with every tool at their disposal. They need training and support, and ideally they have the budgetary resources to command such support just as their staffs receive professional training in aspects of archives methodology. Obvious as this may be, however, trainers, counselors, coaches, and mentors in program management and leadership are typically beyond the budget of most archives and therefore unavailable to most program heads.

In reality, most of us learn by doing. We respond instinctively to situations, and over time we build a patterned response that becomes our unique style in the workplace. Over time we can measure the impact of our actions, determining what produces positive results and what seems to work against us. Over time and with effort, we can modify our behavior and strengthen our skills. We can reduce the number of occasions that we foster negative results and increase our ratio of success. Perfection is not possible, but improvement is within everyone's reach.

Carrying your staff and program forward is a difficult undertaking, and this archivist has experienced her share of disappointments. There are no perfect program heads, only evolving leaders and managers. Every day brings new opportunities for learning, and the observant will learn from others as well as from personal experience. Regardless of your position on the supervisory scale, or your place on an imagined "learning curve," remember to see the value in your efforts and the importance of your work. We all make mistakes, we all have successes, and we all can improve. Value yourself, believe in yourself, and work consciously to improve your management and leadership abilities. Good program heads are the product of time, experience, and of lessons learned.

Chapter 9

Stranger in a Strange Land: The Archivist and the Corporation

Philip F. Mooney

INTRODUCTION: GROWING NUMBERS OF CORPORATE ARCHIVES

One of the smaller subsets of the archival professionals includes those who manage historical records for North American businesses. These corporate archivists have unique opportunities but also face unique challenges in building successful programs. In early 2007, the Web site of the Society of American Archivists listed 342 members of its 3,100 individual members as affiliated with Business Archives. The current *Directory of Corporate Archives in the United States and Canada* counts slightly more than 300 American companies maintaining some form of corporate archives. Compared with previous surveys of historical operations in American corporations, these numbers are encouraging and seem to signal an increased interest in the preservation of business records. In 1969, 133 companies reported a functioning archival program employing 13 full-time archivists. By 1980, the numbers had grown to 200 programs maintained by 60 archivists. The statistical evidence suggests that corporations have an increasing interest in the preservation of their history and are willing to invest in it. Growth in corporate archives has not been spectacular over the past quarter century, but in an environment that is ahistorical in the main, the increase may suggest expanded opportunities for the archival profession.[1]

WHY CORPORATE ARCHIVAL PROGRAMS BEGIN

The factors that influence a corporation to establish an archives are varied, but they tend to fall into distinct categories: anniversaries and special events, litigation, a significant management initiative, or an identified information gap. The looming anniversary has always been a motivator for assembling a historical collection. As companies approach key milestones, they want to document progress and mark highlights in some tangible fashion—a book, an exhibit, or splashy audiovisual presentation. All of these products require historical documentation and someone with the analytical skills to interpret the materials and present the results in an informative and compelling way. The creation of the first corporate archives at the Firestone Tire and Rubber Company in 1943 provided the historical framework for the firm's fiftieth-anniversary celebration some seven years later. Anniversaries provide a single opportunity when the focus of the parent organization is in the past. Many archival programs have been formed to support "the book," "the film," or "the exhibit."[2]

Such celebratory milestones underscore the importance of historical records as a resource for the parent organization and provide a rationale for a more permanent and ongoing internal information center. Moving the archives from an event-driven consulting arm to an ongoing business-support unit is a model that has been repeated dozens of times over the past half century.

Closely linked, if not intertwined, with the anniversary driver is the desire of corporate executives to document the legacy of their tenure. In many cases the founding family or entrepreneurial leader desires to document his or her work and create a corporate culture based on the principles that made the business successful. Most business leaders feel that their contributions have positively impacted the greater society, but without records, the achievement of the enterprise could be discounted, misinterpreted, or forgotten. The creation of a company archives guarantees that the next generation of leaders will understand and appreciate the foundational building blocks that enabled the business to achieve a unique position in the marketplace.

As senior managers come to the end of their business careers the realization often emerges that documentation of their administration is incomplete, fragmented, or nonexistent. In this environment, the creation of a corporate archives offers an opportunity to institutionalize the philosophies, strategies, and mission of the parent organization. At the same time, a designated archives becomes the central repository for records of enduring value that exist in scattered locations with no administrative structure to govern them. The centralization of a records program then enables the production of publications, exhibitions, publicity programs, internal communications and films and videos that perpetuate the legacy and define and shape the corporate culture.

One additional factor should be noted for businesses that form corporate archives. All of them are successful operations with strong cash flow and bottom-line financials. History appeals to the fiscally secure who can afford the luxury of an operation that will not contribute significantly to the revenue stream.

Therein lies the basic challenge that every business archives faces. From its very inception, the positioning of the department is viewed as overhead and tangential to the core mission of the organization. Only a small number of businesses actively sponsor an archival program within their walls, and the sustained existence of the function is totally dependent on the organization's continued financial success. Personality-driven and events-focused archives stand on perilous ground when new management teams appear and when the focus on high-profile celebrations shifts.

From a legal perspective, records offer great value to the corporation and the lack of records can endanger its intellectual property rights, its standing with regulatory agencies, and its reputation with the public. The inability to locate and produce documentation when required can result in significant expense and highlight the need for organized record keeping. While it is generally not the deciding factor for the establishment of an archives, litigation support remains one of the compelling reasons to professionally manage records.[3]

Corporations rely on documentation to protect their rights and to defend the organization from the claims of others. Trademarks, slogans, patents, advertising concepts, and promotional ideas require extensive documentation to assert the owners' rights in a court of law. Failure to do so can result in asset losses in the millions of dollars. Relatively speaking, the costs of an archival program are insignificant compared with the devastating impact of a negative legal decision. In an era of increased public scrutiny, the archives assumes an even larger role in the corporate structure in providing support for compliance and governance issues. An emphasis on a strong records program marks the program as a relevant and critical contributor to the business. A commitment to the professional management of the corporate record signals to regulators that an organization has placed a strong emphasis on the proper care of those materials and that history has a long-term value to the entire workforce.

Very occasionally, an archival program emerges because the business recognizes that the organization has an information gap requiring action. The lack of a managed historical collection can result in expensive work repetition, missed marketing opportunities, factually incorrect data, passive and underutilized resources, and a crumbling corporate identity. Visionary managers will recognize how an archival program can bridge those gaps and make the organization more effective and efficient.[4] Regretfully, this proactive recognition of the positive value of records seldom takes root. Managers, obsessed with delivering results quarter by quarter, spend little time contemplating the significance of heritage in fulfilling goals and objectives.

WHY CORPORATE ARCHIVAL PROGRAMS FAIL

In one very important respect, business and archives make strange bedfellows. A discipline that continually looks to the past for insight, answers and perspective on contemporary issues butts heads with an ingrained philosophy that suggests that only the future matters. Past successes, financial results and leadership models have little relevance in a world that values innovation, lean organizational units and a larger focus on delivering increasing returns to shareholders. In this operating environment, it is not surprising that many archival programs at high profile companies fail in the long term.[5]

The two primary reasons for the elimination of archives are declining economics and leadership change. Just as archival programs are birthed in organizations with a solid financial base, so, too, are they jettisoned when an economic downtown impacts the profit and loss statement. When the budget cuts begin, the archives is exposed as a "nice to have" function, but one that is pure overhead, negatively impacting the balance sheet. The arguments around corporate culture and the significance of heritage in the organizational DNA become much more difficult to justify as management is pressured by investors and analysts to reduce operating costs and improve cash flow.

Management change can also trigger a reevaluation of the archival function. When programs are funded to preserve the legacy of a previous administration, the arrival of a new management team can prove life-threatening. In the political arena, a new president or governor will want to craft a team loyal to his or her programs. In business circles, the new leader frequently desires to change the culture and to foster an organization that embraces change and is willing to move to a new operational structure. There is little interest in reflective thinking or looking to the past for inspiration. The actions of previous leaders are irrelevant in a contemporary society that demands forward-looking leaders. For an archives linked to a specific individual, the challenge for survival begins the day a successor is named.

In these situations, the best strategy is to develop an aggressive public relations campaign that sells the benefits of maintaining an archival program. Creating reports that document the archival contribution, soliciting endorsements from satisfied customers and enlisting support from other operating units can help develop a business case for the retention of the function. All of these techniques should be incorporated into the normal operational procedures of the archives, but in times of crisis, they take on heightened importance.

SELLING HISTORY TO MANAGEMENT

Whatever the reason for the initial creation of an archives, that administrative action only represents the very first step in an evolving process. For an archives to flourish over a long period of time, the concept of maintaining a historical records collection must be visibly communicated to all levels of the organization. An important early action would be to establish the authority of the archives to collect, maintain, and organize records on behalf of the organization. This document, crafted by the archivist, should provide the broadest mandate for the definition of which classes of records will be considered "historical."[6] A policy statement issued from senior management to all employees formalizes that responsibility and provides the executive support that will be required to bring the organization into compliance. Still, a single document will not serve the ongoing needs of the archives. The policy should be restated at regular intervals and incorporated into institutional policies and procedures.

With a collecting policy in place, creating a mission statement for the archives becomes the next critical step. This document should clearly define the role of the function within the corporation. It defines the activities, roles, and responsibilities of the unit; the scope and limitations of its collecting policies. Once the document has been approved by management, it becomes the template from which all business plans are developed and the activities of the archives are measured and evaluated.

The policy statement and mission document represent the building blocks for the program. They secure the initial executive support so critical in developing a program, but, more importantly, they establish a two-way communications process that keeps the archives relevant to the business and at the top of the mind. A third technique to foster management involvement is the creation of an archives advisory board that involves managers from diverse functional areas in helping the archives to collect records and design programs that adequately document the activities of the corporation. These boards need not be highly structured bodies. They can be as formal or informal as they need to be. The end result is to expand the support network for the archives beyond the executive wing to create a constituent base that values and supports archival work.

The use of regular reports to mark progress against the mission further advances a broader understanding, appreciation, and endorsement of archival work. Whether the documents are weekly, monthly, or quarterly, they should be concise summaries that emphasize results. Business leaders receive large amounts of information on a daily basis and need to process it quickly. Business archivists need to find a communications style that mirrors internal information flow and presents the salient points in a compelling, succinct fashion. Storytelling techniques are particularly effective tools to use here. Identify the client, services provided, and benefits received by the corporation. If a project can be linked to financial results, the report takes on added significance, but productivity gains, positive public relations activities, and strong support of other functions are also meaningful contributions.

INTEGRATING ARCHIVES INTO THE BUSINESS PLAN

There is not a natural placement for an archives in the typical organization chart for a corporation. Should it be part of the Communications Group because of its utility as a source of stories, or is it better placed with Legal, where compliance issues rest? Would the Corporate Secretary's Office provide a good home as it already keeps vital records for the corporation, or should it be dropped into Administrative Services with other odd functions like Security, Food Service and Maintenance? There are no right answers to these questions, as every business sees history and its value through a slightly different lens. However, the key point is that the fit will not be a natural one, and the archivist needs to adapt to the cultural values and processes manifested in the workplace.

Although the archives is "different" from other functions, minimizing those differences is critical. The archivist must not retreat into a remote corner of the business, quietly processing collections and hoping for recognition for professionally managing the records. Instead, the archivist must creatively work to mainstream programs and make history a relevant tool in the corporate arsenal. The very first step in this process is to create a business plan that mirrors the submissions of other groups and departments. This document should clearly communicate the role of the archives in the organization and should list objectives targeted for the fiscal year.

Most corporations have an annual business review cycle where the various functions present their business plans and budgets for the upcoming year and request the necessary resources to achieve their stated objectives. Management will then evaluate all of the requests and prioritize budget allocations against the overall corporate strategies. Not all projects will make the cut. Only those requests that are closely aligned with the broad organizational goals and that promise a return on the investment will find a receptive audience.

Using the approved mission statement for the program as the overriding framework, the archives' annual business plan should list key objectives for the calendar year. The objectives should be measurable, realistic, specific, and time bound. They should also be linked closely to the objectives of the functional area where the archives resides. For instance, a communications group might have one of its objectives: "To generate at least six positive stories about the company in the first nine months of the year." Building on that objective, the archives might list the following: "Identify three to six story ideas based on heritage that could be pitched to national media." In this example, the links between functions are clear, the archives becomes an active rather than a passive asset, and the company starts to see some benefits from its funding.

Resource allocators are seldom influenced by reports on reference requests serviced, cubic feet of processed collections, and numbers of finding aids created. Of greater impact is how the collections positively impact the business, its customers, and public opinion. Whenever progress can be quantified in those categories, the archival program gets closer to the business and connected to its values. The more the archivist thinks and acts like businesspeople, the more successful the program will be.

MARKETING THE ARCHIVES

When most archivists think of outreach, they concentrate on audiences outside their institution. They look to engage and inform the community, the media, educators, and academics about the collections they hold and have available for research. For the business archivist, the situation is reversed. Most corporate collections are closed to outside research and holdings are not reported to national databases. Rather, the corporate archivist strives to publicize the collection to potential internal clients to broaden the support base for the function and to promote the collections as a resource for a broad constituency.

With initiatives both big and small, there are a multitude of opportunities that help to gain greater visibility for the archives. The following are some areas of outreach which have applications for all archivists regardless of their institutional affiliation but which are particularly important for business archivists to consider.

Anniversaries and Special Events

Earlier in this chapter, the importance of anniversaries was cited as one of the primary reasons to establish an archives. In many instances, the formation of the program is linked directly to the publication of a book. These histories can be "coffee table" publications rich in illustrations and compelling graphics, or more serious academic tomes that attempt to understand and interpret the major decisions that have shaped the corporation. Regardless of format, extensive records will be required to support the publications process.

For both the fledgling program and the established archives, key milestones focus the entire organization's attention on a specific time frame and release resources that are not normally available. Anniversaries are invitations to celebrate the past and to honor the achievement of previous generations. It is also a time to help create a culture that will define the organization moving forward. A published history reinforces both of these objectives and provides a permanent reference tool for associates, customers, and academics to consider and study.

Whether the publication is internally or externally generated, the archives becomes the most important resource in the organization, and the archivist becomes a critical member of the publications team. Both the neophyte and the veteran can directly impact the quality of the finished pieces. A newly hired archivist will have the broadest mandate from management to collect records from all corners of the organization to support the publication, while a seasoned archivist has the institution knowledge to identify which records, photographs, and audiovisual materials will best tell the story, providing timely cost-effective consulting services to the project. The finished product not only becomes a remembrance of the celebration, it also functions as a visible reminder of an archival presence.

An anniversary frequently stimulates a demand for souvenir items that capture vignettes of history. Postcards, calendars, nostalgia packaging, reproduction advertising and documents capture corporate imagery and provide meaningful keepsakes for associates and constituents, but their creation is dependent on the availability of original documents. Similarly, for consumer goods corporations, such as The Coca-Cola Company, Kraft, and Procter & Gamble, history can become an important marketing tool through the creation of colorful, limited edition packaging for their brands that capitalize on anniversary themes.

Oral histories and time capsules can add depth to the historical presence any time, but anniversaries give them more prominence. Employees at all levels of the organization are eager to tell their stories and recount their personal experiences when the spotlight is on, and when an archivist is present to conduct the interviews, the quality of the information elicited improves because of the special role of the position. The archivist is a fellow associate that the interviewee trusts with sensitive information, believing that the conversation will be handled in a sympathetic fashion. A journalist or outside interviewer would not enjoy the same level of trust and would receive filtered information from a guarded interviewee. Homecoming gatherings of current and retired employees offer extraordinary opportunities for gathering information that would not be captured in other documentary formats.

Time capsules are a more populist form of creating a permanent historical record. While most archivists would cringe at the thought of placing documents into a sealed container that would have exposure to climactic and environmental changes, the placement of a capsule into a building cornerstone or other significantly important physical location puts history in the forefront of corporate thinking. Through the creative use of reproduction and duplicate materials, the public relations objectives can be achieved without threat to original records.

Publications

Once management blesses the creation of the archives with an official proclamation, many would feel that advocacy is no longer required to support the program, but the exact opposite is true. As the excitement of an anniversary fades, the organization reverts to its normal operational mode—focused on the future. To maintain relevancy and to engage associates, many archivists use pamphlets, brochures, and booklets to heighten awareness of their programs. Such publications can be as simple or elaborate as the budget will allow, but their overall intent is to raise consciousness and recruit new users.

One of the most popular tools is an informational pamphlet that explains the role of the archives and outlines the service it provides. It may also become a solicitation tool by defining collection priorities and outlining subject areas requiring additional documentation. Some include samples of research projects completed, quotes from satisfied clients, the mission statement for the program, and the critical contact information for research requests. To be effective, promotional pieces need to employ strong graphics that immediately capture the attention of the reader and encourage further exploration. They should be inexpensive enough to allow wide dissemination through mass mailings and other forms of continuous distribution. Nobody who visits the archives or engages with a staff member should leave without one.

Other popular publications include brand histories, historical timelines, biographical sketches, and photographic compilations. The corporate birthday may justify a book, but every year is an anniversary for some product, service, or region, thereby creating an opportunity for the archives to demonstrate its expertise. In today's mobile workforce, where managers move regularly from one company to another, the archives becomes the living corporate memory that allows minihistories to be produced. Brand managers may inherit products that have been in the marketplace for decades. A history of the brand and its positioning over time will provide useful guidance for future marketing efforts and may prevent a costly "reinvention of the wheel." In addition to the internal relevance, these applications have extended value as a resource for educators, journalists, students, and the general public.

Most corporations produce magazines and newsletters on a regular basis as internal communications tools both for active employees and retirees. These publications require a steady flow of content that the archives can support. Columns that highlight past innovations, mark specific corporate milestones, or provide focus on a given topic spotlight the significance of the archives as a resource. Question-and-answer features, trivia games, compilations of significant photographs, or the inclusion of an oral history all raise consciousness about the program and imbed heritage as a natural element in normal communications flow.

As technology has exploded and changes the way we communicate as a society, archival programs have embraced these new opportunities to share their resources and trumpet their capabilities. Electronic publishing allows programs to design, produce, and distribute a wide range of materials to a mass market for a fraction of the cost of print. Additionally, company intranets and the Internet offer endless possibilities for global organizations and the general public to access archival holdings with a single keystroke.

Company intranet sites facilitate information sharing across national and international boundaries and make the concept of a "virtual archives" a reality. Thousands of photographs, documents, and videos are accessible on-demand and can be downloaded in a matter of minutes to users in far-flung locations. No longer are patrons required to adhere to standard office hours to access collections and make reference requests. The archives is always open and ready to service its clients. These intranet sites also allow the archivist to create an internal information desk where a wide variety of historical data can reside. From biographies of corporate leadership to product and brand histories, the intranet becomes the logical place for associates to find answers to their questions. In a world where people seeking information turn to search engines like Google and Yahoo! to access data of personal relevance instantaneously, the expectation is that the archives will have similar tools to service their business needs for information—easily and quickly.

For the general population, a segment of the corporate internet site dedicated to heritage provides educational content in an easy-to-use format. A well-designed section will encourage visitors to experience history in a very personal way. From downloadable graphics to interactive games to engaging narratives and factoids, the site becomes a significant asset in framing public opinion.

Exhibitions

Creating exhibitions based on archival holdings provides continuous visibility for the program and gives its mission statement validity to the workforce. From a single display case to a dedicated space in a headquarters building to a full-fledged museum, exhibits manifest the wide range of the collection and formalize the importance of history to the parent body. Over time, the archives becomes a vital cog in an employee communications program, providing the links between past and present that define corporate identity. As new products and services are introduced, they are married to their predecessors in creative displays that allow the viewer to connect the dots.

For sales centers, branches, and subsidiaries located away from the corporate center, traveling shows are an excellent means of communicating principles and values in a way that handbooks and publications do not. They are a three-dimensional manifestation of the actions and events that shaped the corporation and established the core values that guide the business today. Similarly, exhibitions can be a powerful initiative to shape public opinion and to make the business relevant to the broader community. They tell the corporate story in engaging formats that convey key messages in a compact presentation. Venues can range from shopping malls and civic centers to libraries, banks, and historical societies depending on the complexity of the exhibit structure, but they enjoy one common element: They provide the business with a tool to engage stakeholders in environments where they do not normally have a presence.

Audiovisual Productions

One advantage of funding an archives is to centralize the collection of records in a single location, rather than having resources scattered throughout the organization with no custodial responsibility. As audiovisual materials come into the collection from different functions and groups, so do opportunities for developing presentations that have wide application. With a little creativity and strong partnerships with other groups, the concept of a "presentation in a box" can become a reality.

The most obvious and broadest-reaching need would be a history of the business. For years the standard format for this type of presentation was the slide show or the video but technology today makes the task much easier. Programs such as PowerPoint empower the archivist to create a template that is general enough to be relevant to the entire organization but allows easy customization at the local level. These electronic presentations are easily transmitted around the globe and have the further advantage of allowing change or updating at a moment's notice. They enhance employee orientation and training programs and are the prefect choice to satisfy requests from educators, service clubs, fraternal groups, and the general public for a business overview.

Next in importance is a presentation on the archives itself. Selling the program, its resources and benefits is an ongoing part of the archivists' job description. Even if they know of its existence, most of the firm's associates will have a very superficial understanding of what the archives does and how it benefits the business. A presentation that describes the program in detail, outlines collecting areas, and documents completed projects will engender greater understanding and may recruit new users. It should be heavily populated with visual references and clearly embody the department's mission statement. The successful archivist will treat this presentation as a campaigning politician would treat the media. There is never an audience too small to hear and be influenced by the party message.

Other prepackaged programs could be compilations of advertising jingles, television commercials, famous speeches, news clips, radio broadcasts, and popular photographs. By having a series of programs "on demand," the department will be able to respond to those last-minute requests that inevitably come to disrupt daily routines. By slowly building a resource base of "best in class" programming in the course of normal work, the emergency requests can be satisfied in a qualitative fashion.

Public Relations

One of the few natural allies for an archives is the public relations function. It is an organizational unit whose lifeblood is information, and the ability to gather and disseminate it quickly is critical. The intersection of the two functions marries complementary skill sets. Public relations staff deal with reporters on deadline, while the archivist is used to providing information on a time-sensitive basis. This commonality of purpose often links the groups together either organizationally or on a workflow basis.

The archives provides the fodder that generates stories about the company whether in the form of facts for press releases, illustrations for textbooks, or film and video for the electronic media. Much of the work is reactive, responding to inquiries flowing into the business, but there are opportunities for the archivist to take a more proactive role in creating news. Creating lists of anniversaries and special events on a regular basis can generate public relations programs that were not scheduled. Similarly, sharing photographs, documents, and other records can add perspective to a contemporary issue. For instance, the launch of a new product may have parallels in history that media relations professionals might not recognize but which would add substance and color to the story. A strong interrelationship between the groups makes this type of exchange mutually beneficial.

The archivist enjoys a special position within the corporation that may have greater respect outside the organization than it does internally. From the perspective of the press corps, the archivist has credibility when speaking about the history of the firm and is considered favorably when offered for interviews. Not every person is comfortable in this role, but for those who are willing to conduct television, radio, and newspaper interviews, they significantly enhance the positioning of the archives as a corporate resource. The archivist becomes a de facto member of the public relations team and elevates the visibility of the archives. To the outside world, an archivist is an interesting and unusual job in a business setting. Capitalizing on that interest, whether directly or indirectly, should be an imperative.

Other Marketing Ideas

Marketing is more of a mind-set and approach to daily work than a series of high-impact events that spotlight the archives. A good manager will look for little opportunities every day to get more recognition for the program and to position it as a mainstream element in the business. Build on the success of a small project and larger ones will gradually emerge. Listed below are some principles that will help build a successful program if executed properly:

1. *Insist on quality work at all times and a commitment to service.* There is an old adage that states that you have only one opportunity to make a good first impression. Businesses are built on results, not promises. Every client is a potential supporter or detractor depending on the quality of the experience. Even for the most established programs, most researchers approach the archives because of word-of-mouth endorsement. A quality work product delivered accurately and on time to meet the client's needs will enhance archival reputation, but a bad experience will inflict serious damage that can jeopardize the entire operation.

2. *Focus on the routine and the obvious.* Perception quickly can become reality from both positive and negative perspective. Everything communicates a message about the archival program, from the physical environment where the archives is located to the lighting, furnishings, and signage used in the space. All of the equipment used in the archives should be of the same quality as that used throughout the business, and managers should lobby for a physical location visible to the general population. Without regular contact with other business units, the archives can quickly fade from active consideration.

   Within the archival walls, the workplace should be clean and orderly, the records well cared for, and the setting open and welcoming. Here, the manager must establish that corporate records are valued and are being preserved by skilled professionals dedicated to the information needs of the business.

3. *Prioritize work against projects that will yield the highest return.* In the corporate world, not all records have equal value, nor should

they receive equal attention. In a consumer goods company, the advertising and marketing files will generally be used more frequently than other records, while banks and insurance companies would rely more heavily on financial records. Over time, the archivist will see these patterns emerge.

With limited staff and resources, the archivist must make choices regarding the records that have long-term value to the business; use will drive those decisions. Those record groups requested most often will garner the lion's share of the resources. They provide the justification for the program and yield tangible results that the entire corporation can see. The archivist is encouraged to enhance those collections and the relationships they represent. Going for the low-hanging fruit is the only strategy to follow when building a program.

THE IMPORTANCE OF RELATIONSHIPS

In the long term, no corporate archives can exist without partners. The initial support of the CEO can carry the program for a while but the program must forge alliances with other operating units if it is to survive. The archivist needs to develop propositions that provide benefits to both parties and that create a broader understanding of the relevance of the historical record. It is a role that requires the archivist to be proactive in surfacing ideas to business associates. While the initiative may occasionally come from the business, most will need to be self-generated. The normal flow of business rarely looks for a historical perspective before launching a new project or program.

Because the archives services the entire organization, the archivist often has cross-functional interactions that provide an opportunity to suggest enterprisewide information solutions. Combined with the historical understanding of the decision-making process and a knowledge of information management tools and techniques, the archivist can properly assume a consulting role in a number of functional areas. Previous sections of this chapter have outlined the value of archives in supporting legal and public relations groups through partnerships that are mutually beneficial. That same model, extended to other parts of the business, builds broad-based partnerships that create joint dependency.

Many corporations today are searching for a technical solution to help manage creative assets, advertising, graphics, Web sites, photography, and audiovisual material. Archivists have embraced early forms of such technologies for years and have been among the early adapters of digital asset management systems. In searching for enterprise-wide solutions, the archivist can partner with the IT and marketing organizations to identify a product or products that will deliver the desired results.

Although marketing plans tend to be forward looking, managers need to understand the brand positioning from a historical perspective, and agencies need to appreciate the role that advertising has played in developing brand image. Ignoring history risks "reinventing the wheel" with the resulting expenditure of large amounts of capital. By enlisting the archives as a partner in the process of orienting agencies and staff, new creative work will benefit from the accumulated knowledge that preceded it. Similarly, the human relations function can incorporate archival elements into its orientation, training, and retiree programs.

The critical element in all of these programs is the archivist presenting these ideas to the function. As obvious as the relationships appear to be, business managers do not naturally think of the archives as a partner in daily work. The archivist needs to make those connections and impose regular quality control checks to be sure the links are still intact.

MEASURING THE VALUE

In looking at the role of the archives in a corporate setting, the financial impact of the function cannot be ignored. It costs money to hire staff, provide space and equipment, and procure supplies for the operation. Corporations like to quantify everything that exists as a cost center, and the archives certainly falls into that category. What then is the return on this investment and how can it be measured?

Most archival programs do not generate revenue streams to offset their expenses but there are a few examples of positive money flow. Companies like Coca-Cola with powerful trademarks license those marks to be used by third parties in return for a royalty fee. Those fees can amount to millions of dollars and a formula can be created to isolate the archival contribution. Reproductions of classic advertising and promotional materials, books, and stationery items, nostalgic packaging and limited-edition collectibles are major product categories that mine the archives for contemporary applications. In some cases, the royalty fees received more than offset the entire operational cost of the program.

In a related area, some companies will charge licensing fees for the use of archival assets in publication projects and documentary production. By charging photography and clips fees to outside vendors, costs for archives operations can be reduced or eliminated. Still another approach is to implement an internal chargeback system for archival services. These charges can be assessed across the entire organization as a general fee in the manner in which utility expenses are shared, or a specific formula can be developed to charge only those groups using the archives.

The more common approach to measuring the archival contribution to the bottom line is to focus on the products and services provided and apply the value of those services against operational costs. For instance, if the archives provides documentation in a trademark or intellectual property case, it is possible to calculate the costs the corporation would assume if outside counsel had been hired to do the same work. Another approach would be to look at the economic impact of a negative court ruling because supporting documentation could not be located. Admittedly, these are soft-dollar projections that are open to dispute, but they may be the only way to develop a measurement tool for management review.

If the archives creates a Web site or prepares an orientation program, or organizes an exhibition, the costs of completing these assignments using outside consultants can be determined. The greatest unknown factor in making these projections is the actual time required for an outsider to deliver finished product to the quality standards of the corporation. The internal archivist obviously has a deep understanding of the organization that allows operational efficiencies.

Good service can generate a support network that can be marshaled to endorse the value of archival services. While the archives itself does not normally generate a large revenue stream, the information it provides may directly impact the profitability of the organization. Compile those e-mails and memos that praise the archival contribution to a successful initiative. Solicit endorsements from satisfied customers and ask those clients to convey their positive commentary to management. The overall weight of a broad-based "friends" group will powerfully link the archives to the core business.

Public relations work has industry measurement standards that can be applied to archival work. When a story appears in a newspaper or runs on local or national television, the costs of advertising in those media will be the standard against which value is determined. The larger the media outlet, the more valuable the placement becomes. A story carried by one of the wire services or broadcast by a national network could cover the entire yearly operating costs of the program.

Finally, there is the value of information itself. What costs would the corporation be willing to assume for information delivered in a timely, confidential manner with historical perspective? Online systems like Lexis/Nexis offer some parameters for comparison, but they fall short on delivering real value. The unfortunate reality is that most of these numbers are very speculative but they do suggest a mode of thinking and evaluation that needs to be communicated to management.

THE LEADERSHIP FACTOR

Administering an archival program within a corporation is a unique undertaking. The position does not fit easily into the classification schemes businesses use in developing job descriptions. An archives department is not a core function, and there may be difficulties in finding a proper placement in the organization. In fact, most corporate programs will change reporting structures numerous times over the years in an effort to find a harmonious marriage. For the archivist, it can be uncomfortable moving from one part of the company to another, requiring great flexibility and strong interpersonal skills. Understanding and appreciating the special contributions of corporate archives while recognizing the inherent contradiction in mainstreaming history help put the function in perspective.

In analyzing successful corporate programs over the past three decades, a few key principles emerge that could serve as guidelines for long-term success:

1. *Never link the archives to a single function.* The ultimate success of a program rests on service to multiple constituencies. The reality of corporate life is that things will change, the relative importance of groups and departments will rise and fall, and managers

will not remain in one role for a long time. Consequently, archivists need to cultivate a broad portfolio of users to mitigate the potential impact of reorganization or shifting business priorities.

Many archivists would not consider sales and marketing to be areas of expertise, or even interest, in their daily lives, but in the corporate world these skills are required elements for success. Every day, the archivist needs to focus on new approaches for selling the program and making it relevant for other business units. When the transitions come, as they inevitably will, the department will find a welcome home in another part of the organization.

2. *Use escalating success stories to build up programs.* One of the biggest mistakes an archivist can make is to attempt to implement a broad range of programs simultaneously. Such an approach is almost certainly doomed from the start. Given the limited resources available both in terms of staff and budget, the inevitable results will disappoint clients and erode critical bases of support.

Rather, archival programs should be strategic, focused, and visible. Manage expectations from start to finish and overdeliver on them. Programs that can easily be measured and that track against larger corporate goals should take precedence over projects that are not as well defined. Resource allocators love initiatives that make good on their promises and have tangible results. When the next cycle of approvals rolls around, programs with proven track records reap the benefit and procure increased budget and staff. Success will increase the level of trust with management and allow the program to grow, but the reverse is also true. A failure to meet objectives and provide measurable returns makes the archival proposition harder to justify and support.

3. *Be an activist archivist.* Strong business leaders have a vision for their business that drives them to move the enterprise from its comfort zone, to seize new growth opportunities and to challenge the status quo. They place a premium on innovation, creative thinking, and a willingness to test boundaries; they are always discontented, haunted by the notion that their consumers might look to other companies to better serve their needs and provide them with the services they desire. While it may be a bit uncomfortable and unnatural to think of archival work in those terms, the archivist must be willing to embrace those attitudes and values to sell the program. Waiting for the phone to ring or the e-

mail request to arrive is a dangerous approach for a service organization that is corporate overhead. The archivist needs to actively look for business propositions that would benefit from the
archival record and then offer resources that will enhance the
quality of the work. To integrate archives into the soul of the business requires the archivist to step forward and package information into relevant modules.

One of the defining characteristics of the modern corporation
is the ever-changing composition of the workforce. People no
longer expect to remain in one job for a lifetime. They want new
experiences in different settings to allow for personal growth and
development. People enter and leave the firm in high numbers,
creating constant "churn" and the need to capture and pass on
knowledge and documentation. Coupled with high employee
turnover is another trend that places a premium on keeping a
lean overall head count. When contractors fill positions previously occupied by full-time associates, the inevitable result is a loss
of corporate memory and inability to use lessons from the past.
Without an archival program in place, the information gap will
widen, exposing the corporation to significant financial and intellectual loss.

The one person in the organization who can fill some of these
gaps is the archivist. More than ever, the role requires an individual who understands the past and is capable of seeing how
previous case studies could influence current practices. Even
more important, the archivist must share this knowledge and put
relevant documentation in the hands of those who need it but
may not even know of its existence. The days of quietly processing collections and hoping someone will recognize the work are
gone. Making archival records an ongoing part of the business
is the only path to take.

CONCLUSION: LEADERSHIP IS THE KEY

Some six decades after the first corporate archives came into existence,
the preservation of business records remains one of the most undocumented aspects of American society. Relatively few public historical
agencies have attached much importance to collecting and preserving
such material, and the private sector has displayed a similar lack of

enthusiasm. Only the 300 corporations that have allocated resources to this function offer some hope that history can become a discipline that has relevance and worth in serving the information needs of the organization.

By far, the most important factor in determining whether an archives has a role in the corporate world is the individual selected as archivist. More than in any other segment of the profession, the corporate archivist must demonstrate managerial and communications skills that rival those of business associates while bringing a new set of technical skills into an environment not well-equipped to receive them. Where programs have succeeded, success is directly linked to individuals who saw opportunities for archival applications in the business and aggressively pursued them. While no two situations are exactly alike, the common thread for successful management is a thought process that moves "outside the box" to identify and capitalize on relevancy in an ahistorical world.

NOTES

1. The Web site of the Society of American Archivists offers current data on the makeup of the profession. The Business Archives Section of SAA provides information on the state of business archives in the United States and current projects supported by the Section. There is a link at the section site to the Directory of Corporate Archives in the United States and Canada, an online resource managed by Greg Hunter, a professor at Long Island University and a consultant in archives and records management. The data I used came from the Section Web site and the Hunter directory (available: www.archivists.org).

2. Many of the leading business archives programs today had their start because of an anniversary or CEO initiative. The programs at Ford Motor Company, Cargill, IBM, J.P. Morgan/Chase, the Royal Bank of Canada, Scotiabank, and the Gap trace their roots to one or both of these initiatives.

3. The initial collection of records that formed the nucleus of the archives at The Coca-Cola Company was created because of a lawsuit between Coca-Cola and The Pepsi-Cola Company in the 1940s.

4. The archives at Kraft Foods, Inc., probably fits this model better than any other program. Management decided to establish an ar-

chives because information was being lost or underutilized (e-mail to the author by Becky Tousey, Senior Manager, Global Archives. January 18, 2007).

5. Among the archival casualties are Bank of America, Texas Instruments, Mobil-Exxon, the J. Walter Thompson Agency, Unisys, Eastman Kodak, and even Firestone.

6. Only records with long-term historical value for the firm would be considered archival. In most organizations, such records would comprise no more than 2 to 3 percent of all records generated by the corporation. The vast majority of business records would be destroyed in the course of normal records retention schedules.

Chapter 10

Managing Change at the Vermont State Archives: A Continuing Issue

Gregory Sanford and Tanya Marshall

INTRODUCTION

During the past quarter century, the Vermont State Archives evolved from a small, outdated office to a modern, robust program that serves state government, carries out a full range of archival functions, has been recognized through awards, and has plans for continuing progress. Four major strategic approaches, discussed in detail below, have helped propel this development:

1. reintroduce the evidentiary/accountability function of archives;
2. present records-based information in ways that would be useful to decision makers;
3. gain statutory authorities to actively manage records and information across government; and
4. integrate records and archival management functions.

Retroactively attempting to give shape to those goals suggests a consistent framework of strategies and tactics that simply did not exist. Instead, the past 24 years were marked by trial and error and the gradual articulation of a program that began as a series of inchoate ideas. Those ideas had their roots in the Archives' past. We needed to restore awareness of the Archives' long-forgotten evidentiary role and return to an earlier vision of putting the Archives within the reach of the people.

In 1982, the Archives within the Vermont Secretary of State's Office was known as the State Papers Division. The division head was variously identified as the state historian or editor of state papers. The latter title, which I inherited when I was appointed head of the division in 1982, reflected the division's archaic focus on annotating and publishing eighteenth-century government records.

The Archives included a basement vault in the Montpelier flood plain, penetrated by sewer and high-pressure water lines, and an almost complete dearth of any intellectual control over whatever records had managed to find their way to that vault. Many of the records, while long-term, were not archival and reflected the interests of other Secretary of State divisions in storing such records outside their offices.

The main "finding aid" was a card index created between 1925 and 1950 by a predecessor who wrote down every name she found on the eighteenth- and early nineteenth-century records. The primary "appraisal" was by another predecessor who wrote, in felt-tip pen, "This is an important document" on communications from such figures as George Washington and Thomas Jefferson.

The degree of cultural change needed to establish the Archives as an important government function became apparent when I sought to add an archivist to what was, in early 1984, a one-person shop. I carefully crafted a position description for an archivist. The state's personnel office responded by sending me, as a mandatory reduction-in-force hire, an art therapist. I managed to get that candidate withdrawn, only to be sent, as another reduction-in-force candidate, a prison guard. The rationale was that just as I kept a secure, locked vault, the prison guard had experience locking things up. Though I finally succeeded in hiring a professionally trained archivist, I clearly confronted an immense challenge in reshaping cultural assumptions about government record keeping.

By 2007, significant elements of that challenge were met. The State Archives is identified as such in statute and the state archivist is required to have professional training and experience. The Archives has legal authorities for the appraisal, management, and accessibility of public records. It is viewed as an institutional resource able to provide information management services, context to current issues, and informed advice on Vermont's public records and right-to-know laws.

Its efforts received widespread recognition, including the State of Vermont Team Public Service Award, the New England Archivists' Distinguished Service Award, and the Society of American Archivists' Hamer-Kegan Award.

The context and environment in which change had to occur are not unique to Vermont and, in various degrees, will be familiar across archival communities at the state and national level. Many archival programs have had to address the historical drift in how their functions and activities are defined and perceived. Many programs had to respond to the belief that records management was the retroactive application of approaches to reducing the volume of paper records; many had to confront institutional perceptions that archival management only served the historical community.

HISTORY OF THE VERMONT STATE ARCHIVES

In 1777, Vermont created itself as an independent republic, a status that lasted until it became the fourteenth state in 1791. The territory that became Vermont was claimed by New York and New Hampshire, clouding titles to lands. New Hampshire eventually relinquished its claims, but Albany's policies toward Vermont created distrust as the settlers found their land titles uncertain and the government unresponsive and distant.

Therefore, when Vermont declared its independence and established a government, the control and accessibility of government records was a vital concern. The 1777 Vermont Constitution, for example, required that all deeds and conveyances of land be recorded locally at the town clerk's office. In 1782 the Vermont General Assembly instructed the secretary of state on what records to preserve and keep accessible. The types of records identified—town charters, laws, and other legislative records—demonstrated the general assembly's view of the Archives as a repository of essential evidence.

In 1823, Secretary of State William Slade expanded the Archives' evidentiary function to include providing context for public dialogues. In publishing a compilation of Vermont state papers, Slade wrote:

> Every government . . . should possess, and should place within the reach of the people, a complete history of its own legislation. Without the possession of such a history, and a practical regard to the

lessons it inculcates, legislation will be, at best, but a succession of *experiments*, and, as a necessary consequence, every operation of government will be characterized with instability and want of wisdom. (Slade, 1823: xv)

Slade's commitment to putting the archival record within the reach of the people was not sustained and the publication program ceased with his 1823 volume. The evidentiary function, however, remained broadly understood and the legislature periodically identified additional records to be preserved by the secretary of state.

In 1902, the evidentiary and publication functions briefly merged. In that year, while trying to locate the New York-Vermont boundary line, the legislature realized that many of Vermont's early surveyor-general records were in New York and enacted legislation for their return and admission as evidence in any court. These surveys of state and town lines were seen of sufficient legal importance that legislation passed in 1906 funded their indexing and publication. The publication appeared in 1918.

In 1913, however, the Archives' evidentiary role began to weaken when the legislature broadened the secretary's scope of publication to archival records of a "general historical interest." After the publication of town land grant charters in 1922, the Archives began publishing volumes of more historical, than evidentiary, value. From 1924 to 1969, when publications temporarily ceased, every volume of the state papers provided annotated transcripts of eighteenth-century laws, legislative journals, and other early records.

The misidentification of the archival function was exacerbated in 1937 with the creation of the Public Records Commission. The commission was charged with managing the burgeoning volume of paper records associated with expanding government services and, later, with office technologies that facilitated the creation of multiple copies. While the secretary of state served on the commission there was no effort to link archival and records management.

The commission became a free-standing division within the executive branch in 1960, charged with approving agency record management plans and with maintaining a records center for little-used departmental records awaiting disposition. By at least the 1970s the Public Records Division had become narrowly identified with managing the physical space consumed by paper records rather than the appraisal and management of content. Consequently, agencies did not seek the division's advice until records became a space problem, long after the records were created.

Conversely, the Public Records Division narrowed the scope of its responsibilities to managing the records center, including a micrographics program to reduce the volume of records at the center. The statutory requirement for comprehensive agency records management plans was not pursued. Instead the division responded, on an ad-hoc, case-by-case basis, to requests to store or film individual sets of agency records. Record series were only established for records accepted at the records center and no comprehensive agency, much less state, approach to records management was developed. Though in the following pages we occasionally use public records and records management interchangeably, the reality was that Vermont lacked a full-service records management program.

Through a series of reorganizations, the Public Records Division moved from being an independent division within the Agency of Administration to a subunit within the central services division of the Department of Buildings and General Services, where it remains today. The link to the state buildings program reflected the identification of records management with the management of office space.

The bifurcated records programs became more distant and the Archives more isolated. By the 1970s the Public Records Division was acquiring archival records primarily through its microfilming program, which required agencies wishing to store records longer than ten years to miniaturize their records (the division rarely, if ever, appraised records as archival and never scheduled records for deposit with the Archives; microfilmed records were not appraised or assigned disposition dates and, by default, became "permanent"). The Archives, still known as State Papers, was content to work on its eighteenth-century records, even when there were statutory mandates for transferring modern records to the program. The statute addressing gubernatorial records, for example, was amended so that the records would be microfilmed, the originals disposed of, and the film kept by the records management program.

Thus, by 1982, the Archives "function" was seen as historical publication and I was hired not for my work at the University of Vermont's Special Collections or the Institute Archives at the Massachusetts Institute of Technology but for my research on Vermont political history. My charge was to create greater visibility for the division, primarily through restoring the publication program.

Although this conflation of archival management with history initially worked to my personal advantage, I quickly realized that the function and purpose of "archives" was obscured not only by an emphasis on publishing records of a general historical interest but also by the failure to appraise and acquire archival records associated with the expanding activities of government. The broad understanding of the Archives' functional role in preserving and keeping accessible evidence of key government transactions was long forgotten.

My initial vision was shaped by the directive to restart the publication program and to increase the Archives' visibility. In order to meet that expectation, my first steps focused on gaining intellectual control over the holdings to identify which records were most suitable for publication. I also thought it essential to move the emphasis away from eighteenth-century records and to publish the newly developed finding aids to broaden understanding of what we held. A 1984 relocation of the secretary of state's office solved one pressing problem by moving the Archives off the flood plain. The limits of my initial vision, however, became clear as the published finding aids failed to enhance either the use or visibility of the Archives. By 1985, we began to explore the historic institutional roots of the Archives and its roles in providing evidence of government transactions.

REINTRODUCING THE EVIDENTIARY/ACCOUNTABILITY FUNCTION OF ARCHIVES

When I was hired in 1982 there was an accumulation of distinct state mandates directing that certain records documenting key government transactions be regularly deposited with the Archives. The Archives still received legislative acts, first designated for deposit in 1782. It still received legislative committee minutes under the general assembly's rules established in 1917. While it had given up physical custody of gubernatorial records, it still retained legal custody as set by an 1864 law. State and municipal boundary surveys continued to be deposited; by the 1960s the Archives' 1782 responsibility for holding town land grant charters had been expanded to include municipal governance charters.

Though limited in their scope, these records underscored the Archives' original mandate to preserve evidence of core government transactions. I decided to use these records to reinvigorate awareness of the Archives' *institutional* function of preserving evidence and, by

extension, meeting the constitutional mandate for government accountability. Each set of records that remained linked to the Archives
evidentiary role offered promise for changing perceptions of our institutional function. Specifically, I looked at the legislative, gubernatorial, and municipal records as the way to leverage change.

Legislative Records

Vermont is a legislative-intent state; that is, if the plain meaning or
statutory context of a law leaves its intent open to interpretation, then
lawyers and the courts can look at bill files, committee testimony, and
other records to seek clarification. The original legislative acts, which
show all changes to a bill voted during its passage, support legislative-
intent research. So do the legislative committee minutes. Both sets of
records were underutilized; indeed, few people knew they existed. We
began to highlight the records, in part through traditional finding aids,
but primarily by initiating contacts with legislators. If a legislator or
committee was considering a high-visibility bill, we researched committee minutes on earlier bills or acts germane to the current proposal.
We then sent unsolicited copies to the legislator. As evidence of the intent of antecedent laws, the records helped shaped bill drafting and
committee discussion.

   Despite a focus on high-visibility bills and legislators, our contacts
were frequently idiosyncratic: how did we determine "high visibility";
was there sufficient documentation to warrant initiating contact; which
legislators or committees might be most responsive; and how could we
achieve political balance to avoid charges of partisan bias? Though we
never developed consistent answers to these questions we experienced
enough success to gain wider attention to our legislative holdings and
we began to receive more legislative-intent researchers.

   In the end, however, this effort did not succeed in the way we envisioned. The failure stemmed from Vermont's bifurcated records programs that left the Archives without records of strong evidentiary
value. In the late 1960s, the general assembly created a legislative
council to provide bill drafting and other support services. Public
Records appraised the council's records as "permanent" (not archival)
and scheduled them for deposit at the records center, not the Archives.
The council records, including bill files, tapes, and transcripts of committee testimony, are a richer source for legislative intent than what
the Archives held. The committee minutes held by the Archives, for

example, were created by legislators elected as clerks of their committee. Feeling that minute taking detracted from full committee participation, legislators often took only rudimentary notes. The legislative council initiated the tape recording of testimony, further diminishing the content of the clerks' minutes (why keep minutes when everything is being recorded?).

Consequently, legislative-intent research at the Archives experienced a high rate of failure as researchers encountered incomplete or even incoherent minutes. Researchers began to focus their efforts on the records held by Public Records. The effort did gain us some attention with the legislature and laid the ground work for later success.

Gubernatorial Records

In 1984 we regained physical custody of gubernatorial records though we had to do so by purchasing microfilm copies from Public Records. We assumed that gubernatorial records had a high research value and would attract users. This effort failed even more completely than the legislative intent work. While many governors left certain evidentiary records such as appointments, pardons, and executive orders, records documenting policy development were less consistently preserved. In addition, Vermont lacked an active research community so, despite outreach, the records remained largely unused. Outreach was further complicated when we discovered that many of the microfilms were substandard and illegible and came with only the most rudimentary of finding aids. This made the use of the records even more problematic. Researchers who did show up were often disappointed by the gulf between our outreach and finding aids and the actual content and accessibility of gubernatorial records. Though a failure on some levels, this effort also laid the groundwork for future success.

One consequence of reacquiring gubernatorial records was the return of the Archives' publication program. Unlike past efforts, however, we did not publish annotated historic texts. Instead, in 1985, we published a guide to the records of Vermont's governors, identifying not only what we held, but also gubernatorial records held by other repositories. This established relationships with those repositories and caught the attention of the governor's office. Within four years we would be asked to help create an indexing system for a sitting governor.

Municipal Records

It was the municipal records that really began to reintegrate the Archives' evidentiary role. In fulfilling our assigned duty to prepare proposed municipal charter changes for submission to the legislature it became clear that few municipalities had consistently updated their charters to reflect changes over time. This was not only a problem for the municipalities, but also for the legislative council that had to put proposed amendments into bill form. Council members did not know the context or structure (chapters and sections) of the charters being amended.

Since the Archives had a record of municipal charter changes, we published, in 1986, an index to municipal charters and special acts. Summer interns used the index to cut and paste special municipal acts into what each municipality's charter currently looked like. We provided copies of these (literally) cut and paste charters to the legislative council and to any municipality requesting one.

The legislative council saw the utility of the index as a key to finding evidence needed to draft municipal acts. The council eventually took ownership of this effort and in 1996 added, and maintains, an appendix to the *Vermont Statutes Annotated* containing the texts of municipal charters. Council members acknowledged the impact of the Archives' municipal index on their decision to create this appendix. One early acknowledgment, linked as well to our work with committee minutes, was the council's invitation for the Archives to participate in the orientation of new committee clerks. By 1999 this invitation was expanded and the Archives regularly participates in the council's orientation program for all new legislators, not just clerks.

Beyond our work with legislative, gubernatorial, and municipal records we explored other ways to reaffirm our evidentiary role. In 1991, we provided a traditional annotated historical text while further anchoring our evidentiary role. In that year we published the annotated journals of the Vermont Council of Censors. The council, which lasted from 1777 until 1870, was the sole body authorized to propose amendments to the Vermont Constitution. Its journals, long inaccessible, provided the only source for understanding the intent of proposals of amendment. The publication became a resource for the Vermont Supreme Court, which often cites the journals in judicial review cases.

During these early years, the staff became active in a variety of professional archival organizations. Ironically, the limited archival record we inherited allowed us time to take leadership positions within these organizations. This involved staff in some of the emerging professional dialogues occasioned by new information technologies.

It was participation in the dialogues, some quite vigorous, over preserving "electronic evidence" that helped reassociate the Archives with preserving evidence. Professional participation led to the Archives receiving an electronic records grant from the National Historical Publications and Records Commission in 1994. The grant allowed the Archives to participate in Governor Richard Snelling's Vermont Information Strategy Plan (VISP) that used functional analysis to understand and improve how information flowed within government. By arguing that information technologies required a focus on records, and on records as evidence, the Archives gained a place within VISP.

This was perhaps our most successful failure in terms of relinking the Archives with accountability and evidentiary responsibilities. VISP did not long survive the Snelling administration, but it attracted legislative attention to the need to update Vermont's record laws. Our participation in VISP led the House Government Operations Committee to use the Archives as support staff as it studied the record laws in 1995–1996.

It was during this legislative work that we came to understand the limitations of a focus on evidence. Many legislators associated "evidence" with "*gotcha* journalism." Records often have a negative connotation to elected officials who experience attacks based on records that in some cases are pulled out of context. We had to deemphasize evidence and focus on record content and context.

These short-term failures laid the groundwork for long-term success. The Archives established a sustained relationship with the legislature's government operations committees. Without VISP, we lacked the resources and authority to implement an electronic records program, but we became perceived as having a valuable perspective on managing electronic records. In the eyes of the press, the Archives, because of its work on the public records law, began to be viewed as an important advocate for open government.

PRESENTING RECORDS-BASED INFORMATION TO DECISION MAKERS

William Slade's notion of linking records to informing legislative deliberations and public dialogues promised a better fulcrum for leveraging cultural change. Our records were too fragmentary to meet consistently the rules of evidence. Even where the records clearly met those standards (legislative acts, deeds, etc.), the user base was too small to affect change. There was, however, a sufficient record to provide context to current public dialogues.

The leap the Archives made was tying the definition of archival records as having "continuing value" to the idea that there were "continuing issues" of government and governance. Each generation had to confront, within its own social expectations and fiscal realities, such continuing issues as education, taxation, crime and punishment, economic development and the environment. If we could present those earlier discussions and actions as useful context to current issues, the Archives' institutional role would be enhanced.

We needed to understand what information, in what form, was most likely to be used by such target audiences as the general assembly and the news media. In an "information age," simply providing more undifferentiated information was unlikely to have much of an impact. Our previous efforts confirmed that no matter how many professional standard finding aids we created, few legislators had the time, training, or inclination to come to the Archives and go through boxes of material. The same held for true for reporters working against deadline.

The first systematic effort at linking archival records as context to current issues was made during Vermont's statehood bicentennial in 1991. We developed a "state capitals" program as part of the celebrations through which we identified key issues currently before the legislature—educational funding, term limits, and capital punishment, for example—and located records on these topics from past deliberations. Scholars were contracted to synthesize those records into 20-minute overviews of how a particular issue evolved. We then held public programs in each of the 14 municipalities that served as seats of Vermont state government before Montpelier became the capital in 1805. One topic was discussed at each location. Government officials associated with the selected topics were invited to attend, along with the general public. After the scholars' presentations, the audience was given the current bill addressing the selected topic and invited to discuss, amend, approve, or reject it based on what they had heard.

While audience size varied among sites, participation was always lively. The audiences came to understand that "current issues" had historical antecedents and gained direct experience with how archival records can inform public dialogues.

The success of the bicentennial project encouraged further exploration of "continuing issues." The key was finding a vehicle for the broadest possible presentation of the issues. Initially, we simply reverted to idiosyncratic contacts with legislators, public officials, and reporters. If we learned of a current issue for which we had substantive archival documentation, we sent unsolicited copies of selected records to legislators, the governor's office, or reporters. The recipients came to see a value in the Archives to their ongoing work and began contacting us for background on issues. In some cases we were asked to testify on the background of an issue; in other cases reporters called in search of brief context for stories.

The breakthrough in presenting continuing issues came in 1996 when the secretary of state's office first launched its Web site. Within a few years every state office, and every legislative committee room had Web access. This created opportunities for moving beyond idiosyncratic individual contacts as well as moving the concept of Archives as a place where research had to be conducted into a constantly available online resource. The Archives' Web site (http://vermont-archives. org) became the vehicle for presenting the *Continuing Issues of Government and Governance* series. The series built upon our previous development of the *Continuing Issues* idea but with the potential for reaching a wider audience. More important, given the goal of *Continuing Issues* to link archival records and information to the need of policymakers to take action, we could reach all potential players engaged in a particular issue (Sanford, 2003).

If the Web was the vehicle for presenting the *Continuing Issues* series, there were still the questions of what issues and how to present them. Here the experience we gained through past efforts proved crucial. First, we had come to realize that a *broad* goal of effecting cultural change was too unfocused to succeed. Rather than attempting to convince everyone of the Archives' valuable institutional role, it was better to focus on a few key individuals who asserted formal or informal leadership. If we could demonstrate our value to those few individuals, that experience could be conveyed through their networks until a tipping point was achieved. We therefore sought input from legislative leaders and reporters on which issues were likely to emerge during the legislative session.

Through previous committee testimony and contacts with individual legislators, we also had a better understanding of how information was used. Simply providing extensive documentation was not effective. Observation and personal contacts made it clear that brief summaries, not reams of archival copies, were more likely to be used. For most people, summaries were sufficient, though in a few cases, notably with bill sponsors, more extensive documentation was appreciated in order to build a case.

Observation also suggested that issues associated with *specific* institutional processes were better to document than broad concepts. Documenting the context of governmental processes offered fewer opportunities for being perceived as promoting a political perspective. Conversely, to attempt to document divisive social issues carried political risks. For that reason we did not offer a *Continuing Issues* package on the history of marriage in Vermont during the gay marriage/civil union debates. The range of perspectives was too complex and the emotions too high. Instead we documented three processes that attracted attention during the civil union debates: judicial review, referendum, and impeachment.

The first online *Continuing Issue*, put up in 2000, looked at the direct primary. Low voter turnout, cross-party voting (Vermont does not require party registration), and growing costs led to a public reexamination of the primary system. We had a 1914 legislative document that set out in columns the respective arguments for the existing caucus system for selecting candidates and for the proposed direct primary bill. The document readily lent itself for judging, from the perspective of 80 years of experience, how the various arguments played out over time. Since the document had been laid out specifically for legislators (brief, contrasting pros and cons) we simply presented it online and alerted the individuals we had identified as leaders.

The other issues we decided to present could not be captured through a single, information-rich document. We therefore created layered online presentations. For a history of amending the Vermont Constitution, which had become a legislative responsibility in 1870, we broke the presentations into a series of short sections. One simply laid out the history of the amendment process. Another provided an overview of proposals, identifying the most common proposals since 1870.

Another section addressed procedural questions (could the House amend proposals, which under the constitution originated in the Senate?). And finally, all post-1870 proposals were listed by year of introduction with a link to the actual language, and fate, of each.

A similar pattern was followed for subsequent presentations in the *Continuing Issues* series. The layered presentations allowed a user to determine what level of information was needed to act. For reporters, the overviews allowed quick contextual information so they could, for example, note that 10 percent of all proposed amendments since 1870 sought to extend the terms of office of either or both legislative and executive offices. Amendment sponsors, on the other hand, could use the language of previous proposals as drafting guides.

The *Continuing Issues* Web site is, to date, our most successful effort to create awareness of the archives' institutional role. Its success was, in part, based on linking records-based information to the need of officials to act; it was a tool that officials could, and did, use. Its success also stemmed from how the information was presented; users could simply select the level of information they needed. Finally, it succeeded because we took the time to find out what the potential users' needs were. This was perhaps the single most consistent lesson from all our efforts: you cannot effect change by staying within your archives or by only talking with archivists. On some levels, *Continuing Issues* is a realization of Slade's dream of putting the archival record within the reach of not just the people, but the people who can use those records to act.

GAINING STATUTORY AUTHORITY TO ACTIVELY MANAGE RECORDS AND INFORMATION ACROSS GOVERNMENT

As with many bifurcated records programs, a certain level of rivalry emerged that retarded efforts to establish cooperation between records and archival management. In Vermont that tension was perhaps exacerbated because Public Records had been acquiring archival records. Divided archival series, coupled with overlapping responsibilities, promoted competition over coordination. By 1983, a competitive environment, occasionally marked by outright opposition, was firmly in place.

Although there were a variety of initiatives designed to build a working relationship between the programs, better coordination was only achieved because of the flexibility to respond to unanticipated opportunities. In 2001, the records program aggressively testified in committee against an archives bill. The new secretary of state responded by getting the two programs to submit to outside mediation to resolve their long-standing problems. Mediation resulted in the hiring of a professional archival consultant, Dr. Bruce Dearstyne, to examine both programs and make recommendations on how to move forward. His report provided a neutral framework that the programs used to present a plan to the legislature that led, in 2003, to enactment of a new archives law.

The new law (3 *Vermont Statutes Annotated* §117), provided the Archives, for the first time, with authorities to manage records, including the sole authority to appraise. The law retained the bifurcated system, though it identified specific areas for coordination. Effective July 2003, the Archives and the Division of Public Records were charged with coordinating in two areas: approving agency records management programs against a statutorily prescribed set of requirements and scheduling records for later disposition, including the transfer of records to the Archives. In both areas, the Archives' scope was limited to "archival records" with the disposition of "public records" remaining under the administrative control of the commissioner of Buildings and General Services/Public Records Division. The new authority over "archival records" also meant the Archives became the legal custodian of records accessioned over the years by the Public Records Division as "permanent." These accessions represented double the volume of records in our own vault, but less than 5 percent of the total volume of records stored at the records center. Many of the "permanent" records were in the microfilming queue and none had ever been appraised to determine whether they were truly archival.

Although we lacked the space to bring any additional records into our physical custody, we were successful in hiring a part-time, temporary archivist to instill some intellectual control over the public records accessions. Yet, in late 2003, when the temporary archivist began her work, we were grappling with the how to coordinate our work with the Public Records Division. How, for example, would we appraise records of state agencies? What would an approved agency records program look like? What would we be approving? The new archivist had an MLS with an archival concentration from the University of Maryland and doctoral work beyond that. She brought to our work professional skills, untainted by the previous internecine battles between records and archival management. Whereas the mediator provided the framework for coordination, the new archivist, who was eventually hired as an assistant state archivist, provided us with the program for integration, although at the time, this was neither the plan nor a goal.

INTEGRATING RECORDS AND ARCHIVAL MANAGEMENT FUNCTIONS

Initially the Archives' goal was to pursue the familiar steps of creating a traditional appraisal plan that was largely retroactive rather than prospective. It appeared to be the logical step for getting a handle on what archival records were currently held in the State Records Center and how, or if, they related to records already in the Archives. The abandonment of this approach, however, came almost as fast as it had been developed. It was clear that we could never, and would never, succeed if we proceeded as many others like us had before. We needed to be at the beginning of the records life cycle, not at the end.

Consequently, the Archives spent much of 2004 and 2005 documenting the current records environment and trying to understand the records and information management needs of state agencies. Our initial partners, including the Vermont courts, sought us out under their traditional belief that archival and records management were concerned with reducing the volume of paper records. While some partners were also motivated by the implementation of new information technology systems, there was widespread belief that digital records obviated the need for management since they consumed less physical space. Whatever the motives of our partners, we were invited to observe and document their record-keeping practices. This entry was facilitated, in many ways, by the Division of Public Records, which started directing state agencies to the Archives for records management advice and guidance.

Using a relational database program and a faceted classification scheme, we started integrating data collected from agencies with agency histories, existing archival record series descriptions, legal requirements, and analyses of government functions. This allowed us to see patterns that could be used for archival appraisal as well as business process management. We effectively bridged archival management with records management and, for the first time, could see how government records, functions, and responsibilities fit together now and in the past. Thereafter, it became apparent that the integration of *information about records*, not the divisions responsible for records, would be the key to future progress.

By 2006, the Archives had not only amassed a large collection of information about state government but also had developed a unique viewpoint of government functions and their relationship to record keeping, a viewpoint that did not go unnoticed by the legislative and executive branches. The state legislature asked us and the secretary of administration to study the record-keeping needs of the executive branch and our report became the impetus for growing interest among legislators and state agencies to "get it right" (Vermont Secretary of Administration and Vermont State Archivist, 2006).

The report offered a strategic plan for developing comprehensive records programs and addressed the benefits of records management, but also highlighted how the division between archival and records management would continue to be an issue. A newly appointed commissioner of the Department of Buildings and General Services, whose staff assisted with the study, began to see how problematic the situation was for the state. By the end of the year the Department and the State Archives signed a memorandum of understanding setting out mutually agreed on goals and practices for carrying out the plan outlined in the report.

The state's chief information officer (CIO) also took a strong interest in the report. New to the position and ready to make an effective change in how the state managed its information resources, the CIO asked us to become an active partner with his department's Enterprise Project Management Office (EPMO), which is responsible for managing information technology projects and approving agency requests for proposals. Our role with EPMO is very similar to that of the *Continuing Issues* series: to link records-based information to the needs of officials to act. However, unlike *Continuing Issues*, which focuses on a few key individuals and legislative matters, we are now focusing on the state as whole and how integrated records and archival management can be used to address a variety of governmental issues.

With EPMO, our role has expanded from using records to describe the historical context to also using context to describe the records, specifically the types of records that support different activities of government. This approach has not only given us the opportunity to delve into the full context of records, but has also brought us closer to the beginning of the record life cycle. We are struggling to keep up with the growing interest in record keeping; the new assistant state archivist is responsible for the majority of the workload with the EPMO as well as our continued data collection and analysis. This is an unanticipated, but fully appreciated, opportunity that provides the Archives with both recognition and support.

This recognition and support became overwhelmingly evident early in 2007 when the Senate Government Operations Committee drafted a bill consolidating archival and records management under the Archives. Initial support for the concept of consolidation came from both the head of the records management program and the enterprise project management office. Endorsement of the Archives did not end there, however. In an unprecedented move, the Archives was offered the Division of Public Records in its entirety—building, staff, equipment, and budget—by the commissioner of Buildings and General Services.

At the time of this writing, spring 2007, the senate committee approved the consolidation bill, which will be taken up by the full senate in January 2008. Whether we will become a fully integrated records division in the near future is yet unclear, but there appears to be strong support of consolidation as a good government initiative. In addition the general assembly approved funding to begin construction of a new archives and research facility. Regardless of the fate of these measures, we have clearly come a long way from the days of being offered art therapists and prison guards.

LESSONS LEARNED

To effect change, it is essential to understand the history of the archival function within your institution. Such an understanding, combined with familiarity with current professional practices, defines where change must occur and provides lessons and models for shaping initiatives.

It is important to be able to see the profession above the "box and folder" level. Knowing *why* we do what we do must precede knowing *how* to do it. In a public institution, we must understand the Archives' roles in providing evidence and, equally important, context. Without that awareness it is easy to slip into assumptions such as those that led to annotating historical texts at the cost of managing records.

That entails stepping outside the Archives to establish direct relationships with those who create and use archival records. We began by creating finding aids that met professional standards. It was not, however, until we learned how our targeted audiences performed their responsibilities that we could provide the records in ways they would actually use them.

It is important to step outside the profession to learn the practices and perspectives of other information services, businesses, and disciplines. Learning about social networks, for example, narrowed our initial inchoate sense of how to affect change to identifying where to focus our efforts to achieve the broadest impact. Learning about mediation moved us from confrontation to solutions by providing a structured, neutral framework for resolving long-standing areas of conflict.

Understanding the higher goals of archival management encouraged risk-taking. If we truly believe what we do has an institutional and social value, then taking risks is less daunting. Risks are just that, so we must be prepared to accept, and build upon, failure. It was not easy to make those initial, unsolicited contacts with decision makers. In some cases those contacts were neither understood nor welcomed. The strength to persist was not always easy to sustain; there were moments when we wistfully longed for staying cloistered in the office annotating historic documents.

Persistence also requires flexibility. It is important to constantly evaluate the outcomes you are seeking and be able to change approaches accordingly. It is also important to be flexible enough to take advantage of unanticipated opportunities. The extensive use of the Archives, and the accompanying national attention, associated with Governor Howard Dean's bid for the 2004 Democratic presidential nomination, reinforced some of the negative connotations elected officials held about records. It was an opportunity, however, to demonstrate the value of archival management, the Archives' role in exercising the right to know, and a host of other high-level issues that would never have been raised otherwise.

Last, we need to change how we manage our knowledge about records. Archivists have a wealth of knowledge and information about their institutions and records but we often lack the ability to effectively communicate it to others. It is often said that we live in an information age or information economy. While this is generally perceived in positive terms, we also talk of information overload and of being inundated with more information than we can possibly digest and use. In a time of information glut we, as archivists, are forced to compete

for the attention of those we serve. We cannot do so simply by providing more undifferentiated information or more online records. We
must understand what records- or information-based knowledge our
institution and our society need in order to make informed decisions
and how to deliver this knowledge in useful and meaningful ways. We
must integrate our special knowledge of record keeping, institutional
memory, and of access and preservation into our service to our institutions and the publics they serve. We must understand that there is
no one perfect way to do our work, nor any perfect, immutable solutions. It is a daunting challenge, but one which we should welcome.

REFERENCES

Sanford, Gregory. 2003. "Upon This Gifted Age." Available: http://
    vermont-archives.org/publications/talks/pdf/NEA2003.pdf
Slade, William. 1823. *Vermont State Papers*. Middlebury, VT: J.W.
    Copeland.
Vermont Secretary of Administration and Vermont State Archivist.
    2006. "Executive Agency Records Report: Preliminary Strategic
    Plan" (Required by Sec. 5, Act No. 71 of 2005) (January). Avail-
    able: http://vermont-archives.org/publications/legislative/pdf/
    LegReport06.pdf

Chapter 11

Appraising, Transferring, Preserving, and Making Available Born-Digital Records from Central Government Departments ("Seamless Flow")

Kelvin Smith

In February 2004, The National Archives (TNA) in the United Kingdom commissioned a fundamental review of IT. The review recommended that The National Archives adopt a process-oriented approach to content production with a focus on end-to-end processes, i.e., data and technology architecture to achieve a seamless flow of content and information between all players. The Seamless Flow Programme is TNA's response to this recommendation.

The program represents a further development in TNA's leadership in this area in the United Kingdom. It builds upon experience gained in introducing a digital archive in April 2003 and has led to several changes in the office's management structure, focusing more on project work than hitherto.

BACKGROUND

The program involves the creation of a seamless flow of digital records from creation in government departments, to preservation in the ar-

Figure 11–1. Seamless Flow Process Model

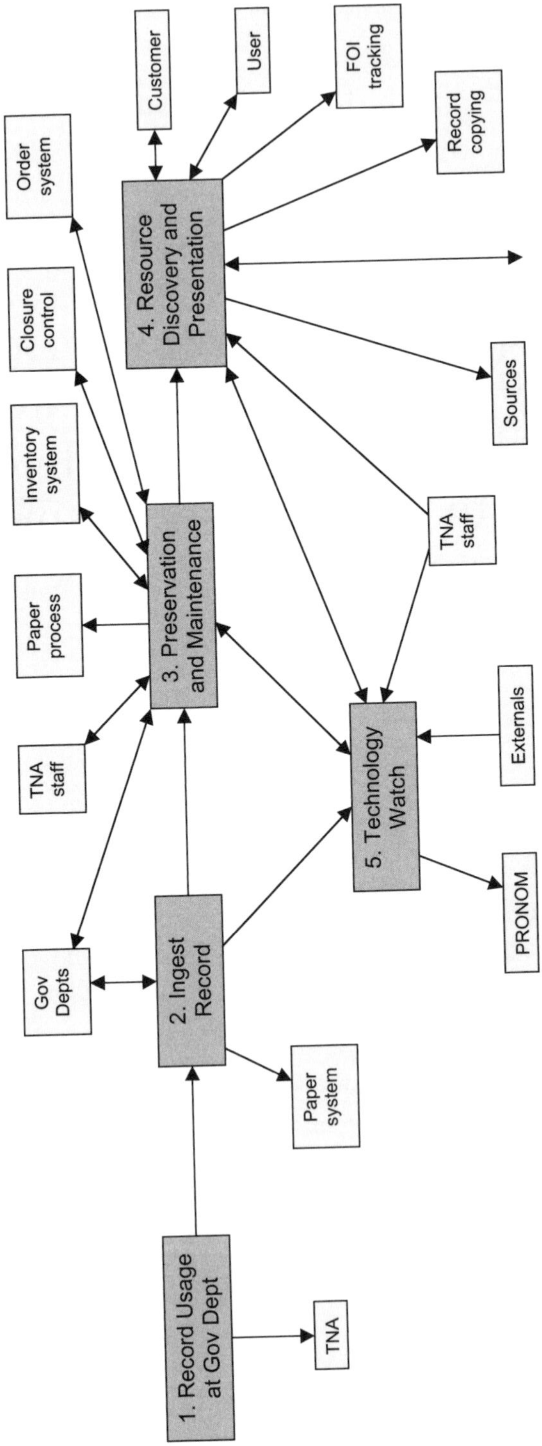

chives, through to delivery on the Internet. The original process model developed in TNA is shown in Figure 11-1. The program is about linking together existing components and automating manual processes. The process of developing the seamless flow approach allows for the review and streamlining of other aspects of TNA architecture—notably catalogs and Web searching. The development of an Internet-based delivery system for digital records is a key component of the response to the U.K. Government's *Modernising Government* target.[1]

The Seamless Flow Programme is divided into a number of projects that progress according to an agreed-upon program plan. The outputs of the individual projects are coordinated by a program manager as part of his Central Programme Development brief. All of the projects have a separate project manager and project board that report into the Programme Board. Eight of the projects are summarized in this section. The ninth project, Business Change and Training, is discussed in more detail in a later section. It is central to the Seamless Flow Programme and also presents some of the most complex management challenges.

Appraisal and Selection

The objective of this project is to develop procedures and selection criteria to guide the appraisal of digital records thus making a contribution to the enablement of the automatic transfer of selected records to TNA. Appraisal, acquisition, and disposition policies[2] are already in place and the methods being adopted for achieving this objective are in accordance with the principles established by those policies. It became very clear, however, early on in the project that new appraisal methodologies would need to be considered. Principally this has centered round the adoption of a macro appraisal approach.

Public Web Search and Resource Discovery

This covers more than the mere searching of digital records. The Seamless Flow Programme as a whole is about linking together existing components and automating manual processes and the overall process allows TNA to review and streamline other aspects of the architecture, most notably catalog and Web searching. Thus the project has identified the need for a more intelligent and accessible global search facility.

Metadata and Cataloging

At every stage in the Seamless Flow process metadata enables the flow of digital records from creation in government departments through preservation in the archive to presentation to users. Thus a standard range of metadata elements is required for the whole program. A store for that metadata, known as the GMMS (Generic Metadata Management Store), has been defined so that metadata for the whole program may be managed and so that it may be supplied to processes and projects as required.

Transfer to The National Archives

This project aims to develop and implement processes for the transfer of electronic records and metadata from government departments to The National Archives and to specify, develop, and implement a set of products that will automate where possible and appropriate all processes involved in transferring records from government departments to the point of loading to a preaccession server. This project is at the heart of the program. It is leading, and will lead, to many changes in business practices in government departments.

Preservation and Maintenance

This project addresses the requirements for permanent and secure storage of digital records and their ongoing preservation. The aim of the project is to make the processes as automated as possible with interaction between business processes as seamless as possible.

Technology Watch

The project is intended to ensure that digital records stored by TNA are capable of being accessed in the long-term, within future technological environments, and to inform sustainability requirements within government departments.

Delivery and Presentation

This project will develop and implement the processes and technologies for the actual delivery and presentation of the born-digital records online and on the Internet wherever possible. A pilot system (Electronic Records Online—EROL) is already running.[3] In some cases the format of the record has been changed for presentation so that it can be viewed online but the content remains the same as the original.

Management and Security

The management and security project was formed to provide policy and guidance on the application of best practice record-handling principles and appropriate security controls consistently across the records life cycle from selection onwards. The advice and guidance will conform to agreed international standards and will help to ensure that digital records are managed appropriately across their life cycle in a manner consistent with their security classification.

THE BUSINESS CHANGE AND TRAINING PROJECT

At the center of the management and leadership issues of Seamless Flow is the Business Change and Training Project. Not long after the various Seamless Flow projects were under way, it was recognized that there were highly significant business change implications for all the processes and procedures. Training was considered a key element within these.

The initiative relating to business change and training became a ninth project within Seamless Flow. In management terms it works in the same way as the other projects—using standard devices such as highlight reports, issues logs and risks logs—but differs from them in that it deals with issues that affect the whole program. For example, the impact assessment (discussed below) addresses all the processes in the program. The staff involved in the project are nontechnical, examining more the business policies and procedures affected by implementation of systems, but they have easy access to technical advice from TNA's Digital Preservation Department.

Methodology

The work of the project team in the initial stages of the project has been to come to grips with just how much change to business practice will result from this major program. It is probably fair to say that, for most team members, this has exceeded expectations. Eight main areas were identified for particular attention and a team member made responsible for leading on those areas:

1. Transfer of records from government departments to TNA
2. Cataloguing of records
3. Accessioning—the processes and documentation necessary between transfer and preservation in the digital archive
4. Software user documentation
5. Training plans
6. Training delivery
7. Freedom of information—the effect on the implementation of the Freedom of Information Act 2000 (which came into effect on January 1, 2005)
8. Redaction of digital records in response to requests under the Freedom of Information Act

In addition, there were significant business changes resulting from changes in a ninth area—that of appraisal policy and methodology. These were felt to have wider implications beyond Seamless Flow and are being dealt with as a specific function within TNA's Records Management and Cataloguing Department.

The process for managing the areas of work was divided into seven stages:

1. Identify the scope
2. Develop new processes and procedures
3. Undertake an impact assessment
4. Compile and agree business change plans
5. Implement the business change plans
6. Obtain feedback and revise as necessary
7. Implement revised plans

Impact Assessment

A key element of the process for managing these areas is the impact assessment. There are many examples of such assessments but, while there are certain generic aspects to them, any particular undertaking has to be tailored specifically for the procedure(s) being assessed. Each project is likely to have a different impact on working practices. When carried out successfully, an impact assessment will help to identify the resources and skills an organization needs to meet its clients' needs. Above all, it will contribute significantly to strategic planning and the identification of training needs.

An important preliminary to undertaking a full assessment is the gathering of relevant information. There may be areas indirectly related to the process that need to be taken into consideration in effecting any business change arising from the assessment. For example (in the program here being discussed), what is the organization's overall information services strategy? Are there plans to purchase new software or hardware in the next few years? Are staffing levels likely to be maintained in the near future? Are there wider government initiatives that have an influence?

Sources for this information need to be identified. In the Seamless Flow Programme, a vital contact in government departments and agencies (the client base) is the departmental record officer (in effect the records manager for the organization who, under a directive dating back to 1957, is responsible for the management of his/her department's records from the moment they are created to their ultimate disposal). Typically, they have wide knowledge of their organization and can either answer or direct the enquirer accordingly.

In the Seamless Flow Programme, the major impact will be on government departments and agencies that transfer records to TNA. For the purposes of this discussion, therefore, it would be useful to examine the impact assessment for the transfer of records from other government departments. It should be recognized, of course, that there are significant impacts from this and the other projects on the work of TNA itself. The transfer impact assessment has been framed as follows:

Introduction

A succinct statement of what the key purpose of the Seamless Flow Programme is and of what the transfer project is intended to achieve.

Questions on current information technology infrastructure. For example;

- Broad ICT architecture
- Software systems used (is there an electronic records management system or a local area network, etc.?)

- What is the staffing structure for the ICT discipline, including required qualifications at particular levels?

Impact

What previous consultations have taken place?

What major impacts are identified?

- On software
- On hardware
- On IT infrastructure generally
- On staff/staffing
- On current policies and practices
- On users and stakeholders
- On finance/budgets

Other enquiries

As a result of the assessment, identify other persons or organizations that should be consulted. (For example, are there any experts who should be contacted?)

Has the assessment identified any additional evidence or information that is required?

Follow-up to the Assessment

ACTION PLAN

An action plan needs to indicate clearly the issues, proposed actions, who is leading the plan, resource implications, timetable, and objectives. The plan should include processes that will monitor the implementation and the outcomes.

WIDER IMPLICATIONS

Are there any issues, strategies, or procedures that have emerged from the assessment and which will have relevance for a wider audience?

REPORT AND FEEDBACK

The results of the assessment and the suggested changes to business procedures (for both government departments and TNA) will be reported and circulated to the clients. Feedback will be encouraged and any modifications to the action plan will be considered and implemented.

PROJECT TEAMWORK

Most of the business change work undertaken by the project falls under the heading "work in progress." The following descriptions cover the major issues that the teams are currently grappling with.

Transfer of Records from Government Departments to TNA

TNA has provided government departments and agencies that transfer records with a software application that will enable them to package transfers in accordance with the OAIS (Open Archive Information Systems) standard.[4] Prior to opening the new transfer application, staff in government departments are not expected to undertake any additional function over and above what they are required to do as part of their current duties. These duties, of course, are changing rapidly as the implementation and use of electronic records management systems become the norm in government organizations. Currently, records staff in government departments catalog, declassify, redact, and prepare records for transfer to TNA. This will continue with digital records. The major change will be the acquisition of new skills and knowledge to understand and operate systems that will undertake these functions more or less automatically.

Records staff will use the transfer application to prepare the SIP (Submission Information Package). This will require familiarity with the transfer application. TNA staff will draw up a program of training for these staff. At present, its own personnel who are involved in the transfer process are testing and familiarizing themselves with the application.

Records staff will use the transfer application to input available system metadata. This is perhaps the greatest departure from current practices in an electronic environment and will require some changes to work procedures. Metadata used in the transferring department's system will need to be converted from existing schema to the schema used in TNA's system. Initially this was expected to be an automated process but so far this has not been possible.

Staff in TNA will liaise with records staff in the government department to examine, approve, or modify the archival description so that it meets the standards required by TNA. It is expected that this will be undertaken as part of the functionality of the transfer application.

Software User Documentation

There are several areas where procedures are being formulated and recorded so that they can be made available to different types of users. Essentially there are three levels:

1. *Standard operating procedures*: for the technical documentation required internally by TNA
2. *General procedures*: a document describing, in simple terms, the procedures for appraising, transferring, cataloguing, preserving, and making available digital records (i.e., the whole Seamless Flow process)
3. *User manuals:* step-by-step guidance for users of the transfer application software

It is the last of these on which the business change team is concentrating. There are three manuals—aimed at the users in government departments and the users in TNA (one using a metadata editing application). These are being drafted by consultants who have designed the transfer system and are currently waiting completion. It is expected that other software user documentation will be drafted as the program develops.

Training Plans

Training plans have begun with a training needs analysis. A questionnaire was sent to business change team leaders. Later this will be modified and also sent to government departments and agencies. Once training plans have been drawn up on the basis of the results of the analysis, the key players will need to agree on a plan. Training schedules will need to be drawn up and, of course, the training needs to be delivered.

REDACTION OF DIGITAL RECORDS IN RESPONSE TO
REQUESTS UNDER THE FREEDOM OF INFORMATION ACT

The issue of redaction also posed significant management challenges. The Freedom of Information Act 2000, which came fully into effect on January 1, 2005, emphasizes the statutory right of access to information, rather than documents or records. The Code of Practice on the Management of Records under Freedom of Information states that where a complete document cannot be made available "Authorities should consider whether parts of records might be released if the sensitive information were blanked out."[5] Redaction has therefore become an important and sensitive issue since the introduction of Freedom of Information. While important principles have been established in the paper environment, some modification has to be made to procedures in a digital environment. Much of the guidance currently available to public authorities in the United Kingdom can be found on the Web site of The National Archives.[6]

Current Best Practice for Redacting Electronic Records

The redaction of digital records is a relatively new area of records management practice, and raises unique issues and potential risks. It has therefore featured strongly in the business change project under the Seamless Flow Programme. A number of different approaches to electronic redaction have been examined as part of the Seamless Flow development.

TRADITIONAL REDACTION

For electronic records, which can be printed as a hard copy, traditional redaction techniques (blacking out, cutting out, etc.) can be applied. Either the record may be printed and redaction carried out on the printed copy, or the information may be redacted from an electronic copy, which is then printed. If the redacted copy is required in electronic format, this can be created by scanning the redacted paper copy into an appropriate format, such as Adobe Portable Document Format (PDF).

FORMAT REDACTION

Records may be redacted electronically in their original format. This may be carried out either using deletion tools within the creating software, or by using specialized redaction software. This approach must be treated with extreme caution, due to the possibility that deleted information may still be recoverable, and the potential for information to remain hidden within nondisplayable portions of the bitstream.

CONVERSION

An electronic record may be redacted through a combination of information deletion and conversion to a different format. Certain formats, such as plain ASCII text files, contain displayable information only. Conversion to this format will therefore eliminate any information that may be hidden in nondisplayable portions of a bitstream.

ROUNDTRIP REDACTION

The redacted record may be required to be made available in its original format, for example, to preserve complex formatting. In such cases, an extension of the conversion approach may be applicable. Round tripping entails the conversion of the record to another format, followed by conversion back to the original format, such that the conversion process removes all evidence of the redacted information. Information deletion may be carried out either prior to conversion, or in the intermediary format. This approach requires a thorough understanding of the formats and conversion processes involved, and the mechanisms by which information is transferred during conversion.

PILOT TRANSFERS

Early on in the planning of the Seamless Flow Programme and, more particularly, in the implementation of the Transfer to TNA project, it was decided to undertake a small number of pilots to tests and procedures prior to formal roll-out. These pilots have now run their course, and it is evident that they have been valuable in identifying changes to business practices. The changes have yet to be formalized and discussed with departments and agencies.

The purpose of the pilots is to demonstrate a successful transfer of digital records from a government department to TNA from the point of completion of the appraisal process through to the records being securely stored in the Digital Object Store and being made available across the Internet. This means, of course, that the developing appraisal procedures have also had to be employed to make the pilots worthwhile and relevant. These procedures involve the production of an appraisal report on the transferring department. This report comprises an investigation of the department's role and functions—its policy, operations and committee structure, and in that context what it does, what it has done, why it did it and its achievements. This investigation is largely undertaken without any appraisal, at this stage, of the records of the department. The aim is to concentrate resources on areas of the file plan of known value and not to examine all branches for material of possible historical value. This macro appraisal approach represents a considerable departure from TNA's current practice and from what government departments are familiar with. All the participants' skills are required to make the changeover successful.

BENEFITS ANALYSIS

The Business Change and Training Project team has recently begun work on the identification of benefits arising from the introduction of the Seamless Flow Programme. This may prove difficult since there is little baseline data on the transfer of digital records from which to analyze the likely benefits. Some preliminary work has been undertaken, however, and data such as the following is being collected:

- Productivity of accessioning staff
- Cost avoidance of staff for accessioning
- Productivity in processing records
- Earlier delivery of records to TNA, reducing costs to government departments and improving the availability of records
- Cost of transfer
- Improved access to records (for public, TNA staff, other government departments and to answer Freedom of Information inquiries)
- Improved record delivery costs
- Safeguarding vital records to support government business

This work derives from a wider study of benefits from electronic records management (ERM), which TNA undertook in September 2004 and which continues to form the basis for much of the work in ERM implementation in government departments.[7] Among the focal points of the study:

- ERM must be related to the strategic context of the organization.

- A risk register and regular review must be done to ensure that expected benefits materialize.
- Effective management of benefits—supporting their achievement and their evaluation and measurement, should be done.
- Categorization of benefits—nonfinancial (sharing and reusing records corporately, long-term sustainability, protection of vital records and historical records, enabling timely responses to Freedom of Information requests) and financial (staff time, space, reduced paper and other purchases, less transport costs) should be undertaken.

CONCLUSION

In reality there is no conclusion to this exercise. When the Seamless Flow Programme is concluded, business change will go on. This is bound to be the case anyway. Technology does not stand still. It will continue to affect and influence business processes. Business change is a constantly evolving issue in the context of an activity (electronic records management) that is itself continually evolving. The advances in technology are inexorable and one of the greatest challenges for records and information managers is to keep pace with them. This brief examination of one element of the process may serve as a timely reminder of what lies in store.

What does the changing world mean for the information management community? We have moved from a predictable world of paper to a volatile world of information of all kinds. Preservation of digital records is a huge new challenge that we need to rise to (as well as dealing with paper legacies—some as long as thirty years). People using our services expect us to deliver, present, and interpret information ever more quickly and intelligently. Such changes affect the role that TNA is playing in the information management community. It is increasingly being required, because of the immediacy of the electronic media, to be at the heart of the creation of information in government. Part of the plans for developing this new role includes the setting up of the Knowledge Council. This is part of the new Transformational Government initiative, which, as its name indicates, will transform our ways of working in the public sector.[8]

What has been learned so far? One obvious point is the need to resource such a massive undertaking adequately. Without that there is a danger that cheap solutions are put forward which will not stand the test of time—and the sustainability of records, metadata, and the Seamless Flow framework itself is crucial to the success of this undertaking.

The acquisition of new skills—not only at TNA but also in transferring departments and agencies—has become an important and urgent necessity. These skills need to be identified at an early stage in a program of this kind. So far, TNA has approached this with a mixture of the importation of such skills (for example, in designing new parts of the system such as access control and preservation) and retraining existing staff. Much of its past work on professional competencies in records management has been modified and repackaged as part of a major initiative by Professional Skills in Government (PSG).[9]

At present, electronic records created by the government are selected and transferred to TNA, where they are stored in the digital archive, by means of a labor-intensive process. Over the next few years it is expected that the volume of electronic records transferred to TNA will increase dramatically. The only way this can be managed is by automating as many of the processes as possible. There will also be a need for the capacity to handle an increased range of document types, databases, DVDs, etc. Above all, it must be possible to preserve records actively, for example to migrate electronic records to new formats as they become obsolete. Digital preservation will be the heart that keeps the TNA body alive.

NOTES

1. A core target in the United Kingdom's White Paper Modernising Government (Cm 4310) stated, "By the year 2004 all newly-created public records will be electronically stored and retrieved."
2. These policies can be seen on the TNA Web site at www.nationalarchives.gov.uk/recordsmanagement/selection/default.htm (accessed January 2007).
3. The pilot version of EROL is available at www.nationalarchives.gov.uk/ero (accessed January 2007).
4. ISO standard 14721 (2003)—a standard common language to discuss digital archiving. This includes the terms:
   - SIP—Submission Information Package, the collection of digital objects and surrounding metadata created for transfer to an archive
   - AIP—Archival Information Package, the collection of digital

objects and surrounding metadata created for permanent archival storage
- DIP—Dissemination Information Package, the collection of digital objects and surrounding metadata created for presentation to users

5. Lord Chancellor's Code of Practice on the Management of Records under section 46 of the Freedom of Information Act 2000, paragraph 11.7.
6. www.nationalarchives.gov.uk/documents/redaction_toolkit.pdf (accessed January 2007).
7. Guidelines on the Realisation of Benefits from Electronic Records Management (TNA, September 2004). See www.national archives.gov.uk/documents/benefits_realisation.pdf (accessed January 2007).
8. See www.cio.gov.uk/transformational_government/index.asp (accessed January 2007).
9. See the Web site for details about the launch of a new set of competencies on information management, available: http://psg.civilservice.gov.uk/ (accessed January 2007).

Chapter 12

Leading from the Middle: Building a University Archives

Leon Stout

INTRODUCTION: MY ROUTE TO PENN STATE ARCHIVIST

This chapter reflects on my leadership experience as a program director, focusing on my work as a university archivist at Penn State University from 1974 to 2001. In particular, the chapter conveys insights about leading from a middle level, where you have a program to lead but also answer to executives above you in the institution's leadership hierarchy. I have to confess, I didn't become an archivist because I wanted to be a manager, let alone a leader. In fact, in my younger days I only knew I wanted to do something connected with history such as teaching in high school or, later, at the college or university level. I proceeded through bachelor's and master's degrees at Penn State University focusing on eighteenth-century China. In 1972, I wanted to try my hand at teaching before committing to a doctoral program. The dry academic job market of the early 1970s ended that dream fairly quickly, but I heard of an opening in the University Library, in archives. Didn't that have something to do with history?

So the rest was not history, but archives. I accidentally discovered a career I hadn't realized existed. A crash refresher in American History quickly began as I assumed my duties at Penn State's Historical Collections and Labor Archives (HCLA). At the same time, I discovered that there was some carryover from my previous work. My specialty had been institutional history, the study of the Qing Dynasty emperors and their government, one of the world's great premodern bureaucracies. The study of institutions turned out to be the perfect training for archival work. I understood record keeping and record making, how organizations communicated, made decisions and documented their activities—this I would later discover was the core of archival science.

In short order, I decided to change directions. Instead of a doctoral program in history, I undertook a master's in library science part-time at the University of Pittsburgh while working in HCLA at Penn State. By the time my degree program was wrapping up at Pitt, I found myself the successful candidate for the position of "Penn State Archivist" in 1974.[1] I thus entered the world of university archives, not knowing quite what to expect. But I discovered I had something to manage and a staff to lead.

My domain was not yet the University Archives, despite my new title. It was the Penn State Room, a collection of university-related history materials begun 70 years previous to support a succession of college historians and curators. The first, a philosophy professor, doubled as the college librarian and had started the "Statiana Alcove" in 1904, a year before Penn State's fiftieth anniversary. He collected publications, photographs, early college memorabilia, correspondence of early trustees and faculty, and the core of the first president's papers. He wrote alumni magazine articles about the college's history and drafted a book-length history of the college which did not find publication. His successor as college historian was a professor of Pennsylvania history who spent much of the war years writing a new history of the college, which was published in 1946.

The curators who followed over the next thirty years were more librarians than archivists. They added more publications, created vertical files, indexed college and town periodicals, but collected few unpublished materials other than some additional presidential papers and more random manuscripts. The university librarian for a time had the additional title of archivist, but it had no purpose and was dropped. One curator, while on a fact-finding road trip in the early 1950s, came back reporting she had been to Yale and their university collection was "purely archivistic" and thus held no interest for her. The Penn State Room appeared, to the few aware of its existence, as little more than the university attic. During my interview for the position, I sounded out the dean of libraries about his expectations for me in this position. He responded that anything I did would be an improvement—clearly there was no where to go but up.

Taking over the Archives was still intimidating. I had only supervised students before, while most of my new staff were almost my parents' age. I thought it best to be circumspect at first, and so spent time analyzing the situation. I gradually developed a vision for the Archives from discussions with Dr. Ronald Filippelli, the labor archivist and head of HCLA at Penn State; I also used information from a slim university archives reader (Veysey, 1965; Shipton, 1965), and from archival classics (Schellenberg, 1956; Norton, 1975). I didn't see myself as a leader yet; I adapted to the form of participatory management popularized by Douglas McGregor (McGregor, 1960) and then prevalent at Penn State.

Obviously, leadership is more than management. My purpose in this chapter, by reflecting on my experience, is to examine opportunities for leadership in a mid-level position. The University Archives at Penn State is today a section of a special collections department. As archivist I reported to a department head, who in turn reported to an associate dean for libraries at the main campus. For most of my career, the University Archives was physically separate from the rest of Special Collections and the department head gave me considerable license to develop the Archives as I saw fit. In 2000, the three special collections units—University Archives, Historical Collections and Labor Archives, and Rare Books and Manuscripts—moved into a single facility and have gradually become a more integrated department. Part of that integration is a very gradual move toward functional organization, in part represented by my move to the new position as head of Public Services and Outreach and also by the recent creation of a new position of head of processing. Although my responsibilities have changed in part, I still spend much of my time with university history and archives.

ASSESSING THE ARCHIVES PROGRAM

Initially, I found that the Penn State Room had limited resources and very few goals. Its collections grew slowly as donated materials accumulated—there were no particular collecting initiatives. It had its ways of organizing information to achieve inventory control and provide public service, but these were entirely independent of the library's bibliographic apparatus and not related to standard archival practices. I took some good advice to start slowly and evaluate the situation. I examined the collections, learned what the staff did, burrowed through old files, reports, and documents, and started keeping statistics to measure use and acquisitions.

I soon discovered several things that needed to change and a number of others that seemed to be fine the way they were. The staff was very knowledgeable about Penn State history and competent at what they were doing, but knew nothing about modern archival work and little about basic library functions. There were about 1,200 users that first year, almost two-thirds of them undergraduates, which surprised me because I had rarely seen an undergraduate user in HCLA. I discovered that the periodical indexes and the biographical and subject vertical files seemed to offer them ready access to historical information for papers and speeches. Most of their research could be completed in a day or two. These "nonarchival" efforts would have to continue; we needed to hold on to these users. But there was also an obvious need to expand the numbers of researchers using archival materials.

On the other hand, no archival work as I understood it was being done—no collecting initiatives, appraisal, or processing. The several hundred cubic feet of archival holdings were inventoried through card files. There were no accession records, control folders, deeds of gift, or inventories. I gradually formulated a vision: we needed to become a modern university archives, but we would retain those aspects of the "Penn State Room" that had created and sustained a core constituency of donors and users.

Developing a vision was not a conscious process; there were few planning models to emulate, although I had played a part in the Libraries' Management Review and Analysis Program, a year-long self-study sponsored by the ARL's Office of Management Services (Johnson et al., 1977). As a member of the Organization Task Force, I'd spent the better part of a year reading organizational study and program evaluation literature. My reading in the archival literature and attending a college and university archives workshop at my first SAA meeting at Philadelphia in 1975 also had an impact. Articulating the "vision" evolved gradually through work with the staff and colleagues.

However, implementing it was not to be easy because there seemed to be little or no institutional consciousness of the value of a university archives. The university's administration was unaware of the need;

faculty were not yet advocates because they did not understand the potential benefit for teaching; students for the most part were unaware of our existence. Penn State is a "state-related" institution, an ill-defined status that ultimately makes us something of a private institution with a public character—an "instrumentality of the state" as the lawyers put it. The state's public record laws did not apply to us—there would be no opportunity to point to a legal mandate to persuade reluctant records holders to do the right thing. Moreover, space rarely seemed an issue on a campus that sprawled over a rural landscape with hundreds of buildings on thousands of acres. Nor was there a records management program of any kind. Central record-keeping offices understood their legal responsibilities, but there was no policy or procedural guidance for any other offices.

The one thing I had in my favor, although I didn't realize it at the time, was that Penn State had a historical consciousness. It was one of the first of the Land Grant Universities, and had pioneered in a number of academic program areas. It had an attractive campus and very loyal alumni, who were becoming increasingly excited about Penn State thanks to the successes of a unique football coach named Joe Paterno. This was fertile ground and I took to outreach as a means of building that consciousness of history *and* archives.

TAKING ADVANTAGE OF OPPORTUNITIES

During the next several years, I helped bring recognition and support for the program through taking advantage of opportunities in university history in outreach, service to the university, and leadership of a significant initiative involving the university's central files. These are described below.

University History and Outreach

I started with historical exhibits about campus buildings, events, institutions, and personalities. We staged receptions and always invited Alumni Association leadership. In the late 1970s, they asked if I could do slide shows for alumni club meetings around the state, and so I developed a series of programs on the history of student life, the campus, Greek life, and the general history of the Penn State in various periods. These presentations were intended to be fun and entertaining, but I always focused as much as possible on the history and, in addition to images, showed actual documents. Every show was preceded by several slides showing the Archives, and concluded with an explanation of our collections and how people used them.

Gradually, community and student groups asked to see these shows. Student honorary groups and the Lion Ambassadors, the student auxiliary to the Alumni Association, and the leaders of campus tours for prospective students became regular audiences. Then, with slight changes, faculty began to ask me to present versions of this program in classes where students could learn something of the university history and archival materials that could be relevant to class projects. Classes in architecture and landscape architecture were the most frequent users of our resources, but classes in sport history, social studies education, journalism, historical geography, art education, and English came along too in time.

Service to the University

At the same time, it was necessary to build a consciousness in the *administration* for the Archives. Historical outreach helped in this effort, but other tactics would as well. One of the primary opportunities was an indirect benefit of our academic status. Penn State librarians had faculty status and I was thus a member of the faculty. Service to the university and the profession was highly valued in our promotion and tenure process. A vacancy arose among the libraries' faculty senate representatives; I ran and was elected in 1984. As with most such bodies, the real work is done in committee and I soon managed to join the Admissions, Records, and Scheduling Committee, the academic advisory body to the director of admissions and the Registrar. Through consistent effort and being an always-willing volunteer, I became vice chair and then chair of the committee.

This gave me formal access to two of the major record-keeping officers of the university, and to assistant deans in all of the colleges, several of whom also served on the committee. Additionally, it enabled me to work closely with the executive secretary of the Senate, who played important roles in a variety of curricular processes, and who was later helpful in positioning me to be elected to the University Promotion and Tenure Committee, and to the Faculty Rights and Responsibilities Committee. This latter committee, which I also eventually chaired, placed me in a key role in helping to solve academic personnel problems with college deans, department heads, and the provost's office. These experiences led to roles in administrative program review committees, search committees, and even building planning committees. All of these experiences were, of course, time-consuming and took me away from daily duties in the Archives. However, the networking opportunities were invaluable in building visibility and support for our program.

I had recognized early on that being the archivist carried little or no weight in the university, and thus the Archives was not taken seriously. If I wanted the Archives to be considered at the appropriate times, if I wanted to be invited to the tables where decisions were made that would ultimately impact the Archives, I had to first prove my competence. I had to demonstrate that the Archives, as embodied by me the archivist, had something to contribute to the benefit of the university and the offices these people represented. Otherwise, we would be waiting on the sidelines for those occasions when people needed historical documents or information. Perhaps I was impatient, but I was unwilling to wait; we had to prove the Archives had value as both a source of historical information and a service to administration for managing the archival record.

Central Administrative Files Project

Another opportunity for service came in the mid-1980s. The university was in one of its periodic budget crunches; ways were being sought to save money. The Board of Trustees' office called me to advise on one of their responsibilities—the Central Administrative Files, which had been created some twenty years earlier when the administration was far smaller, to centralize the records of the Board of Trustees, the president, and his vice presidents. It consisted of 75 file cabinets of materials dating from the 1920s to the present. The two staff members in charge of it were nearing retirement. The trustees' office was considering converting it to a computer assisted retrieval (CAR) system. Computer assisted retrieval of microfilmed records was, at the time, considered state-of-the-art automation in business record retrieval. The vendor proposed filming all the documents on 16mm film, placing them in cartridges, and blip indexing each item for nearly instant retrieval on a computer-driven reader/printer.

I immediately pointed out the flaw—there were probably over a half-million pages in those cabinets; item indexing each one would take at least two minutes with even the most minimal subject analysis. Assuming top speed and no breaks, it would take the two staff members more than five years each to complete the indexing. This was hardly what the trustees' office wanted to hear. I was asked to come up with an alternative, and with a systems analyst from information technology, we crafted a filming solution with indexing at the folder level that would include only documents from the 1950s on. The indexing work was reduced by more than two-thirds and the index was produced on COM microfiche by a keyword-out-of-context (KWOC) program (this predated the microcomputer and its easy-to-use database programs). This effort proved successful enough that the Board asked us to adapt the process to index their minute books and funded a new archival staff member to index over 125 years of minutes. It also positioned us for the next step—records management.

Archival Infrastructure

As usage and recognition increased, we also improved the policies and approaches of the program. Internally, we gradually began to develop the infrastructure of an archives, collecting initiatives for university records and faculty members' papers, a consciousness of proper preservation techniques, an organizational structure of record groups and finding aids based on archival principles of arrangement and description, and a more consistent pattern of reference service and tracking of use. Statistics showed consistent growth over time with an unmistakable upward trend.

Part of the evolution came through careful development of new initiatives through staff training and planning efforts. While our budgets were, if anything, shrinking in real dollars, I was also teaching an introductory archives course beginning in 1979, and class projects in arrangement and description also began to supplement the efforts of regular staff, wage employees, and work-study students.

RECORDS MANAGEMENT AND UNIVERSITY ARCHIVES

In the late 1970s and early 1980s, the university continued to grow in enrollments and staff, but not in buildings. The administration was renting more space and moving staff into town from a variety of departments. At one point the vice president for business circulated a campus-wide memo saying that space was at a premium now and that offices should not waste it storing old, useless records, among other things. This was my opportunity. I immediately sent a response saying: good memo but there's lots of important information in those old records, as well as legal requirements that have to be followed; we ought to take a systematic look at what to save and when to discard it. This resulted in the creation of a committee to study the problem with the archivist as chair.

The resulting report, issued in 1985, recommended the creation of a records management program and the designation of the Penn State Room as the University Archives, with an official archives policy as a foundation for its operation. The president and the provost, both relatively new, had each come from institutions with archives and records management programs and confessed surprise we didn't have them. They approved the report completely, but urged us to try to get a grant to start records management. This we were successful in doing through a regrant program for Pennsylvania colleges and universities that had been funded by the National Historical Publications and Records Commission (NHPRC).[2]

With over 1,000 offices at Penn State's 24 campuses, a comprehensive office-by-office survey was impossible, but we opted to survey major records offices, such as the registrar, physical plant, accounting operations, and other top-level business offices. We then sampled a variety of colleges, departments, research centers, and administrative offices on several campuses. We established a Records Management Advisory Committee of representatives from the major record-keeping offices, the president's office, internal auditing, and administrative computing. From these activities, we developed, with the committee, an administrative policy for archives and records management and general records schedules for common administrative records and financial records. Every office we approached received a letter from the president requesting that they cooperate with us. In many cases, our reception surprised us. Instead of being obstructed by secretive bureaucrats, we were welcomed as the people who would finally tell them it was all right to throw away old records. Most offices, we found, were not discarding willy-nilly, but rather were saving everything "just in case" since there was no one to give them credible advice on disposition.

The records management project helped us to establish a continuing relationship with all the major record-keeping offices. The survey work was vital to creating general records schedules and identifying archival records for transfer. Ironically, working with senior administrators also opened up a connection to the Intercollegiate Athletics department, which resulted in a major transfer of athletic records and the creation of a Sports Archives initiative within the University Archives. This brought us additional collections and endowments, as well as positioned us to assist with the creation of the University's sports museum. Overall, the records management project was fundamental to helping the Archives become identified as an effective administrative service in dealing with records issues.

OPPORTUNITIES IN ELECTRONIC RECORDS

Records management also happened to provide our entrée to electronic records. I was looking for opportunities to serve the archives profession, something that I also found intellectually appealing. I became active in both the Mid-Atlantic Regional Archives Conference, eventually serving as chair in 1989–1991, and in the Society of American Archivists, eventually serving as treasurer in 1994–1997, and vice president and president in 1999–2001.

However, some of my earliest involvement in SAA came in the Automated Records and Techniques Task Force, starting in 1980. I had been fascinated by computers since working on my MLS degree and experimented through the 1970s with mainframe computer software for text processing, statistical analysis, and database management. My first publication in the *American Archivist* was a survey of automation in college and university archives (Stout and Baird, 1984), and I began teaching computer workshops at archival meetings in 1984. However, the leaders of the Task Force—Harold Naugler of the National Archives of Canada, Carolyn Geda of the Interuniversity Consortium for Political and Social Research at the University of Michigan, David Bearman, and Charles Dollar, Bruce Ambacher, and Tom Brown from the U.S. National Archives—were all more concerned with the machine-readable record, as it was called then. I gradually learned about electronic records from the experts.

When our records management grant ended in 1986, the university continued the records management program, retaining the project archivist and the advisory committee. One of the members of that committee was involved in institutional computing, and listened with interest as I described the work of the two national archives on electronic records. He had helped us incorporate electronic records into our records management surveys. We decided to begin addressing electronic records, and crafted an NHPRC (National Historical Publications and Records Commission) grant proposal that would enable us to survey and appraise some 3,000 "administrative computing history datasets." These were files originating in a variety of academic and administrative legacy systems, and were most often snapshots of databases captured at regular intervals. Some went back to the late 1960s, but most were less than ten years old. We hired a data archivist and followed the standard procedures developed at the National Archives to review, appraise, and preserve these datasets.

The results of this 1991–1993 grant project seemed ambiguous to some. Few datasets could be identified as "archival" and preserved. On the other hand, there had rarely been a clearer demonstration that electronic records could not be left to sit for years and then taken up, appraised, and preserved with any likelihood of success. It was irrefutable proof that archivists needed to be involved with electronic records at the time of their creation, and that the policy environment and role of archivists would have to change dramatically with electronic records. The project report resulted in several important procedural changes in administrative computing and raised the consciousness there to the larger issue, but did not yield the most desired result, an ongoing program, for which the university did not seem to be ready to endorse (Stout, 1995).

In the following years, there were several opportunities for the Archives to participate in electronic records issues. As a part of the development of the university's integrated business system, I was invited to participate in a study of the archiving needs of the electronic approval system (EASY) function, by which e-forms were moved through the administrative chain for approvals of changes in employees' status, e.g., hiring, promotions, raises, changes in title, etc. Though the "electronic personnel record" was essentially a collection of databases, changes to records in it were accomplished through the EASY system, with the electronic forms then retained as an archival record of the changes. The problem was that they were accumulating far faster than expected and their retention became an issue. Increased storage was the solution, although several offline options were also evaluated.

Another opportunity presented itself with the development of imaging systems and the growing interest in various departments in imaging paper records for various reasons. The administration chose to

draw a committee together to study this phenomenon rather than allow units to jump into projects on their own. As a member of this committee, I was able to link archives and records management to decision
making about business imaging. We strongly discouraged any imaging implementation that did not require considerable sharing of
records among staff or between offices, and also any project that simply aimed to reduce paper storage by reformatting. We encouraged a
full business process analysis and possible reengineering before any
major investment in imaging. Nevertheless, as the cost of scanners
came down, we could not prevent offices from doing some imaging
but major projects to convert were largely avoided when unnecessary.

PROMOTING AWARENESS OF ARCHIVES

Although I have focused almost exclusively on the development of the
Archives' role and position in the university as a whole, the development of the Archives in the awareness of our library colleagues was
also necessary. In coordination with the other two special collections
units, the Archives has built collections that are recognized beyond
Penn State, including oral history projects, preserving archival records
of scholarly and professional associations, and collections of papers of
distinguished Penn State alumni. The Archives became an early participant and supporter of the libraries' development activities along
with the rest of Special Collections, with our long experience with donor relations and the solicitation of gifts.

Over time we developed a homegrown database for collection management that will become the basis for implementing a public Web-
based search program for EAD finding aids. This database began in
the University Archives and now encompasses all archival and manuscript holdings in Special Collections. Its further development is being hosted by the libraries' information technology services working
together with Special Collections. Over the years, we also gradually
persuaded the library cataloging department to add first our books
and serials, and now all of our archival and manuscript, map, picto-
rial, and audiovisual collections to the libraries' online public access
catalog.

Naturally, outreach through exhibits, publications, public programs,
and instructional sessions remains a strong focus of the Archives and
all of Special Collections. Over the years I have presented several hun-

dred slide slows and other programs, taught numerous classes, written a monthly magazine column, the "Penn State Diary," since 1990, and served as a resource for the media in many ways. The Archives and its staff were major players in the celebration of Penn State's 125th and 150th anniversaries, the design and creation of a university sports museum, and the conception and construction of numerous exhibits, books, and articles commemorating many other anniversaries of significance and community events. All of these efforts reflect a strategic approach to our work that includes continual education, calling attention to our holdings, and encouraging their use in imaginative, creative ways.

Although at one time Special Collections, and perhaps Archives in particular, were looked at as expendable luxuries in academic libraries, the picture has changed generally—especially at Penn State. As library databases, full-text journals, and e-books have become more commonly shared, research libraries have come to recognize that it is their special collections materials that really distinguish them from their peer institutions. It is the archives, manuscripts, and rare books that will draw scholars from around the world to visit. But it is not only collections that have given us greater respect in the libraries. We have also gained this by being willing to participate in the governance of the larger library by committee and task force service. As I look back, my list of committees seems endless, and my chairmanships numerous. We have been good citizens and this too has made the Archives more real to the rest of the library as well.

IS IT ME OR IS IT THE ARCHIVES? INSTITUTIONALIZING ARCHIVAL SUCCESS

These examples encompass nearly 30 years of work as university archivist. In 2002, I stepped aside to accept a newly created position in Special Collections as head of Public Service and Outreach. My former assistant, Jackie Esposito, was promoted to university archivist and has continued to build on the foundations that I laid and has moved the Archives even further along. On the whole, we have succeeded in positioning the Archives in the consciousness of the administrative and academic leadership of the university.

But will our success continue? Many small businesses fail, mostly because of the poor business planning and decision making of their proprietors. But another group is of greater interest to me: the ones that become successful and grow. A founder's ideals, industriousness, and smart decisions propel a business to the point where it seems poised for greatness. Then the founder leaves, dies, retires, is bought out, or forced out. It's a critical point for many businesses. How much of the essence of what made the company successful did the founder manage to institutionalize versus how much did he or she hold in his or her own hands? In the latter case, the successors may not have the vision, or be able to control the basic technology, or truly understand the market niche of the business. Many such small companies simply fail and close after a traumatic transition.

There is a school of organizational theorists who believe that businesses, like living organisms, have a life cycle (Adizes, 1988). They're born, they grow, they age, and they die. After 35 years of observing the ways of university bureaucracy, and 25 years of consulting in archives for other colleges and universities, historical societies, governments, and both profit and nonprofit corporate bodies, I've come to believe that something similar happens in the not-for-profit sector as well.

I recall a Penn State political scientist who transformed his interest in the politics and government of Australia and New Zealand into a "studies" program and then a research center. He had a staff, an office suite, visiting dignitaries, lecture series, cultural events, a newsletter, a publications series, graduate students, library collecting initiatives, and all the other accoutrements of a successful academic small business. However, he retired, moved away, and died not long after. He wasn't replaced with a similar academic specialist, let alone an entrepreneur like himself, and soon the center and all of its assets had disappeared.

Even in the library, I recall language and area subject specialists who built their own thriving little centers based around their collections, only to have their growing enterprises nipped in the bud upon their departure. They were, in essence, unable to institutionalize their visions to make their collections the heart of an important programmatic initiative in the library. The collections remain, but they have faded into the stacks; there are no more bibliographies, public programs, exhibits, renowned visiting scholars, or donors being courted for endowments to further build collections and programs.

Clearly this could happen in the Archives too. I have no qualms admitting that I have been an archival entrepreneur. I did not sit quietly in my office processing collections and answering reference questions all day. I took the initiative and built a functioning, institutional archives out of the library's "attic." As I near retirement, I hear many comments like, "You can't be replaced," and "They don't know how much they'll miss you." While personally gratifying, I don't necessarily regard these as measures of success.

Years ago Clifford Shipton wrote of a faculty meeting at Harvard where budget cuts were being considered. Department heads said, "You can't cut the Archives budget; it would cost us more to do the work they are doing for us" (Shipton, 1965: 68). That idea embodied one of my main goals as university archivist: to be seen as indispensable. No law mandates our existence; we have to prove our worth every day, so that no one will think to ask, "Why do we need an archives?"

If anything can establish the conditions for continuity, it is consistent performance and the development of a solid staff that routinely meets or exceeds the expectations of our constituencies within the university. An institutional archives' number one customer and priority is *the institution itself*. The academic library culture we live in stresses the educational and research needs of students and faculty, but the archives' constituency must also include the administrators and staff of the university.

Being a resource for historical information is of inestimable value. "Archives" is no longer seen as a synonym for useless heirlooms no one can part with. But administrative service through records management has also become a vital need. Though it begins with the archivist providing the services, offices gradually come to see the Archives as the source of skills and knowledge as more archival staff members become known to them and valued as service providers. Let's examine this dual mission in more detail.

The Usable Past

Penn State, with over 450,000 living alumni and 165,000 members in its alumni association, has one of the most loyal bases in the nation. They care about the traditions and embrace the history of the university as an important part of feeling that they are still "Penn Staters." There are conscious reminders of that past all over the University Park Campus. The built environment is the key and its history is recognized by two National Register Districts on campus. This physical presence is further elaborated with over fifty historical markers commemorating faculty achievements as well as campus landmarks and traditions. Visitors learn about that past with the Penn State Historical Map, which shows the districts and markers and also provides brief descriptions of the contributing structures.

The historical bibliography continues to grow as well. Forty years ago, there wasn't a historical book about Penn State in print. A Penn State guidebook (*This Is Penn State*, 2006) provides historical essays and interesting facts about the campus. The most recent general history of the university is out of print but its text and images are freely available on the Archives' Web site (Bezilla, 1985). Besides numerous historical volumes documenting individual colleges, departments, and campuses, histories of the Nittany Lion mascot (Esposito and Herb, 1997), and the Penn State Blue Band (Range and Smith, 1999) were published by the university press. Alumni and local magazines regularly include historical articles.

The University Archives has contributed to all of these developments and products that explain and associate the university's history with the institutional self-concept. As archivist, I served as a reader for a number of the history books, all of which drew on the Archives for source materials. I was the author of the lead essay on the history of the campus in the above-mentioned guidebook, and also wrote many of the magazine articles about campus history. I was a member of the committee which selected the historical markers for creation, and wrote the text of some of them. In addition, much of the imagery and some of the objects on display in the university's sports museum came from the archives, and I also served on the university committee overseeing the planning and design of the museum.

I believe the Archives has become solidly placed in the consciousness of the university as a historical resource and authority. I have worked diligently to reinforce that concept, and continue to do so. But in most cases, it is to the Archives and the current archivist that people within and without the institution turn when they need historical information and access to historical records. I call that a success.

Archives as Administrative Service

European traditions of archival science have always pointed to archives as an administrative *service*. In spite of the dominance of historians in the founding and development of most governmental archival repositories, our fundamental principles of archival organization and core functions still draw on the European traditional foundations of archival work. Thus it is hardly surprising that we seek recognition of the value of archives to the administration of our institutions for both preserving the archival records and managing the disposition of the remainder. The National Archives' mission statement, for example, reflects both the historical and administrative service elements (National Archives and Records Administration, 2006).

But that administrative service is not simply a housekeeping function; "continuing access to the essential documentation of the rights of American citizens and the actions of their government" sums up the function of the archives in preserving and making accessible the "essential evidence" of government actions (National Archives and Records Administration, *Preserving the Past*: ix) Obviously, a private institution does not have the legal requirement to preserve and open its records as a matter of statute or governmental regulation. But today's nongovernmental organizations are subject to many laws and regulations with records retention requirements, not to mention auditing standards for financial records. At the very least, organizations may be subject to discovery in litigation, and thus effective records management and archival policies are increasingly seen as necessary, if not in the institution's vital interests. However, a quasipublic institution like Penn State also must maintain a certain degree of public accountability, and thus record keeping must be a serious concern for both risk management and public perceptions.

Have we succeeded in institutionalizing the Archives at Penn State as an administrative service? I believe that we have to a degree, and that the key to that success has been the records management program. Records management touches every administrative and academic unit of the university and impacts the work of every staff member. But many archivists whom I have known shied away from records management. They preferred to deal with the archival records, their organization and preservation, and the users of those records, especially the scholarly user. Perhaps this is because of their educational background as historians, or their library training. Perhaps they simply didn't want to work in the records trenches helping offices deal with all the records that were going to be discarded, feeling that this work simply carried too high a degree of tedium. However, as has been asserted in the Australian Records Continuum model, I have increasingly come to believe that records management and archives are inseparable (for example, in Pederson, 2004). The evolution of electronic record making and record keeping only seems to make that concept more inescapable. To capitalize on this aspect of institutionalization, archivists need to embrace records management as a core part of their mission.

Our records management program has developed as primarily one of education and guidance. Our general schedules have continued to evolve over the past 15 years, and our records management staff of two (part-time) regularly offers educational programs on records management to university staff all over the system. In collaboration with the Archives, the university's business services unit opened an inactive records center, providing shredding services for confidential documents. Although the program lacks some of the control elements present in other organizations' records management programs, the Records Management Advisory Committee continues to meet regularly and provides strong oversight to the program.

In addition, at the committee's urging, the vice provost for Information Technology and CIO and the dean of libraries are jointly sponsoring a task force on digital preservation at the direction of the executive vice president and provost and the senior vice president for finance and operations. The task force, which includes the university archivist, has issued a preliminary report recommending a digital repository as an initial step in preserving electronic records of archival value. Although there is still much to be done, the university is aware of the recent changes in federal rules of evidence and their potential impact on litigation. This is only the latest addition to the list of concerns about the longevity of functional and reliable electronic records, which has resulted in the university now actively seeking strategies to preserve digital objects of enduring value. This has been a goal of the University Archives for the past 15 years for which the time may finally have arrived.

Archives in Our Future

ARCHIVES AND ADMINISTRATION

Probably the largest archival challenge awaiting the university is the long-term viability of records from the two enterprisewide systems of business and student records, which have been locally designed, implemented, and updated since the mid-1980s. Penn State's 24 campuses and World Campus of Distance Education programs are highly integrated; we are truly one university, geographically dispersed. As such, we are particularly dependent on telecommunications and information technology to manage the academic and business processes of the institution. At some point in the future, these systems will have to migrate to newer hardware and software platforms. The Archives must play a role in helping with the planning for these changes to ensure that electronic student and business records of long-term value are preserved for future use; older analog versions have been preserved in the Archives. These are issues that may only be on the radar screens of the most forward-looking IT administrators. But, archivists need to raise and define the archival and records management issues, advance solutions, and work with IT administrators and others to ensure that archival considerations are taken into account.

Another significant concern for the administration is the continued pressure from the state legislature to make the university subject to "open records" laws in Pennsylvania. Although the Commonwealth has antiquated open records laws, there is growing pressure in the state legislature to update them. Much of the record reform legislation, which is being strongly supported by the Pennsylvania Newspaper Publishers Association, includes provisions to end Penn State's exemption from the freedom of information laws. The university, on its own initiative, long ago opened its Board of Trustees meetings and minutes to the public, and has drastically expanded its "open budget" documentation online (launched in a ceremony and press conference held in the University Archives in the 1990s when the first open budget was made available) (Pennsylvania State University, 2007). However, this does not satisfy the media critics, who have never been happy with Penn State's quasipublic, state-related status when it came to sharing information. Although the state appropriation to Penn State now accounts for less than 10 percent of the university's income, it is still the largest appropriation to any educational institution in the state.

Does this represent another opportunity for the Archives? With our enterprise-wide perspective and the archival ethic of being honest brokers, can we lend expertise on this issue, or help to clarify how much university information really is open to the public through the Archives? To some degree, this would require the media to change its perspective, as much as it would require the Archives to stand up and offer to play a leadership role. Perhaps this is an example of an opportunity to take a public stand, to offer educated professional commentary and analysis on an issue of public controversy, the type of activity which Professor Richard Cox of the University of Pittsburgh often takes us (as a profession) to task for *not* doing (Cox, 2005). Can we be successful here, can we shed light and reduce the heat of controversy in this area of public policy? Taking a leadership role in this complicated access issue might help to advance the image of archives as not just being all about dusty old records.

ARCHIVAL AUTONOMY IN THE LIBRARY

Managing our program's status within the university library was another leadership challenge. With the physical unification of archival and rare book units in one Special Collections Library space in 2000, the Archives gave up some of its autonomy. We did this willingly to enhance the flexibility with which we could staff our various functions, with one reference room for all, a shared exhibit space, and all staff together in adjacent offices where we can pitch in and help one another in urgent situations of need with collections or classes. There have been other benefits as we have been able to collaborate on efficiencies in information systems development, Web page development, and digitization projects, along with the special expertise we could afford to develop as a department, which would have been more unlikely alone, such as with audiovisual collections resources.

At the same time, there are sometimes compromises that one may have to make. There can be subtle, and sometimes not-so-subtle, tensions with the libraries' development operations. Potential donors can entice with gifts of materials that may not quite be what you are seeking, or money for projects that are not really very high on the priority list of things that need to be done. But perhaps the greatest tension is with the role of the Archives in providing records services to university administrators.

I have seen college and university archivists at other institutions who are prevented by more senior library administrators from "going outside the chain of command" to talk to senior administrators in other university offices to arrange the transfer of records. I have seen a library administrator in another institution usurp the collection development function of the archivist by accepting a major collection that was out of scope, and virtually unsupportable given their budget, without any consultation or recourse, simply for the prestige its announcement gave the institution. I have seen pressure exerted to limit an archives from engaging in records management because the library didn't see service to the administrative staff as part of its mission. This last situation has been ameliorated by the Archives' explanation that records management was its collection development process, and thus it was vital for the archives in building its collections. I have even seen a college president, who had been a historian, reject the idea of a college archives; he couldn't imagine scholars coming there for research on college records because "nothing of any importance ever happened here."

Fortunately, none of these things happened to me or to the Penn State University Archives (although I have resorted to the "records management as collection development" idea at times to clarify why it was important to other librarians). We have been remarkably fortunate, surviving through two heads of Special Collections, three deans of libraries, and four presidents over the past 33 years. But the job is never done or complete. The environment is continually changing. Universities are remarkably fluid—new administrators, faculty, staff, students, library and archival staff are coming all the time. Many have little or no appreciation of either Penn State's history or of the role and functions of archives.

So the challenge is continuous. We try and be good at both tasks— to safeguard and preserve the records of the university, ensuring that the people can discover, use, and learn from this documentary heritage, and ensuring continuing access to the essential evidence of the work of Penn State students, alumni, and staff and to enable us all to hold the university accountable for its actions (to paraphrase the National Archives mission statement). That is the leadership challenge for the archivist: build the consciousness in the university for the presence and function of the archives as both research resource and expert in record-keeping issues.

CONCLUSION

My career as an archivist has been rewarding and endlessly interesting. In these pages, I have illustrated some of the qualities that were important to me as I led the Archives. Warren G. Bennis and Robert J. Thomas (2007) delineate the characteristics that have been important to leaders through the past two generations. The first they call "adaptive capacity," e.g., resilience and openness to learning from your experiences and being open to ambiguous situations and new things (Bennis and Thomas, 2007: xi-xii). Others might call this the good for-

tune to work in a "learning organization." My opportunities to serve
and build networks were clearly all opportunities to learn new things
as well as to proselytize for the Archives. While the university had no
executive education program for me as a middle manager, I did have
the good fortune to be selected for the Mellon Fellowship program at
the Bentley Library, University of Michigan, in 1988. This had been
preceded by a three-month sabbatical during which I did research in
archival history. The final month at Michigan enabled me to read
more, and most importantly converse daily with my fellow fellows,
whom I still consider to be among the brightest minds in the field. The
opportunity to explore and think hard about the archival enterprise,
first from a historical standpoint, and then from a social science perspective was invaluable to me as a teacher, an archivist, and a budding
leader.

A second basic quality according to Bennis and Thomas is "engaging others through shared meaning." "Quite often, effective leaders
are accomplished storytellers" (Bennis and Thomas, 2007: xii). Perhaps
it was my niche, my talent, or simply my predilection, but I have always been a storyteller. I have spread the gospel of both archives and
Penn State history whenever I had the opportunity. But this cannot
be one-way communication. I have worked very hard to also be a good
listener—to understand people who didn't seem to be interested in my
stories, to hear why what I wanted to do wouldn't work and what
would in its place. I was not always comfortable with bald candor, but
I did my best to hear it. Whether it was in the Faculty Senate where
my proposed legislation was being ripped to shreds on the floor, or
in Faculty Rights and Responsibilities when a faculty member appealed
to me to try and reverse the injustice of his negative tenure decision,
I've listened, tried to appreciate what I was hearing, and acted in my
best judgment.

This leads to Bennis and Thomas's third point, "voice"—self-knowl-
edge—knowing what you stand for, being comfortable in your own
skin. Archives is, if nothing else, a values-laden profession. The idea
of protecting people's rights and holding your organization accountable through the record still brings a chill down my spine. We deal
with copyright, privacy and confidentiality, and the integrity of the
record, concepts that are not just words in print, but rather issues we
must confront on a daily basis.

Finally, there is integrity. Bennis and Thomas argue there are "three
elements of integrity: technical competence, ambition, and a strong

moral compass" (Bennis and Thomas, 2007: xiv). I have amply described how important demonstrating competence was to my efforts. Ambition is hard for me to judge; I don't consider myself brazenly competitive, but I seek opportunities to serve, in part to advance the cause of the Archives and in part to meet my personal goals. While I have had little formal mentoring, I have tried to emulate people whom I admire for their dedication and skills. Unlike some of our worst-case examples in public life today, I have had the good fortune to be influenced by men and women with a passion for doing the right things in their work and their lives.

Bennis and Thomas also state that leaders have had to work through "defining crises," a "crucible" moment that shapes them for the future. Although I can't say that I have ever faced a true "crucible" situation in my career, I have seen times of crisis and great uncertainty. Leadership requires that we meet those crises and work through them, doing the best we can for those who depend on us.

NOTES

1. Since my appointment in 1974, the University Archives has been a part of the Special Collections Department of the University Libraries. The University Libraries provides library services to all 24 Penn State campuses across the state. Likewise the Archives documents the history of and maintains archival collections for all campuses.
2. The archivist initially approached NHPRC and the State Archives about a direct grant. However, the State Archives was planning to apply for a regrant and thus the archivist was hired as a consultant and wrote much of the successful regrant proposal for the State Archives.

REFERENCES

Adizes, Ichak. 1988. *Corporate Lifecycles: How and Why Corporations Grow and Die and What to Do About It.* Englewood Cliffs, NJ: Prentice Hall.
Bennis, Warren G. and Robert J. Thomas. 2007. *Leading for a Lifetime: How Defining Moments Shape the Leaders of Today and Tomorrow.* Boston: Harvard Business School Press.

Bezilla, Michael. 1985. *Penn State: An Illustrated History*. University Park, PA: Pennsylvania State University Press. Available: www.libraries. psu.edu/speccolls/psua/psgeneralhistory/bezillapshistory/index.htm (accessed August 2007).

Cox, Richard J. 2005. "Why Records Professionals Need to Explain Themselves." In *Archives & Archivists in the Information Age*. New York: Neal-Schuman. 91-118.

Esposito, Jackie R. and Steven L. Herb. 1997. *The Nittany Lion: An Illustrated Tale*. University Park, PA: Pennsylvania State University Press.

Johnson, Edward R., Stuart H. Mann, and Carol Whiting. 1977. *An Assessment of the Impact of the Management Review and Analysis Program (MRAP)*. University Park, PA: Pennsylvania State University.

McGregor, Douglas. 1960. *The Human Side of Enterprise*. New York: McGraw-Hill.

National Archives and Records Administration. 2006. *Mission*. Available: www.archives.gov/about/plans-reports/strategic-plan/2007/ nara-strategic-plan-2006-2016.pdf (accessed August 2007).

National Archives and Records Administration. *Preserving the Past to Protect the Future: The Strategic Plan of The National Archives and Records Administration, 2006–2016*. Available: www.archives.gov/ about/plans-reports/strategic-plan/2007/nara-strategic-plan-2006- 2016.pdf (accessed February 3, 2008).

Norton, Margaret Cross. 1975. *Norton on Archives: The Writings of Margaret Cross Norton on Archival & Records Management*. Edited by Thornton W. Mitchell. Carbondale, IL: Southern Illinois University Press.

Pederson, Ann. 2004. "Australian Ideas and Management Models: The Records Continuum." In *Understanding Society Through Its Records*. Available: http://john.curtin.edu.au/society/australia/index.html (accessed August 2007).

Pennsylvania State University. 2007. *University Budget Office*. Available: www.budget.psu.edu/ (accessed August 2007).

Range, Thomas E. and Sean Patrick Smith. 1999. *The Penn State Blue Band: A Century of Pride and Precision*. University Park, PA: Pennsylvania State University Press.

Schellenberg, Theodore R. 1956. *Modern Archives: Principles and Techniques*. Chicago: University of Chicago Press.

Shipton, Clifford K. 1965. "The Reference Use of Archives." In *Allerton Park Institute. 1965. University Archives: Papers Presented at an Institute Conducted by the University of Illinois Graduate School of Library Science, November 1-4, 1964*, 68–81. Edited by Rolland E. Stevens. Champaign, IL: Distributed by Illini Union Bookstore.

Stout, Leon J. and Baird, Donald A. 1984. "Automation in North American College and University Archives: A Survey." *American Archivist* 47, no. 4: 394–404.

Stout, Leon J. 1995. "The Role of the University Archives in the Campus Information Environment." *American Archivist* 58, no. 2: 124–140.

This Is Penn State: An Insider's Guide to the University Park Campus. 2006. University Park, PA: Pennsylvania State University Press.

Veysey, Laurence R. 1965. "A Scholar's View of University Archives." In *Allerton Park Institute. 1965. University Archives: Papers Presented at an Institute Conducted by the University of Illinois Graduate School of Library Science, November 1-4, 1964,* 82–93. Edited by Rolland E. Stevens. Champaign, IL : Distributed by Illini Union Bookstore.

Chapter 13

The State Archives, Education, and Politics in New York

Christine Ward

INTRODUCTION

The New York State Archives is one of only four state archives in the country that exists within an agency whose mandate is education. This chapter will consider the Archives' evolving role in education as well as its more traditional records management and archival responsibilities and how its placement within an education agency—the New York State Education Department with all of its organizational complexities and peculiarities—affects its ability to accomplish its mission. It will also consider this issue in light of recent changes in statewide education policy and in New York's state government leadership.

The New York State Archives is one of the youngest state archives in the nation. Established by statute in 1971 within the New York State Education Department's Office of Cultural Education, the program is located in a storage and research facility that also houses the New York State Museum and New York State Library. In 1978, the Archives opened to the public and from that point forward, undertook a period of rapid and continual program expansion and growth, much of which was dependent upon identifying and seizing strategic opportunities as they occurred and developing strategic partnerships statewide. The Archives' original mandate was to identify, acquire, preserve, and make available New York's state government archival records; responsibility to oversee local government records programs were added in 1976. By 1992, however, under the leadership of State Archivist Larry J. Hackman, it had assumed the records management function for state government; expanded and established a permanent funding source for its local government records function; created the Documentary Heritage Program to provide technical advice and grants to private historical records repositories across the state; and built a not-for-profit fund-raising organization, the Archives Partnership Trust, to raise supplementary resources for the state records archival program.

Because of its placement within New York's educational leadership structure, the State Archives has both an organizational and an ideological interest in education. Although an education function is not specifically referenced in its enabling legislation, the Archives has made education an integral part of its mission. Our basis for asserting this link derives from our belief that archives, and cultural institutions in general, have much to contribute to the educational process. During the Archives' early years, its leaders focused their energy and resources on building the programs described above; education was not a priority. Given the archival program's late start and the significant needs of New York State's archival records, our highest priority had to be the creation of a structure that would ensure the preservation and accessibility of those records; this work was necessary as a precursor to educational outreach. Nonetheless, without establishing a formal education program, the Archives gradually developed, and found creative ways to support, a small program of education-related activities that included projects carried out both in-house and across the state. Several initiatives were undertaken that required minimal resources, but that laid the groundwork for what would become an important function, and 20 years later a key component, of the State Archives Program.

Strategies to obtain resources for these activities included: reallocation of line items in the State Archives operations budget (for example, using funds originally intended to support local government records services to fund the writing and publication of *Consider the Source*, a manual on educational uses of archival records, which, in fact, provided a real service to local governments, including school districts); establishment of an *educational uses* category for grants to local governments from our Local Government Records Management Improvement Fund;[1] and acquisition of grants and donations from external sources to support education projects. During those early years a number of initiatives were started, including: student awards for use of historical records; educational uses grants from the Local Government Records Management Improvement Fund; several publications; and hiring a part-time educational coordinator. These initiatives will be discussed in more detail later in the chapter.

Because the State Archives' budget has never had the capacity to provide more than limited support for education, the Archives Partnership Trust has, since the late 1990s, become the primary source of support for educational activities and projects. The Trust raises private funds from foundations and corporate and individual donors. These funds are directed to an endowment that includes several named education funds (e.g., the Littauer Education Fund, the Hearst Education Fund) or to special projects as designated by the donor (e.g., the Verizon Literacy Project, the Time-Warner *Esquela Electronica*). Since its establishment in 1992, the Trust has raised an endowment of close to $4 million and over $1 million to support projects to improve access to and preserve State Archives' holdings, promote their use, carry out educational initiatives, and raise the visibility of archives and history around the state. Without the Archives' creative early efforts to establish elements of an educational program and the Trust's success in securing the necessary resources to build on that foundation, beginning under the leadership of State Archivist V. Chapman-Smith in 1996, the New York State Archives would have been unable to develop the strong array of programs that today mark our association with education in New York State.

The State Archives' mission is to lead efforts, on behalf of all New Yorkers, to manage, preserve, ensure open access to, and promote the extensive use of, records that support information needs and document the history, governments, events, and peoples of our state. An organization-wide strategic planning effort in 2007 defined four priorities, summarized below, for the coming five years. These priorities were selected because they are essential to carry out our mandate. Just as important, however, is their timeliness in light of the current political and social climate in both New York and the nation, which offers strategic opportunities for moving the State Archives' agenda forward. The four priorities are to:

1. Ensure that all records of New York State government, including those of the executive and the legislature, are effectively and appropriately managed.[2]

2. Establish a fully functioning program to address the challenge of managing the electronic records of government.
3. Build capacity in records repositories across the state to protect their collections and facilities from both natural and manmade disasters.
4. Become a provider of training and information about using historical records for educational purposes as well as a key provider of historical content by making historical records and teaching materials widely accessible.

Now that the State Archives' archival and records management programs have reached a mature stage of development, it is time to embrace education as one of its strategic priorities, i.e., the meaning of the fourth new priority. It will build on the past but is a significant new, expanded initiative for which we are seeking appropriate additional resources. This means that in the next five years, we are making a commitment to build on the advances we have made over the years to support our educational mission, and will actively seek from state government the resources necessary to expand and sustain educational programming. Two of many factors influencing our decision to take this step at this time are: (1) a change in the political climate in New York under a new gubernatorial administration with a keen interest in education; and (2) a concomitant broadening of state educational policy to embrace cultural institutions as partners in the effort to improve education and raise student achievement.

In New York State, the State Education Department (SED) is the only executive department that does not report directly to the governor. The Board of Regents oversees the department and is appointed by the state legislature. The State Education Commissioner is appointed by, and serves at the pleasure of, the Board of Regents. This situation works both for and against the department. Department leadership is stable because it does not change with gubernatorial administrations and education policy is not subject to politics. On the other hand, the state budget is developed and managed by the Division of the Budget, part of the Executive Department. This means that the governor's staff exercise significant control over the operations of the Education Department by controlling its proverbial purse strings. However, this situation can lead to the department's inability to implement policy if the necessary resources are withheld. It is therefore imperative that the Board of Regents and the Education Department maintain open communications and a strong alliance with the governor even though there is not a formal reporting relationship. As a program of the Education Department, the Archives' position is parallel. The ability of the State Archives to carry out its mandates regarding state and local government records is dependent upon the goodwill and active support of the Division of the Budget, the Executive Office, and the state legislature. We, of course, need the support of our parent organization, the Education Department, to secure and maintain the support of all these controlling organizations.

THE NEW YORK STATE ARCHIVES AND EDUCATION

New York's educational system is among the largest and most complex in the country. As a program of the SED, the State Archives functions within the structure and rules of that organization as well as those of the government of the New York State. The Board of Regents and the SED govern education from pre-kindergarten to graduate school and have an oversight role, through the University of the State of New York (USNY), for both continuing professional education and more informal lifelong learning. The Board of Regents oversees the University of the State of New York, the most complete, interconnected system of educational services in the United States. USNY includes: public and private schools; colleges and universities; vocational and educational services for adults and children with disabilities; libraries, museums, archives, and records programs in state agencies and local governments; public broadcasting stations; professionals practicing in 39 licensed professions; and certified public school teachers, counselors, and administrators.

Although USNY has existed for many years, not all of the entities that comprise USNY, including many of New York's cultural institutions, have traditionally thought of themselves as part of New York's educational enterprise. Within the past several years, the Board of Regents has attempted to change those notions, mobilizing the capacity of USNY to raise the educational achievement in the state. The concept of USNY and its potential impact on education is reflected in its statement of purpose: "USNY means education. The pathways to a good education in New York State are through its institutions . . . USNY is about potential—to collaborate, innovate and create new knowledge."[3] This all-encompassing view has focused new and welcome attention on the role that cultural, including archival, resources and institutions in New York can play to enhance and support this effort. The State Archives has, since its inception, considered research and lifelong learning to be important objectives of its program. Archival exhibits, public programs, and publications offer content and interpretation that lead to a better understanding of New York's history, society, and culture. A competitive research fellowship program supported by the Archives Partnership Trust (and now over ten years old) encourages, and provides stipends for, research in the New York State Archives. The trust also invites broad dissemination of the results of that research through sponsorship and support of two annual conferences on New York history as well as support for other historical meetings and conferences in the state. A quarterly magazine, *New York Archives*, is in its seventh year of publication and offers a popular review of New York history through use of archival sources in repositories throughout the state.[4] A very popular program that introduces millions of travelers to New York's history are the *History Happened Here* kiosks located at travel plazas along the New York State Thruway. Each kiosk, produced in partnership with the Thruway Authority and local cultural institutions, and funded by the Archives Partnership Trust, local organizations, and commercial vendors at the plazas, highlights the history and archival resources of the region in which it is located and encourages travelers to visit that region's archival repositories.

We see ourselves as educators and purveyors of New York's history, through encouragement, support, and dissemination of scholarly research as well as through promotion of a more popular (and perhaps more easily understandable to a lay audience), rendition of New York's past. We know that much of our nation's history is closely aligned with issues and events that occurred in New York and we are committed to sharing with every New York citizen our state's proud, but largely unappreciated, heritage. We approach this responsibility on many levels and believe that in order to reach the broad and diverse audience of New Yorkers, we need to provide multiple avenues to learning and offer information in a variety of ways—both traditional and nonconventional.

Since the passage in 1989 of a Local Government Records Management Improvement law, the New York State Archives has been involved in adult education programs through in-service training for state and local government officials and staff in historical records repositories. Each year, about 200 workshops are held around the state on topics in records management, archival programming, disaster preparedness and risk management, use of historical records in the classroom, and many more. Educators' Roundtables and workshops for local historians and staff of historical records repositories who carry out education programming introduce them to New York's learning standards and assessments and help them understand how they can support teachers in the use of historical records. The Archives also sponsors seminars and special programs to acquaint potential researchers, including local historians, genealogists, and teachers, with the wealth of documentation in the holdings of the State Archives; the seminars also introduce researchers to our services, and explain the research process to those who are new to the task.

We also have a long history of interest in traditional K–12 education, promoting teaching methodologies that integrate historical records into the curriculum, and creating tools to help teachers employ historical records to enhance their lessons. During its early years, the Archives established a small unit within its office of public programs and outreach to oversee educational initiatives. This unit was initially staffed by a part-time person (now full-time), whose role is to develop and coordinate aspects of the archives program that provide services to, and resources for, teachers and students. The unit is responsible for activities related to: working with teachers who apply for our Student Research Awards; advising applicants for educational uses of historical records grants; monitoring educational projects receiving grant awards; presenting information on educational uses of historical records at conferences around the state and nationally; acting as liaison to the SED's offices and committees; managing Archives education projects such as publications and Web sites; overseeing education project interns; coordinating the Archives' role in National History Day; and coordinating work on the *History Happened Here* kiosks.

The Archives' placement within the SED should have created a natural bridge between the Archives and the educational system in New York State. Unfortunately, this was not the case until quite recently because cultural resources and organizations such as archives, museums, and libraries traditionally have been considered by all but a few educators to be tangential to the learning environment. Something to be "added on" if there was time and inclination, they were not perceived to be integral to the educational process. "Enrichment" was a commonly used term to describe the interaction between students and cultural institutions and materials.

276 LEADING AND MANAGING ARCHIVES AND RECORDS PROGRAMS

In the late 1970s, the SED issued a new fourth-grade curriculum that focused on local history. At that time, there were no textbooks available for teachers to use and State Archivist Edward Weldon seized this opportunity to promote the use of historical records to fill the void. Understanding that use of primary materials in the classroom could bring history "to life" for students, the New York State Archives became one of the first archives in the nation to promulgate the concept of incorporating historical records into the educational curriculum. In 1981, the State Archives published *Teaching with Historical Records* and then, in 1985, *Researching the History of Your School*, both by Kathleen Roe. These publications were intended to promote the use of local historical records in education, provide guidance to teachers and students in using historical records, and give students an opportunity to become intimately involved in the past. Both had an immediate and seminal impact on a small segment of New York's educational community. Unfortunately, their impact was limited to those teachers who understood their value and found them to be useful pedagogical tools. Inhibiting factors included the lack of easily accessible and widely available training for teachers and the cost to school districts of developing a curriculum incorporating local archival sources and specific to their regions. A fourth-grade-level New York state history text that provided general guidance on teaching community history was finally published in 1984 and offered a simple solution for many districts. We received only limited support from the SED in marketing the concepts and expanding the reach of *Teaching with Historical Records* and *Researching the History of Your School*. Yet, it is likely that our placement within the SED offered us some credibility among teachers and made possible access to practitioners that would have been otherwise difficult to obtain.

Another early attempt to link archives with education in New York State were the State Archives' Educational Uses Grants to local governments. Beginning in 1991, the second year of New York's innovative Local Government Records Management Grants Program, a special category of grants for educational uses was established. These grants may be used for projects that employ local government records as teaching tools in the classroom and in the community including: teacher training workshops, development of curriculum materials, community walking tours, and local history brochures and exhibits. These programs have been very popular and continue today. Over the past 16 years the grants program has awarded more than $4 million for a total of 279 projects in local governments around the state. Following are some examples of successful projects:

- *Liberty High School in New York City*: This school for immigrant students developed two sets of curricula, one for Spanish-speaking and the other for Chinese-speaking students, both based on historical records from their communities to which the students could relate. Project goals included helping students: learn to speak and read English, learn how others assimilated into the culture of the United States, and boost their self-esteem. The curricula were later expanded into two Web sites and became the basis for a statewide literacy initiative called the *Legacies Project*, funded in 2002 by the Verizon Foundation through the Archives Partnership Trust (available: www.archives.nysed.gov/projects/legacies).
- *Holland Patent Central School District in Upstate New York*: This district and its teacher center created continuous interdisciplinary K–12 curricula and learning materials. In preparation for fifth-grade social studies assessments, the teachers developed a "Survival Guide" to prepare students for the tests beginning in the earliest grades. Assessment results for this district were outstanding, supporting the case that use of historical records is not just an "enriching" activity but actually helps students develop critical thinking and analytic skills that better prepare them not only for a test but for life (available: www.oneida-boces.org/ppd/resources_teachers_soc_studies.htm).
- *Northern Westchester-Putnam Teacher Center in Downstate New York*: This was one of many grants to teacher centers throughout New York to develop and undertake teacher training programs. Training grants are an excellent "turnkey" approach to developing a cadre of trained teachers across the state. In all of our grant-supported teacher training projects, participating teachers develop learning materials for their classrooms. This project created perennially popular and useful teaching materials including document packets on the Harlem Hellfighters of World War I fame and Sarah Bishop, the topic of a local legend from the Revolutionary War period.

In some cases, these grants were used by their recipients to leverage funds from other sources, encouraging broad local involvement and building local interest in educational programs that use histori-cal records. Lacking the capacity to offer more than minimal resources for educational projects around the state, the State Archives' strategy has been to support many small projects and to encourage grant re-cipients to promote the successes of these projects through local me-dia coverage and advocacy in the state legislature. The Archives has also built visibility for these and all of our local government grants through the media and in the legislature. We routinely provide press releases about grants to legislators to announce awards in their dis-tricts. This has brought not only the local projects, but also the whole program, to the attention of legislators. In 2005, the legislature voted to remove a "sunset" provision from the Local Government Records Management Improvement Fund that had been included in the origi-nal law. It determined that, after 15 years, the program had been suc-cessful and should be permanent. We believe that, over time, visibility creates goodwill, brings attention to innovative programs, and even-tually will generate additional resources for such programs.

In 1995, the Archives published its third groundbreaking resource for teachers, *Consider the Source: Historical Records in the Classroom*, by Julie Daniels. This volume, which has gone through two printings (in-cluding a CD) and will soon be revised and updated to be made avail-able on the Internet, has become the standard for use of historical records in New York's classrooms. Because actual teachers contributed to the publication, it speaks to teachers' needs and is in great demand by teachers all over the country. As the recipient of awards from the American Association for State and Local History, the Society of Ameri-can Archivists, and the National Association of Government Commu-nicators, it is used in at least two undergraduate educational methodology courses and several in-service training programs in New York State. Colleges in other states are also using it as is the teacher training program of the National Council for History Education.

Consider the Source offers lesson plans and other suggestions to help teachers integrate historical records into their lessons. The SED rec-ommends it to teachers who request information on how to incorpo-rate historical records into their curricula, but there has been limited formal effort by the department to promote this tool on a proactive basis. Next year the publication will be prepared for Internet distri-bution and linked to the state's learning standards. We are hopeful that there will be more active promotion via the department's Web site at that time.

The reasons for the department's seeming lack of active effort in this regard are complicated. Although the department may well be willing to recommend and promote tools to help teachers do their jobs, it cannot require the use of any methodology because New York is a "home rule" state in its relationship between the state and local governments. The SED does not play a hands-on role with regard to the way in which school districts educate their children. The SED promulgates educational standards that school districts must ensure their students meet and it assesses student progress toward achievement of those standards. It does not, however, develop or enforce a statewide curricula, require specific texts for classroom use, or tell districts or teachers how to do their jobs. This leaves the process for achieving the required outcomes up to each district.

Statewide K–12 learning standards were first issued in 1997. Fueled by a national movement for accountability of school districts, teachers, and students, the standards set a minimum level of achievement that all students must reach. Students educated in New York State must now be prepared for life and work in the global and fast-paced economy of the twenty-first century. Students must be able to think analytically and creatively; to recognize points of view and bias; to question and to posit hypotheses; to draw conclusions and solve problems; to identify and evaluate sources of information to employ in this process; and to develop confidence in their ability to acquire knowledge. The pedagogical methods that use historical records as the objects of analysis make it possible to instill these skills; document-based questions (DBQs)—until recently used only on advanced placement exams—are now employed to assess content knowledge and skills development. In 2001, the department began to measure progress toward the new standards through a series of statewide assessments or tests. The social studies assessments are given in the fifth and eighth grades and, for the first time, include document-based questions that require the student to read, analyze, and respond to questions about a primary resource.

The promulgation of the new standards and assessments resulted in an immediate and acute need to help teachers appropriately select and use records in the classroom to help their students build the required skills. There is a great need for both preservice and in-service teacher training in methodologies relating to educational uses of historical records and other cultural resources. Many teachers find it difficult to change their practices and most don't know how to begin to incorporate historical documents into their lessons. Most undergraduate methodology courses don't teach use of historical records in the classroom and many teachers do not have a history or research background from which to draw upon.

As mentioned earlier, while the SED creates and enforces the standards and administers the assessments, it relies on other entities within the University of the State of New York to provide teacher training. A new partnership is evolving between the Archives and the SED's Office of Higher Education which oversees higher education institutions in New York State. We are hopeful that this will eventually give us access to teacher training programs in colleges and universities in the state so we can promote teaching with historical records as a methodology that these institutions should incorporate into their undergraduate and graduate programs. In a bureaucracy as large and complex as New York's educational system, there are many layers of interests that have to be persuaded of the efficacy of our approach and enlisted as partners before we will be in a position to approach the college and university programs directly. As we seek allies within the department and attempt to synchronize our efforts with ongoing discussions, we will rely upon the assistance, advice, and insights of our deputy commissioner for cultural education who is programmatically responsible for the State Archives, State Library, and State Museum and has direct access to the leaders of the department's major programs areas, including Higher Education.

With only minimal resources available for educational activities during our formative years, we made a conscious decision to stretch the impact of those limited resources by focusing on training teachers rather than students. The traditional museum model of turning the institution itself into a classroom, bringing groups of schoolchildren to the State Archives site in Albany to interact with staff and with the collections, was simply not feasible. Space and staffing constraints also made it impossible to host large numbers of visitors. However, the two-dimensional nature of most archival material lends itself to the production of realistic copies of documents, including facsimiles and digital images. With the proper training in use of historical records, teachers can bring "documents" right into their own classrooms and incorporate them into their lessons. This seemed to be a way to get the "biggest bang for the buck" and today continues to be the smartest way to use our educational resources.

The State Archives began offering teacher training with the publication of *Teaching with Historical Records* in 1981 but abandoned the effort after a short time because of limited staff resources. In the early 1990s, we began again to promote teacher training by encouraging and supporting others to do it. Through Local Government Records Management Improvement Fund grants for educational uses of historical records, we encouraged applications for teacher training projects. This approach provides grant funds to support the hiring of a teacher consultant/trainer with experience using historical records in the classroom. The training is provided through New York's Teacher Centers; teachers' professional conferences such as the New York State Council for the Social Studies, and regional social studies councils; New York's Boards of Cooperative Educational Services; and individual school districts. The use of classroom teachers as trainers has been a very successful model and an effective means of delivery. Teacher-trainers are able to talk about their "hands-on" experiences, and what classroom techniques worked and what did not. Teachers relate best to someone who understands the classroom environment and can convey personal experiences—"war stories." This approach makes it possible to train significant numbers of teachers with minimal use of Archives' resources.

The New York State Archives has a long-standing policy of involving its customers in decisions about its services. Our educational programs have followed that same model. Teacher focus groups representative of geographic, ethnic, and grade-level diversity were brought together in 1997 and again in 2004 to evaluate our educational resources and services to teachers. They also provided perspective on their needs, obstacles they routinely encounter, and ways in which we might help. Teacher training in using historical records, both preservice and in-service, came up over and over again as a critical need. They also asked for images of documents from the Archives and local records repositories, accompanied by lesson plans and instructional materials. The results of these sessions, which were facilitated by an objective outsider and not attended by Archives staff, have informed our program direction and service development. Because we pay close attention to the interests and concerns of those working in the classroom, we can be sure that our offerings are exactly what New York teachers want and need. Since the education environment in New York is rapidly changing, we expect to hold future focus group sessions more frequently—perhaps every four to five years.

Several educational products created for teachers by the New York

State Archives were developed as a result of recommendations from the teacher focus groups. We created, with funding from JP Morgan Chase, through the Archives Partnership Trust, a book titled *The Erie Canal: New York's Gift to the Nation*, keyed to the fourth- and twelfth-grade curricula, which included lesson plans, copies of archival materials, and historical essays. We also developed online products: *The Erie Canal Time Machine* (www.archives.nysed.gov/projects/eriecanal), *Legacies* (www.archives.nysed.gov/projects/legacies), and *Throughout the Ages* (www.archives.nysed.gov/projects/throughout)—all developed for the Internet in the past five years and all funded through corporate and foundation grants raised by the Archives Partnership Trust. Each new product built on earlier products and incorporated changes in the structure and operation of the system based on feedback from teachers who evaluated preceding products. *Throughout the Ages* is our newest offering, providing more than 400 historical images from the Archives' collections with extensive background material geared to pre-K through sixth grade. It is an innovative and unique tool that offers teachers the opportunity to create customized worksheets and lessons around the primary resource that can be used for an entire classroom or to address individual student needs.

As the State Archives developed and expanded its offerings for teachers, the Archives' staff also kept in close touch with SED staff who advise teachers on implementation of the standards and curriculum alignment. Through these interactions, informal supportive relationships developed between Archives and Education Department staff. Through these relationships, our department colleagues have come to understand and appreciate our efforts on behalf of teachers and eventually began to help us make the right connections within the educational community. Today, we ask them to participate on our advisory committees and they invite us to participate on theirs. We are now presenting together at conferences, with education department staff promoting standards based learning and Archives staff talking about content that supports that learning. We are also working together on special curriculum-development projects such as one for the celebration of the Hudson-Fulton-Champlain Quadricentennial which will occur in 2009. In these efforts, we provide content while education staff ensure alignment to the standards. It is this informal staff-level network that sustained our work for most of the past 20 years and that we are hopeful is now beginning to "pay off" as our colleagues become aware of the contributions that our materials and our methods can make to the effort of raising student achievement in New York State.

NEW OPPORTUNITIES: EDUCATION POLICY CHANGE IN NEW YORK STATE

The New York State Archives has had a significant positive impact in encouraging the educational uses of historical records, bringing teachers and community historical records repositories together, and raising awareness of the value of cultural resources in public education. New educational policy initiatives that recognize the importance of archives and other cultural resources are presenting new opportunities. We believe that this new focus provides a basis for substantially enhanced State Archives initiatives in the area of teaching and learning with historical records. In November 2005, the Board of Regents held a summit that brought together leaders from New York's education, business, cultural, and community service organizations to confront the educational challenges facing the state. The summit, and the resultant Regents' plan for the next stage of education reform, called P–16 (pre-K through college), drew on the strengths of the University of the State of New York, including cultural institutions. The P–16 Plan (http://usny.nysed.gov/summit/p-16ed.htm#aims) recognizes that cultural institutions have a significant role to play in helping to raise the level of educational attainment in New York. Not only are cultural institutions identified as partners in the effort in the Regents' plan, but there is finally acknowledgement that education occurs within these institutions and through their programs. It is now acknowledged that cultural institutions, in fact, can contribute in a real way to individual and collective student achievement.

The Regents' plan maps out the overall direction for education in New York State and identifies the resources necessary to carry out each proposed action. Among the multitude of actions identified in the P–16 Plan, several will be carried out by the State Archives and/or our constituents—local governments and historical records repositories around the state. One very important action in the P–16 Plan is to create standards-aligned content with teacher guides, training material, extensive online resources, and interactive flexibility to fit classroom needs. This year the Regents are supporting a Statewide Internet Library initiative that has a digital component and, if funded, will provide a vehicle for making educational materials available to teachers across the state. Providing access to educational content is something the Archives has done for many years, but if the Statewide Internet Library is funded this year, with a follow-up initiative to develop significant digital collections in the coming years, we could be the recipients of resources that will make it possible to do extensive work in this area, on a scale never before feasible. This would create vast improvements to and expansion of our online offerings and would make a real difference, not just for schoolchildren, but for anyone who wants access to images of materials in the State Archives.

Another aspect of the P–16 Plan that will have significant benefit for the archival and cultural community in New York State is a requirement that cultural institutions chartered by the Board of Regents provide educational programs at no cost to families living in poverty. This action is also linked to a budget initiative for the coming year—the Cultural Education and Museum Act, which, if passed, would provide new resources in the form of state aid and competitive grants to chartered cultural institutions that deliver educational programs aligned with the Regents' learning standards. Historical records repositories such as historical societies, museums, and libraries, many of which already offer educational programs both in-house and in their local schools, would benefit from this initiative. Education programs delivered by cultural institutions are numerous across the state, but vary in quality depending upon the institution's resources. The availability of state aid, which is tied to specific standards of quality and practice that the program must meet in order to qualify, will have an immediate and long-range impact on the ability of cultural institutions in this state to improve and expand their educational offerings. Such programs provide an important enhancement to the traditional classroom lesson, expand the information available to the students, broaden students' experiences, and stimulate students' interest. Museums and other cultural institutions in New York have never received state funding to help support their educational programming. The P–16 Plan recommendation and its associated budget initiative aim to correct this inequity and to assert the Regents' position that cultural institutions are real and valued partners in the educational enterprise in New York.

A number of great benefits can occur in formally connecting the State Archives' educational initiatives with the Regents' plan for education in the state. If funds are made available to support the P–16

Plan, the infusion of new resources to develop and expand Archives' educational programs will have an impact on many of our other programs as well. The technological capability and capacity to deliver online and other types of professional development and training for teachers, once acquired, can be used in any number of our training venues for professional development of local and state government officials and staff of historical records repositories. As we identify, prepare, and scan large numbers of records and images for use by teachers and students, we will create the metadata and other archival tools that will make this material available for other research and uses. Every user of the State Archives will benefit from enhancements to our educational programs and offerings.

Actions in the P–16 Plan that relate to the State Archives, Library, Museum, and our constituents are the result of many years of behind-the-scenes work to convince the Board of Regents, the SED leadership, and resource allocators in the state that we are valuable partners in the education enterprise. We worked through our deputy commissioner for cultural education (who coordinates programs of the State Archives, Library, Museum, and Public Broadcasting) to send that message to the commissioner of education. It was not an overnight phenomenon, but a deliberate, consistent, continual delivery by the deputy, the leadership in the Office of Cultural Education, and leaders of cultural institutions statewide of that message, bolstered by examples of effective programs operating across the state.

The education summit in 2005 was the first indication that the message had been received and appreciated because leaders from cultural organizations were invited to participate. We are now "at the table" and in order to remain a viable partner, we need to demonstrate the value of our programs and the positive impact they have on student achievement. However, measurement of success is difficult; there are no widely accepted scientific studies that measure the impact of using historical records on student achievement. At this point, we have only anecdotal proof that this approach works. We understand that validation of the methodology will depend upon data that can be obtained only from long-term longitudinal studies. We are currently discussing this in the broader context of cultural materials and educational programming carried out in cultural institutions and working with our colleagues in the Office of Cultural Education to figure out ways to get the necessary research done.

NEW OPPORTUNITIES: LEADERSHIP CHANGE IN NEW YORK STATE

Regents policy changes provide one important set of opportunities to garner new resources and move our program forward. We continue our long tradition of capitalizing on other changes and seizing other opportunities as they become apparent. Election of a new governor almost always brings changes, new priorities, and revised policy and budget parameters. In January 2007, Eliot Spitzer took office as governor of New York State. Spitzer promised significant change in state government. Among the administration's many new priorities and initiatives, two are closely aligned with the priorities of the State Archives. One of Spitzer's priorities is education and our department's leadership is working closely with his office to advance a joint vision for education in New York, including the P–16 Plan and associated budget initiatives. A second focus of the new administration represents an area in which the Archives has a vested interest and one that offers significant opportunity for partnership—making government accountable and transparent. Within one month of taking the reins of government, the Governor Spitzer issued several executive orders on the topics of government ethics and open government. The Archives, through its state and local government records management functions, is a key advocate for, and purveyor of services to support, both accountability and transparency while improving government effectiveness and efficiency and keeping costs contained. For example, proper management of the state's records makes it possible to retain those records that must be kept for specific periods of time and legally dispose of those records that are no longer required, thereby reducing the need for storage space and saving the state money and time. Systematically managed records document government decision making and actions and enhance accountability.

The enacted state budget for the last fiscal year contained significant increases for education, including a number of actions that appear in the P–16 Plan. Most of that new educational funding went to support fundamental educational initiatives to raise achievement in reading and math and to ensure strong accountability at all levels throughout the state's educational system. But we are hopeful that there will be funding for P–16 initiatives related to the Archives in future years and, as previously described, are working toward securing that funding in the next budget cycle.

The Regents' budget proposals for fiscal year 2008/2009 were submitted to the Division of the Budget in September 2007 to be considered for inclusion in the executive budget, which was delivered to the legislature in January 2008. In addition to the educational initiatives, we were successful in arguing for inclusion of two new initiatives in the Regents' budget: one to address the management of state and local governments' electronic records and the other to prepare for, and manage, the risks to state and local government records posed by natural and manmade disasters.[5] These initiatives derive directly from our strategic priorities described at the beginning of this chapter and focus on government records as they relate to accountability and "good government" practices.

The executive budget, looking forward to a year of austerity, did not include any of the aforementioned Archives initiatives, but the next phase of advocacy is beginning, as the Regents and SED leadership work to encourage the legislature to add important initiatives into a final budget for the state. In the coming months, most of the SED's and the Regents' attention will be focused on shepherding education initiatives through the budget process in the legislature. It is therefore imperative that the state archivist be closely involved in advocacy for our records initiatives. The initiatives may seem technical in nature and clearly not within the traditional education framework; legislators and their staff may not understand their importance or why they are included within the context of the state education budget. Because of this, there is a strong possibility that they could be lost among the many pressing educational initiatives being presented. We need to familiarize legislators with records issues as they relate to our initiatives so they understand the problems, the need, and the State Archives' role in addressing that need, before they have to decide which of the many initiatives proposed by the department will be incorporated.

Beyond the budget for the coming year, it is important that we continue to advocate within the Executive Chamber and the Division of the Budget for the future. As of this writing, the administration had been in office just over a year. We thought we had a good sense of their priorities and interests, but not enough time had elapsed to gain the attention of a new set of policymakers and resource allocators. Operating in a political environment necessitates being prepared for unexpected change. As this chapter was undergoing final revision, Governor Spitzer suddenly resigned in March 2008 as the result of a scandal. Lt. Governor David Paterson succeeded him. It is still too early to predict the nature of the relationship that must now begin to develop with the new Governor, a man with whom the Archives has had few contacts. We are working to determine which strategic approaches will be successful in putting the State Archives on the administration's agenda and establishing us as the authority to whom they will turn on records issues as well as a partner in creating information policy for New York State. Following is a short summary of the actions we plan to take in the next several months.

We are beginning discussions with staff from the Executive Office, including the governor's staff, the Office for Technology, the chief information officer, and the Division of the Budget. We will make presentations on the services offered by the State Archives and how these can benefit both the state and local governments and New York citizens in general. In our presentations and advocacy materials, we make several points:

- The State Archives' business is records and records are central to government accountability and transparency—two of the administration's stated priorities.
- Good records programs support good government.
- Records also support government efficiency and can save the state money when implemented correctly and consistently.
- All state government agencies and programs, including the governor's own office, need to pay attention to records issues particularly as they create electronic information and develop electronic data systems.
- The records of government in both traditional and digital formats are at great risk statewide from both natural and manmade causes.
- The state's disaster-preparedness and risk-management plans must incorporate records as important government assets and critical components of governmental operations, which are key to reestablishing operations in the wake of any significant interruption or disaster.

Our discussions with administration staff over the next several years will focus on a variety of topics specific to our assessment of records management needs in New York State, including: development of a statewide information policy; scheduling and disposition of the records of the executive office; preservation and assurance of access to electronic records and records requirements in the creation of electronic systems; records issues related to e-mail systems; open meetings and the generation and archiving of meeting Web casts; preservation of state agency Web sites and Web publications; and disaster preparedness and risk management for all records including electronic systems. We are hopeful that the importance of proper records management within the context of government operations will resonate and take hold in the culture of the new administration. At this time, all indications are positive; the culture appears to be welcoming. We have great opportunity and challenge ahead of us and a great deal of work to do.

NOTES

1. The Local Government Records Management Improvement Fund, established in statute in 1989, created a special account funded by fees collected by New York's county clerks that supports records management services to the state's 4,300 local governments, including direct technical advisory services and a competitive grants program. For additional information about services to local governments, go to the New York State Archives Web site at: www.archives.nysed.gov

2. Since its inception, the New York State Archives has had impressive success in gaining control over the records of New York's governmental agencies and the historic records of the state's courts. For a variety of reasons, however, the legislature and Office of the Governor have shown little or no interest to date in working with the State Archives to develop and implement an appropriate management system for their records. With a new gubernatorial administration that has publicly stated their interest in government accountability, we think that the time is now right to reopen the discussion about governor's records. Over the years we have developed a number of key relationships in the state legislature that could also be useful in pushing this issue with that body.

3. University of the State of New York, State Education Department. http://usny.nysed.gov/aboutusny.html (accessed: September 5, 2007).

4. New York has 4,300 local governments and over 3,000 historical records repositories that exist in libraries, museums, historical societies and community organizations. Many of these organizations

have a long history of collecting local history and together these entities hold vast historical resources. New York's Historic Documents Inventory, begun in the 1970s, inventoried most records at the local level. Descriptions of these collections are incorporated in the online catalog of the New York State Archives (www. archives.nysed.gov).

5. Both of these initiatives are consistent with priorities and initiatives of most other state archival agencies and of the National Archives and Records Administration. As we seek to address these problems in New York State, we will be coordinating our efforts with our colleagues in other states and in the federal government to arrive at solutions that serve the entire country.

Chapter 14

Leading Archives and Records Programs: Perspectives and Insights

Bruce W. Dearstyne

THE ESSENTIAL ROLE OF LEADERSHIP

The first chapter in this book introduced some of the issues and challenges that the leaders of archives and records programs face. The subsequent chapters provided an excellent variety of insights into leadership challenges and effective approaches. The issues in archives and records management are complex, the writers in this book are talented and experienced, and the approaches are varied. This chapter considers interpretations of leadership advanced in recent literature and how these insights may apply to archives, records, and related information programs.

It is difficult to summarize all the leadership insights and strategies in the earlier chapters, but they would include:

- An understanding of leadership principles is essential for success, but every leader needs to develop his or her own style, and to modify it over time as circumstances change.
- A great deal of leadership work consists of *communication*—with the program director's boss, boards of trustees and other top officials, customers, staff members, and others.

- The leader needs to align his or her program with the priorities of the parent organization, while, at the same time, operating consistently with commonly accepted archival practices and in accord with ethical guidelines.
- Leaders need to develop measures for program attainment that are meaningful for the decision makers and resource allocators in the organization.
- Defining and constantly articulating the program's mission is a key responsibility of leaders.
- Having a champion or champions in the organization can be immensely helpful.
- Building a network of alliances within the parent organization helps get the program visibility and cooperation and may help the program campaign for more resources.
- Adaptiveness and improvisation are essential leadership skills in leading these programs because of the variety of settings and continual changes in both challenges and opportunities.
- Good leaders stand ready to seize opportunities that may enhance their programs and, at the same time, benefit the parent organization. They occasionally take chances, after thoughtful analysis, to advance their programs.
- Developing and following a consistent decision-making process, including appropriate input and advice from staff members on planning and major decisions, are important factors in successful leadership.
- Persistence may be essential; achieving success may require sustained effort.
- Major projects or significant technological change may be an opportune time for program reexamination and changes in direction or priorities.
- Good leaders care sincerely about the people who report to them and they foster a sense of team spirit and enthusiasm which enhances program productivity.

Archives and records program managers clearly need to develop and apply leadership skills to succeed in their work. Successful information programs need to be *led*, not just *managed*, if they are to surmount challenges and succeed in today's competitive, dynamic organizational settings. Too often, programs are tolerably well managed and deliver acceptable levels of service, but they fall short of their full potential for success and outstanding achievement due to lack of leadership. *Leadership* implies envisioning, changing, inspiring, and transforming. Leaders appeal to and bring out the best in people and programs and link their programs to higher concerns and aspirations of organizations or even society as a whole. It is a process that requires dedication, high energy, flexibility, determination, exceptional communication skills, and exhibition of courage particularly during times of adversity. Leaders take chances (based on sound analysis and discussion); disturb the status quo (but with a clear end game in mind); act decisively (make tough decisions even when others urge hesitation); and put the good of the program above the good of their own careers (out of dedication to the welfare of their organizations and their employees).

Management—getting the job done effectively and the service or product delivered reliably—is difficult enough, but leadership is of a different magnitude because it involves moving the program from its present status toward a new (hopefully better) state of affairs. Leadership is similar to management in some ways and, as a practical matter, program directors may need to play both roles. But it is effective leadership, of the sort exemplified in the other chapters in this book, which sets great programs apart from mediocre ones. Warren Bennis (1989: 45) contrasted leadership with management in his influential book *On Becoming a Leader*:

The Leader . . .	The Manager . . .
Innovates	Administers
Is an original	Is a copy
Focuses on people	Focuses on systems and structure
Inspires trust	Relies on control
Has a long-range perspective	Has a short-range view
Asks *what* and *why*	Asks *how* and *when*
Has his/her eye on the horizon	Has his/her eye on the bottom line
Originates	Imitates
Challenges the status quo	Accepts the status quo
Is his/her own person	Is the classic "good soldier"
Does the right thing	*Does things right*

Leadership is difficult in part because people do not prepare for it, they underestimate its challenges, or they assume that they will gradually rise to the occasion through hard work. New leaders and managers often approach their positions with false assumptions. They assume that their status and authority will automatically convince people to do what the leader wants, that control is important, and that "keeping the operation in working order" is the main challenge. In reality, leaders find that there is a good deal of interdependency in the program; that authority only goes so far, compliance does not equate to real commitment, and trust must be earned; that they need to influence people and groups beyond those that report to them; that communication and negotiation are important aspects of the work and a major responsibility is "initiating changes to enhance the group's performance" (Hill, 2007: 51).

VARIETIES OF LEADERSHIP

Just what is *leadership*? There is no single, narrow definition that explains the nature and impact of leadership for archives and records programs or, for that matter, programs and organizations in general. A number of recent conceptual definitions are useful for consideration because they provide insights into the strengths leaders need and what they need to do. These definitions have some overlap, but they also provide considerable contrast about approaches and needs.

Leadership Is Something That Is Exercised at Several Levels of the Program

When considering the nature of leadership, it is tempting to conclude that leadership is at the top only—the program director or CEO. In fact, there needs to be one leader at the top who has responsibility for direction of the entire program and for keeping it fresh and responsive. As noted in some of the perspectives below, it is particularly important to clarify decision-making authority and responsibilities. But in dynamic organizations and programs, leadership is found and exercised at multiple levels; it is a trait that is encouraged and cultivated by the program director. People may not have command authority but they still find ways to lead that help move the program toward achievement and greatness. Leadership may be exercised on an ad hoc basis and focused on particular issues and problems. Leadership of this type is something that is recognized and acknowledged when it is exercised in a helpful way:

> Leaders are effective when the people around them acknowledge them as leaders. A title does not make a leader; a real leader is set apart by his or her attributes, attitudes, and behaviors. . . . [Most aspiring leaders need relatively mundane virtues, including]: a reputation for hard work, a reputation of integrity, appealing ideas, reliability—someone perceived as having done his homework. Have you always done what you said you'd do? Do your colleagues think of you as someone who always tells the truth and admits his mistakes? Are you the first to figure out what is wrong and to formulate a new approach? (Harvard Business School, 2004: 200)

This notion is particularly helpful in archives and records programs, which are often modestly resourced and challenged by rising expectations, digital technologies, and other issues. Having people at all levels show initiative and leadership helps keep the program innovative and responsive.

Leadership Is About Transformation

The most effective and memorable leaders aim to change their organizations' programs on a grand scale, take them to a new level, and leave a legacy of *transformation*. The institutions are significantly different and stronger at the end of the leader's tenure. In fact, the setting and context in which the program is situated may itself be changed by the strong leader's transformational leadership. Burns (2003: 25) contrasts *transactional* leadership (practical, incremental, making progress, but not fundamental change) with *transforming* leadership which "cuts much more profoundly . . . [causes] a metamorphosis in form or structure, a change in the very condition or nature of a thing, a radical change in outward form or inner character." Archives and records programs need to balance adherence to traditional principles and techniques with the need to adapt and improvise, particularly in meeting the challenge of digital records. While the pace of change is slow in some settings, in others it is much more rapid, and archives and records programs need to be agile and adept at change. Lawler and Worley (2006: 283–311) argue that there is too much stress on stability in modern institutions. The best leadership approach is to develop strategies that maintain a program's fundamental identity and mission but, at the same time, craft temporary advantages and advances.

Leadership Is About Consistency and Clarity of Purpose

Other leadership experts argue that the leader's most important role is to articulate and inspire a clear vision for the future of the organization. Leaders win our loyalty by describing the future state of affairs with great clarity and in vivid terms that we can all understand. The vision becomes both the beckoning star and the light that guides the journey. It appeals to our imagination and our heart and is a source of motivation and inspiration. This, in turn, leads to ingrained clarity of purpose. Buckingham (2005: 197) explains:

> Effective leaders don't have to be passionate. They don't have to be brilliant. They don't have to possess the common touch. They don't have to be great speakers. What they must be is clear. Above all else, they must never forget the truth that of all human universals—our need for security, for community, for clarity, for authority, and for respect—our need for clarity, when met, is most likely to engender in us confidence, persistence, resilience, and creativity.

Clarity of purpose inspires and motivates employees. It helps them make wise, consistent decisions and aids them in seeing where their work fits in with the work of the program as a whole. It encourages cooperation toward common ends. It provides criteria for measuring progress.

Leadership Depends on the Right Set of Traits and Behaviors

From another perspective, leadership depends on the innate character, ability, and skills of the leader. These traits can be developed and refined over time, but they need to be strong for a leader to succeed, whatever the setting. Some of the most interesting recent insights here are derived from study of military leadership; of course, we have to select and interpret to glean insights that are as appropriate to an archives or records program as they are to the battlefield. The U.S.

Army's "Bench Project" is designed to develop the future generation of leaders, who must be strategic, creative, team builders, effective managers, and diplomats. It has developed a number of assessment tools, including "Top Leader Behaviors That Set Apart Exceptional Senior Leaders" (O'Neil et al., 2005: 111):

1. Keeps cool under pressure
2. Clearly explains missions, standards, and priorities
3. Can make tough, sound decisions on time
4. Sees the big picture; provides context and perspective
5. Adapts quickly to new situations and requirements
6. Can handle bad news
7. Gets out of headquarters and visits the troops
8. Knows how to delegate and does not micromanage
9. Sets a high ethical tone and demands honest reporting
10. Builds and supports teamwork within staff and among subordinate units
11. Is positive, encouraging, and realistically optimistic
12. Sets high standards without a "zero defects" mentality"

This list, and others like it, are helpful models for leaders of archives and records programs.

Leadership Requires Engaging Others Through Shared Meaning

Warren Bennis and Robert Thomas have studied leadership traits of both older and younger leaders to identify consistent approaches. One of the most important is the ability to inspire and develop what they call *shared meaning* (Bennis and Thomas, 2007: 121–155). These effective leaders use several techniques: constantly talking about vision (as a way to unify, inspire, and mobilize employees); community-building storytelling (to illustrate points and deepen understanding); extensive and varied communication (including doing a great deal of active listening to understand what people *really* think); and welcoming hard truths (a way of confronting problems before they get out of hand). "Effective leaders don't just impose their vision on others, they recruit others to a shared vision. . . . Especially in our digital age, when power tends to coalesce around ideas, not position, leadership is a partnership" (Bennis and Thomas, 2007: 137).

Leadership Entails Bringing Out the Best in People

In this perspective, what counts most is the potential application of employees' energy and talents. The leader's role is to encourage, foster, facilitate, and encourage, and that depends on the character, integrity, and caring and inspirational nature of the individual leader. It requires "emotional intelligence" and "mindfulness," e.g., deep self-understanding; awareness of people, surroundings, and events around oneself; and manifested feelings of concern, compassion, and hope (Boyatzis and McKee, 2005: 1–12). Leaders inspire trust and model desired behavior through their own energy, dedication, ethics, communication, and other behavior. They are selfless and dedicated to the welfare of the organization or program and the people in it. They empower others to act, clear away red tape and obstacles, educate, inspire, and "encourage the heart" through thoughtful praise, rewards, and recognition. Leaders touch the hearts of followers and work to align their employees' aspirations with those of the program. "Leadership is a relationship between those who aspire to lead and those who choose to follow" (Kouzes and Posner, 2006: 52). One goal of the leader is to foster the work of, creative, innovative people. "A leader protects creative persons from the bureaucracy and legalism so ensconced in our organizations . . . connects creative people to the entire organization . . . [gives them] breadth of opportunity and the assurance of fair treatment rather than hierarchy and control . . . sets an example for openness and imagination and acceptance" (DePree, 2001: 2–5).

Leadership Is About Challenging Your Team

Constancy of purpose is important, giving people the opportunity to show and achieve their best is essential, and continual progress is a worthy goal. In this interpretation, however, good leaders need to go beyond those things and constantly challenge people as a way of developing their capabilities. Leaders constantly challenge, evaluate, coach, and constantly upgrade the capacity of their team. They are a constant presence and they practically exude energy and momentum. They establish trust and candor and probe, push, and question. They inspire risk-taking and learning by setting a good example and challenging and expecting others to do the same. Strategy is important, but action and progress are what count. "When it comes to strategy, ponder less and do more . . . come up with a big *aha* [!] for your business—a smart, realistic relatively fast way to gain sustainable competitive advantage" (Welch and Welch, 2005: 166–167). A list of "What Leaders Do" includes (Welch and Welch, 2005: 63):

- Leaders relentlessly upgrade their team, using every encounter as an opportunity to evaluate, coach, and build self-confidence.
- Leaders make sure people not only see the vision, they live and breathe it.
- Leaders get into everyone's skin, exuding positive energy and optimism.
- Leaders establish trust with candor, transparency, and credit.
- Leaders have the courage to make unpopular decisions and gut calls.
- Leaders probe and push with a curiosity that borders on skepticism, making sure their questions are answered with action.
- Leaders inspire risk taking and learning by setting the example
- Leaders celebrate.

Leadership Is About Careful, Systematic Decision Making

A different perspective on leadership starts with the assumption that the leader's main challenge is to make critical decisions that affect the well-being and destiny of the organization. Decision making is the heart of leadership, in this interpretation, because it is decisions that effect change and progress. Michael Roberto (2005) refers to "strategic decision-making" focused on issues that have high stakes, novelty and ambiguity, and where a decision means a substantial commitment of resources. These would include, for instance, decisions about the vision and mission of the program, major new initiatives, program expansion, and dealing with major threats. Leaders should not make such critical decisions themselves; decision making is a complex process, and the leader's first obligation is to set the parameters for a process, including who will be involved, the type of investigation to be done and discussion to be carried out, the need for contrasting or dissenting opinions, and the process by which the decision will be made. Confronted with the need or opportunity for a decision, the leader "takes a step back and focuses on *how* the organization ought to go about tackling the problem. The leader asks this question: what kind of process should we employ? . . . he does not focus exclusively on finding the right *solution*. Instead, he focuses first on trying to find the right *process*" (Roberto, 2005: 228–229).

Leadership Is About Execution

In this interpretation of leadership, all of the above factors are regarded as important but proponents argue that too often leaders lag after providing a vision, effecting change, bringing out the best in people, and making appropriate decision. They fail at *execution*, e.g., putting the new policy into effect, changing the culture of the program or organization over the long term, effecting reorganizations and structural changes, and carrying out new initiatives. Sometimes, they relish the dramatic, exciting work of setting new directions but are much less interested in the more mundane challenges of making things work. In other cases, they believe that execution can be delegated to others and then are surprised when things don't work out.

The best leaders understand that *execution* of a strategy is a much greater challenge than formulating the strategy in the first place. Execution requires having the right organizational structure, effective coordination and information sharing, managing change (including overcoming resistance), changing the organizational culture, and understanding and building on the sources of power and influence in the organization. It requires sustained leadership attention and engagement over the long run (Hrebiniak, 2005). Effective execution requires a practical, coordinated approach to get things done. Bossidy and Charan (2002: 57–84) assert that effective leaders demonstrate seven "behaviors":

1. *Know your people and your business.* Leaders practically *live* their businesses or programs; they're not detached or distant. They get information firsthand (as well as filtered through employees) They encourage dialogue and try to identify problems that need attention as well as successes.
2. *Insist on realism.* This is essential to execution. Leaders like to hear what's going right but also insist on learning what's going wrong. They insist on realistic assessments.
3. *Set clear goals and priorities.* Having too large a number means focus will be scattered and resources will be stretched.
4. *Follow through on decisions made*, for instance, at meetings. This signals a serious intention to get things done in a timely fashion.

5. *Reward the doers*—the people who produce results. Good leaders link rewards to performance and make it clear that people who excel are likely to be recognized and promoted.
6. *Expand people's capabilities through coaching.* Leaders should foster growth through mentoring, coaching, and other types of development opportunities.
7. *Know yourself.* Finally, the best leaders are self-aware and exhibit such traits as authenticity, self-awareness, self-mastery, and humility."

THREE MODELS FOR DEVELOPING STRONG PROGRAMS

The leadership literature includes many case studies and models for building effective programs that succeed over the long term. Three of the most impressive—(1) *program building through systematic stages of change*; (2) *moving from merely good to truly great*; and (3) *becoming resilient*—are described briefly in the following sections. Some of the elements in these models have reverberations in the leadership work described by the authors in the preceding chapters.

Program Building Through Systematic Stages of Change

John P. Kotter (1996) advanced the notion that deep-seated, lasting change comes by leading through several strategic steps or changes:

- Demonstrating the need and urgency for change
- Building teams to support and guide it
- Leading a process to develop a vision
- Continuously communicating to secure buy-in
- Enabling and encouraging action by change-inclined employees
- Creating short-term wins that show the benefits of the new direction and encourage more change
- Making changes stick by embedding the new ways in the organizational structure and culture

It is often a slow, systematic, gradual process that requires flexibility and a commitment to adjustments along the way but that proceeds inexorably toward a new vision. Leading through the multiple steps involves creating a climate for change, engaging and enabling the whole organization, implementation, and then sustaining the change.

For instance, *increasing urgency* requires building a case that clearly identifies the gap between current organizational performance and desired performance; sources of complacency; probable negative consequences if nothing is done; and the benefits (described in terms people can easily understand) of the desired change (Cohen, 2005: 13–33). This model has been widely recognized over the years for its systematic approach, emphasis on persistence, and advice on not relaxing or declaring victory too soon, before the change is baked into the organization. It is a good model for the gradual but necessary change that is sometimes needed in our programs.

A second helpful, and influential, model has been described by Jim Collins (Collins, 2001 and 2005). Collins cautions that "good" is sometimes the enemy of "great"—we tend to be satisfied with programs that perform acceptably rather than pushing them on to the next level, greatness. Great programs in the not-for-profit arena have three distinctive traits: (1) superior performance—they get results, efficiently, that contribute to the mission; (2) a distinctive impact—they make unique contributions with sustained excellence; and (3) achieve lasting performance—they deliver excellent results over a long period of time and bounce back from adversity. Great programs begin with great leaders, what Collins calls "Level 5 Leadership," the highest level in the leadership hierarchy he describes. "Level 5" leaders build greatness through a blend of personal modesty, even humility, and unbending professional will; an ability to engender trust and persuade people to do what is needed; appropriate decision-making styles; and an ability go get things done in a diffuse power structure that recognizes and harnesses individuals' motivations and abilities. Careful selection and hiring processes are essential—"getting the right people on the bus"—and identifying areas where the organization can excel and deliver exceptional service is also important. Collins also describes the "flywheel concept," i.e., pushing, achieving small gains, pushing some more, reporting on success, continuing to push, and garnering more and more support through successful work. "Success breeds support and commitment, which breeds even greater success, which breeds more support and commitment—round and round the flywheel goes. People like to support winners!" (Collins, 2005: 24).

A third useful model is what the consulting firm of Booz Allen Hamilton characterizes as the *resilient* organization in *Results: Keep What's Good, Fix What's Wrong, and Unlock Great Performance* (Neilson and

Pasternack, 2005: 211–236). This insightful book describes various types of ineffective or less-than-effective organizations including *fits-and-starts* (by turns, passive and overly energetic), *outgrown* (management structure and techniques suited to an earlier, simpler time), and *overmanaged* (too much red tape and bureaucracy). But it also offers an optimal positive model, the *resilient* organization, one that has a coherent but flexible set of strategies that enable it to chart a strategic course and avoid fads and digressions. It is aspirational, "continually entertains the inconceivable" and "keeps moving the goal posts" to define and then meet increasingly ambitious goals. It is based on a culture of commitment and accountability and is characterized by robust information flow to keep everyone informed (and aid decision making and empowerment). *Resilient* organizations are likely to have cross-functional teams, motivations and rewards for productive people, multiple ways of celebrating successes, and an ability to learn from mistakes and bounce back from adversity.

IDENTIFYING AND IMPLEMENTING SUCCESSFUL STRATEGIES

The insights presented by the authors in this book, and the models presented above, all illustrate successful strategies for building robust programs. A few strategies that I believe are particularly useful are summarized below:

1. Define measures of achievement and greatness
2. Demonstrate alignment with/contribution to enterprise mission
3. Build understanding and support at the top
4. Build and work through networks to deliver services and gain influence
5. Keep the program in a learning/adaptive mode
6. Concentrate on people
7. Lead with confidence

Define Measures of Achievement and Greatness

One strategy is to establish benchmarks or expectations for what the program will deliver and achieve. Great programs are often identifiable and distinguished from their mediocre counterparts by what peers (for instance, professional association colleagues) say about them, for example:

- "The program is one of the best in the business."
- "They never seem to lose momentum; they build success on success."
- "They proceed strategically, get support from their company, expand and move on, provide excellent service—and they make it look easy!"
- "Their best people wouldn't consider leaving, they all seem to like working together."
- "They have obvious respect and high regard for the director."

Great programs may also be identified by professional recognition and citations, such as the Society of American Archivists' Distinguished Service Award, the ARMA/Iron Mountain Award for Excellence, or the Center for Digital Government's "Digital States" award. Leaders need to set expectations for excellence and achievement. Leaders build a culture of commitment and continuity, share information, organize cross-functional teams, and provide strong motivation and rewards for productive people. "Resilient" programs also bounce back quickly from adversity; setbacks are used as learning/growing experiences.

Success is difficult to quantify in the absence of business metrics like profit/loss and stock prices. One measure is the degree to which it meets customer/constituent needs and contributes to enterprise mission (see below). Leaders find ways to gauge and report on outputs and impacts:

A great organization is one that delivers superior performance and makes a distinctive impact over a long period of time . . . the critical question is . . . "How effectively do we deliver on our mission and make a distinctive impact, relative to our resources?" [It also] achieves lasting endurance . . . can deliver exceptional results over a long period of time beyond any single leader, great idea, market cycle, or well-funded program. When hit with setbacks, it bounces back stronger than before. . . . What matters is that you rigorously assemble *evidence*—quantitative or qualitative—to track your progress. (Collins, 2005: 5–8)

Demonstrate Alignment with/Contribution to Enterprise Mission

Another leadership strategy is to demonstrate how and why the archives, records, or other information program is important to the institution of which it is a part. Several of the authors in this book emphasize this strategy. This may require constant educating, reporting, citing clear examples of cost avoidances and efficiencies, and getting others to make the case for your program. Clearly supporting the larger mission helps ensure visibility, influence, and resources for the program over the long run and helps insulate against adversity, e.g., business downturns that result in budget reductions and layoffs. Alignment with enterprise mission is important even when it is difficult to do. An institution's archives, for instance, may feel important connections with outside researchers, but it needs to align with its parent company's goals, meet its expectations, and abide by its requirements (for instance, regarding access).

One example of the need to align is in the work of chief information officers, which is often related to records management and to some degree to archives. CIOs used to be primarily information technology custodians and technicians, and their work was regarded as a supporting service. More recently, their role has evolved with growing understanding of the importance of information as the basis for organizational operation. In many settings, CIOs are becoming, in effect, chief information strategists, with expectations that they will find ways to put information to work for the enterprise. In short, they are aligning with the priorities of the enterprise. The top expectations for CIOs now include (Smith, 2006: 220):

1. Learning the business, aligning IT strategies, and thinking outside of the IT box
2. Being a change agent for everything that is wrong with the business
3. Using technology to increase profits
4. Reducing costs, improving efficiencies, and meeting financial targets
5. Securing everything

Build Understanding and Support at the Top

This strategy is tied to alignment with enterprise mission, and to building through peer networks. No archives or records program stands alone; as the other chapters in this book emphasize, every program is a subsidiary part of a business, government, or some other institution. Establishing and maintaining a mutually satisfactory, productive relationship with your boss, board of directors, or board of trustees is essential to secure the visibility, support, resources, and authority that the program needs to get its work done. As Neff and Citrin (2005: 173–174) note:

> . . . the professional-boss relationship is . . . mutually dependent in terms of setting and meeting objectives and aligning how various projects and responsibilities fit into the wider organization. Each party in this partnership needs to know when to be hands-on and when to be hands-off, when to push and when to pull back. . . . [To build a relationship], align expectations; listen and learn about the main concerns affecting the business; explain and establish your modes operandi; delineate your authority; fit into and start to transform the culture; and constantly communicate the reasons for and results of your actions.

In most institutions, the executive who supervises the chief archivist or records manager wants the program to succeed. But, like all executives, he or she is likely to have responsibility for several program areas, so the archivist or records manager needs to compete for time, attention, and resources. It is essential to "educate" the boss in the program's goals, accomplishments, and contributions to the organization's bottom-line priorities; to highlight and dramatize its needs and potential; and to ensure that the boss hears from satisfied customers and, if appropriate, outside interested parties (e.g., members of an advisory committee). Bosses like team players who cooperate with their peers who are directing other programs, and they also value people who support the boss, make his or her job easier, and, indirectly, make the boss look good by producing program results. Bosses want "strong performance, loyalty, and good advice" and a communication style that is consistent with their own (Neff and Citrin, 2005: 197). Building and maintaining understanding and support at the top is one of the key responsibilities of the archival or records program leader.

Build and Work Through Networks to Deliver Services and Gain Influence

Many information programs are modestly resourced and their mandates may be unclear, too limited, or simply difficult to carry out because they often involve getting other programs and offices in the organization to contribute resources, cooperate, or otherwise take action. For that reason, among others, one sound leadership strategy is to build networks within the organization. This strategy dovetails with garnering support from your supervisor. Building peer networks may include other program directors, for instance: bureau chiefs who want to achieve more efficiency through streamlined record keeping and information management; the information technology offices (there is a common interest in managing electronic records); the audit department (well-organized records are essential to financial documentation); counsel's office (records may be needed for litigation); and promotion and marketing (use of archival records to strike historical themes in advertising). Working through a network creates allies and cooperation to the archives or records program, magnifies its resources, gives cooperation in encouraging sound practices, and may help in times of budgetary or other adversity.

The networking strategy has at least one other dimension: securing support for the program from influential individuals and groups beyond the organization who may depend on its services or recognize, and are willing to articulate, the value of what it is doing. People who understand the importance of the work are often honored to have an opportunity to attest to its contribution, and their testimony can be more objective—and therefore more persuasive—than advocacy from the program itself. Leaders should work to:

. . . find influential allies and secure their involvement on behalf of the program. This is crucial to most major change, especially to a meaningful expansion of continuing resources . . . once a handful of allies is found, they will help bring others . . . the first step in most of these relationships is simply to inform the individuals about materials, developments or issues that might be of interest and to probe for possible interest in broader aspects. . . . No program can afford not to regularly increase its circle of friends in high places, and then to bring them to appropriate advocacy on behalf of the program. (Hackman, 2001: 44–45)

Keep the Program in a Learning/Adaptive Mode

One of the traits of most successful programs is that they keep growing and changing. In "learning organizations," people continually seek new information and expand their capacity to achieve new things and, in effect, collective aspiration is fostered and encouraged. People strive to see and understand patterns and the "big picture," not just their own program areas. They continually seek and process information on the field, changes in technology, shifts in the makeup of the customer base and customer expectations, and are characterized by decentralized decision making and widespread availability and sharing of information within the organization. Choo (2006: 1–28) adds a slightly different interpretation: "'Knowing organizations' are ones that have developed deep collective capacity to make sense out of the evidence before them; create actionable information and, in turn, transform that information into knowledge; and use that knowledge to make timely, strategic decisions." Kanter (2001: 320–321) suggests some traits of the culture of such dynamic programs:

People can do anything not explicitly prohibited (as opposed to doing only what is explicitly permitted).

Conflict is seen as creative (as opposed to disruptive).

Ideas that are unusual, controversial, or "different" are strongly encouraged and well received (as opposed to view with skepticism and resistance).

Decisions about significant activities are made almost immediately (as opposed to taking a long time).

Decisions are made by the person with the most knowledge (as opposed to the person with the highest rank).

Departments collaborate (as opposed to stick to themselves).

People shift their job responsibilities in the course of a year (as opposed to sticking with preplanned tasks).

Changes are considered a fact of life, and people take them in stride (as opposed to finding them disruptive and uncomfortable).

Concentrate on People

One of the leader's chief responsibilities is to recruit, orient, train, develop, motivate, and bring out the best in the people who make up the program. This is particularly important in our field, where resource constraints are likely to mean that every employee is needed and must work at his or her full potential. Three areas are particularly important:

1. *Careful recruitment, interviewing, and hiring.* Too often, programs spend insufficient time advertising, recruiting, interviewing, and checking references. The objective is not only to determine whether a candidate is capable doing the job but also more subtle things: How does this candidate feel about the program's mission and the mission of its parent agency? Will this person's aspirations and style be compatible with our culture? How is she likely to do in team situations? Is there an inclination to "stretch" and grow by learning new skills over the years? What about communications and interpersonal skills?

2. *Understand and appeal to what really motivates people.* Surveys by the Gallup organization have shown that people are motivated toward excellence by factors other than salary. When interviewed, employees indicated that what led them to exceptional work included such factors as (Wagner and Harter, 2006: xi–xii):
   - "At work, I have the opportunity to do what I do best every day."
   - "In the last seven days, I have received recognition or praise for doing good work."
   - "My supervisor, or someone at work, seems to care about me as a person."
   - "There is someone at work who encourages my development."
   - "The mission or purpose of my company makes me feel my job is important."

3. *Give particular attention to knowledge workers.* Davenport (2005) explains that knowledge workers "have high degrees of expertise, education, or experience, and the primary purpose of their jobs involves the creation, distribution, or application of knowledge." Knowledge workers are likely to be the most important, productive, and innovative employees in any program. They need robust access to information; they often work, share and create new

knowledge in communities; they bridle at red tape and constraints; and they may prefer flexible work hours and other arrangements. Leaders need to make sure that the conditions exist for organizing communities; developing employees; assessing invisible, hard-to-measure knowledge achievements; and ensure there is a "knowledge-friendly culture" that encourages learning, and makes jobs "fast, flexible, focused, friendly, and fun" to the degree practicable (Davenport, 2005: 10, 187–209).

Lead with Confidence

The final particularly useful insight may be this: leaders need to develop their own style, modify and refine it as they gain more experience, but proceed with a high level of confidence in their own abilities and make critical decisions. They should avoid at all costs the trap of indecisiveness because they feel they lack fully developed leadership skills or lack full confidence in their own decision-making abilities. If a leader is hesitant, indecisive, or tends to revisit his or her decisions too often, the confidence of both his or her boss and staff sags, and the entire program may languish. The best leaders learn and grow with time, and they refine their style and approaches to meet changing settings and needs.

On the other hand, leaders are not perfect and they may make mistakes. Sometimes, it is good to show some modesty and an understanding of the limits of what any leader can accomplish. Pfeffer and Sutton (2006: 187–214) point out that people may expect more of leaders than they can actually deliver; leaders may face constraints that they can't influence such as unforeseen budget problems or long-tenured but unproductive staff who stay on in their positions; and, too much praise for a leader can result in overconfidence, which can result in mistakes in judgment. Take credit but also some blame; keep talking about a vision for the future; don't focus on too many priorities; and "be specific about the few things that matter, and keep repeating them" (Pfeffer and Sutton, 2006: 206).

Above all, keep *leading* and keep your program vibrant and moving! Leadership depends on personal style; it's different for everyone, and it may evolve over time; there are lots of styles and approaches that can be effective. A leader's success is heavily dependent on what people perceive as the leader's values, motivations, aspirations, and ability appeal to people's deepest feelings. "Leadership begins when something grabs hold of us . . . leadership is personal . . . [loyalty] is something people choose to grant to a person who has earned it" (Kouzes and Posner, 2006: 14, 50, 94). The outstanding leaders whose chapters appear in this book illustrate many approaches and styles that are built on individual strengths, tailored to particular circumstances, and, above all, get results and are characterized by sustained achievement.

REFERENCES

Bennis, Warren G. 1989. *On Becoming a Leader.* Boston: Perseus Books.

Bennis, Warren G. and Robert J. Thomas. 2007. *Leading for a Lifetime: How Defining Moments Shape the Leaders of Today and Tomorrow.* Boston: Harvard Business School Press.

Bossidy, Larry and Ram Charan. 2002. *Execution: The Discipline of Getting Things Done.* New York: Crown Business.

Boyatzis, Richard and Annie McKee. 2005. *Resonant Leadership: Renewing Yourself and Connecting with Others Through Mindfulness, Hope, and Compassion.* Boston: Harvard Business School Press.

Buckingham, Marcus. 2005. *The One Thing You Need to Know About Great Managing, Great Leading, and Sustained Individual Success.* New York: Free Press.

Burns, James MacGregor. 2003. *Transforming Leadership: A New Pursuit of Happiness.* New York: Grove Press.

Choo, Chun Wei. 2006. *The Knowing Organization: How Organizations Use Information to Construct Meaning, Create Knowledge, and Make Decisions.* New York: Oxford University Press.

Cohen, Dan S. 2005. *The Heart of Change Field Guide: Tools and Tactics for Leading Change in Your Organization.* Boston: Harvard Business School Press.

Collins, Jim. 2001. *Good to Great: Why Some Companies Make the Leap . . . and Others Don't.* New York: Harper Business.

Collins, Jim. 2005. *Good to Great and the Social Sectors.* Boulder, CO: Jim Collins.

Davenport, Thomas H. 2005. *Thinking for a Living: How to Get Better Performance and Results from Knowledge Workers.* Boston: Harvard Business School Press.

DePree, Max. 2001. "Creative Leadership." *Leader-to-Leader* 29 (Spring). Available: www.leadertoleader.org/knowledgecenter/L2L/spring2001/depree.html

Hackman, Larry J. 2001. "Ways and Means: Thinking and Acting to

Strengthen the Infrastructure of Archival Programs." In *Leadership and Administration of Successful Archival Programs*, 44-45. Edited by Bruce W. Dearstyne. Westport, CT: Greenwood Press.

Harvard Business School. 2004. *Manager's Tool Kit: The 13 Skills Managers Need to Survive*. Boston: Harvard Business School Press.

Hill, Linda A. 2007. "Becoming the Boss." *Harvard Business Review* 85 (January): 51–56.

Hrebiniak, Lawrence G. 2005. *Making Strategy Work: Leading Effective Execution and Change*. Philadelphia: Wharton School Publishing.

Kanter, Rosabeth Moss. 2001. *Evolve! Succeeding in the Digital Culture of Tomorrow*. Boston: Harvard Business School Press.

Kotter, John P. 1996. *Leading Change*. Boston: Harvard Business School Press.

Kouzes, James M. and Barry Z. Posner. 2006. *A Leader's Legacy*. San Francisco: Jossey-Bass.

Lawler, Edward E. III and Christopher G. Worley. 2006. *Built to Change: How to Achieve Organizational Effectiveness*. San Francisco: Jossey-Bass.

Neff, Thomas J. and James M. Citrin. 2005. *You're in Charge: Now What? The 8 Point Plan*. New York: Crown Business.

Neilson, Gary L. and Bruce A. Pasternack. 2005. *Results: Keep What's Good, Fix What's Wrong, and Unlock Great Performance*. New York: Crown Business and Booz Allen Hamilton.

O'Neil, Dennis P., Patrick J. Sweeney, James Ness, and Thomas A. Kolditz. 2007. "Leader Development and Self-Awareness in the U.S. Army Bench Project." In *Leadership Lessons from West Point*, 107-130. Edited by Major Doug Crandall. New York: John Wiley and Sons.

Pfeffer, Jeffrey and Robert I. Sutton. 2006. *Hard Facts, Dangerous Half-Truths, and Total Nonsense: Profiting from Evidence-Based Management*. Boston: Harvard Business School Press.

Roberto, Michael A. 2005. *Why Great Leaders Don't Take Yes for an Answer*. Phildelphia: Wharton School Publishing.

Smith, Gregory S. 2006. *Straight to the Top: Becoming a World-Class CIO*. New York: John Wiley and Sons.

Wagner, Rodd and James K. Harter. 2006. *12: The Elements of Great Managing*. New York: Gallup Press.

Welch, Jack and Susy Welch. 2005. *Winning*. New York: Harper Business.

Chapter 15

Leading Archives and Records Programs: Issues and Sources

Bruce W. Dearstyne

LOOKING TOWARD THE FUTURE

The previous chapters have explored archival and records program leadership and development from several perspectives. This concluding chapter suggests some topics for possible further attention and suggests some sources to explore and delve further into some of the issues raised by the authors of this book. Continuing the discussion, including more publications about leadership, program development, management, and related topics, is an important strategy for strengthening our programs. It is imperative that archives programs remain responsive and resilient, master the complex challenges they will continue to face, and have the capacity to get work done in exemplary fashion but with modest resources. This will require solid research and publication of articles and books; it will also rely on identifying canons of best practice and drawing on the reflections and wisdom of seasoned program directors, as this book does. Even more important, it will mean being aware of, and drawing on, the best leadership and management practices in business, government, education, not-for-profits, and other organizations, and interpreting and applying them to records and archives program settings. Our professional community, broadly defined, needs to give attention to these dynamic issues even as we continue to improve professional techniques, establish new policies, and develop new standards for carrying out records and archives work.

SOME ISSUES FOR FUTURE CONSIDERATION

The previous chapters introduced and discussed a number of issues but they also raised some topics that merit further exploration, and these are discussed here.

Defining and Asserting Program Roles in an Increasingly Complex Digital Arena

Modern institutions, in effect, run on information—it is the basis for customer interaction, competitive advantage, research and development, internal and external communication, and decision making. "Knowledge workers," the key employees in most organizations, need access to information for their work; decision makers need it to make timely, appropriate decisions. There is a trend in management toward more collaboration, for instance, via wikis, which is information intensive.[1] These trends will continue in difficult-to-predict ways, but information, particularly in digital form, will continue to grow in importance. Where will *records* (essentially, *recorded information*) and *archives* (essentially, *records of enduring value*) fit in?

Strengthening Measures of Program Excellence and Attainment

The archives and records fields need better and more robust measures of how well they are doing in order to survive and prosper in institutional settings where there is almost always competition for resources. What are the essential elements of an archives or records program? What are reasonable expectations for resources that are required? How should we measure and report on the value of records management to an organization's "top line" (its mission) or its "bottom line" (for companies, making a profit)?

Defining and Addressing High Visibility Issues

We need leadership and management mechanisms and tools for defining, reacting to, and taking proactive initiatives to address issues that may not be seen as priorities but may attract more attention and eventually come to center stage. One example might be disaster preparedness—always an issue for archivists and records managers but one that took on more importance after the terrorist attacks of 9/11/01 and Hurricane Katrina. Another example is "electronic discovery," an area in which interest rose in the wake of new laws, judicial decisions, and court rulings over the past several years. Another issue might be ethics, another traditional concern in our field but one that intensified in public attention after the Enron scandal and other corporate scandals in recent years. We have heightened attention to our obligations relating to access, support for research, privacy/confidentiality, legal responsibilities, balance of documentation, and, for archivists in particular, obligations to posterity.[2]

Blending Leadership and Management

In most archives and records programs, the director has to carry out some *leadership* (giving direction and momentum to the program) and some *management* (working through others to get the work done). In fact, in addition, he or she may need to actually do some of the work directly. Balancing these two (or, possibly, three) roles is a challenge, particularly for new program directors. What skills are needed? How should a program manager balance his or her time among these roles? What are the consequences if one of the roles is slighted?

Developing Better Approaches to Transitions

A number of the chapters touch on an issue that is often neglected: *transitions*. Programs can sag or lose momentum during the period when a leader is planning to leave; often, there is a search for a replacement, perhaps with someone standing in in an "acting" capacity; a new leader is appointed, but takes some time to get up to speed. More attention is needed in the management of the "transition out" process, ensuring that the program's effectiveness continues during the "interim" period, and developing strategies for new leaders to take charge more expeditiously.[3]

Increasing the Role of Professional Associations

Professional archival and records management associations need to focus more attention on leadership and program development skills, for instance, through articles in journals, books in archives publications programs, and sessions and forums at professional meetings. They also need to better define the set of knowledge, skills, and abilities that are needed by leaders to achieve program success.[4]

Enhancing the Role of Education for Information Professionals

Education for both archivists and records managers helps prepare the program leaders of the future, and also is a source for current leaders to broaden and sharpen their skills. But even in the strongest programs, though *management* courses are common, *leadership* courses are rare. More and better courses are needed. Probably even more critical is the need for postappointment and midcareer seminars, courses, and other development opportunities.

Identifying and Integrating Helpful New Ideas

Just as our fields keep changing, so also do the fields of management and leadership continue to evolve. Hundreds of substantial books on leadership and management are published each year. Some recycle familiar notions; some push flashy new concepts that lack much substance; others are solid and well worth our attention. For instance, concepts of employee collaboration, giving everyone a stake and a "voice" in shaping future program directions, and appealing to socially minded younger workers, all seem to be gaining attention.[5] We need to find mechanisms, probably through professional associations, to identify the best and most relevant, distill their messages, and make sure that program leaders know about them.

SOURCES

As we consider the future of leadership in archives and records management, what are some of the areas to watch and sources to consult? This concluding section discusses three areas: sources in the field, journals, and books, both within the field and beyond it.

Sources in the Field

There are a number of places to look for information and insight on leadership and program development issues, challenges, practices, and problems:

- Sessions at professional association meetings.
- Awards and recognitions for exemplary program practices given by professional associations.

- Speeches by presidents of professional associations, often helpful in defining professional issues and trends.
- Newsletters, announcements, "alerts," and other items that convey information about issues and the contexts in which archives and records programs operate.
- Reports and plans of records and archives programs. These provide insights into how programs are coping strategically with issues, how well they are succeeding, and how they are measuring and representing their accomplishments.
- Listservs dedicated to discussing techniques can also be helpful in sharing best practices and solutions to problems.

Journals

Excellent professional journals such as *Information Management Journal* and *American Archivist* focus mostly on practices and techniques for getting the work done. Their editors and readers may welcome more articles on leadership and management issues.

A number of journals are recognized for their leading-edge coverage of leadership and management issues. They are carefully edited, competitive (a factor that helps ensure quality), and most of the articles are peer-reviewed (another reassuring feature). They include the following:

- *Academy of Management Journal*
- *Academy of Management Review*
- *California Management Review*
- *Harvard Business Review*
- *Journal of Leadership Studies*
- *Leader-to-Leader*
- *Leadership*
- *Leadership Quarterly*
- *Leadership & Organization Development Journal*
- *Management Learning: The Journal for Managerial and Organizational Learning*
- *Public Administration Review*
- *Sloan Management Review*
- *Strategic Management Journal*

Books in the Archives/Records Field

This section, and the ones that follow it, are highly selective; they are meant to convey some suggestions for further consideration rather than a definitive or exhaustive bibliography.

Mary F. Robek et al., in *Information and Records Management: Document-Based Information Systems* (New York: Glencoe, 2000), present insights on program content.

Azad Adam's *Implementing Electronic Document and Record Management Systems* (New York: Auerbach, 2007) includes coverage of business process reengineering and cultural changes in organizations as they transition from paper to electronic systems.

Kelvin Smith's *Planning and Implementing Electronic Records Management* (London: Facet Publishing, 2007) presents a number of management issues, including making the business case.

Michael Kurtz's *Managing Archival and Manuscript Repositories* (Chicago: Society of American Archivists, 2004) covers all aspects of management and includes coverage of leadership.

Caroline Williams's *Managing Archives: Foundations, Principles, and Practice* (United Kingdom: Chandos Publishing, 2006) includes a chapter on program management.

Karen Benedict, in *Ethics and the Archival Profession: Introduction and Case Studies* (Chicago: Society of American Archivists, 2003), offers advice on how archivists resolve moral and ethical issues.

Bruce W. Dearstyne (ed.), in *Leadership and Administration of Successful Archival Programs* (Westport, CT: Greenwood Press, 2001), offers essays by a number of successful archival program directors.

Elizabeth Shepherd and Karen Anderson, in *Management Skills for Archivists and Records Managers* (New York: Neal-Schuman, 2008), combine current thinking and theory with practical advice.

Books in Related Fields

Ann E. Prentice, in *Managing in the Information Age* (Lanham, MD: Scarecrow Press, 2005), provides insights into the management of libraries and information programs.

Sue Roberts and Jennifer Rowley, in *Developing Leadership in Information Services* (London: Facet Publishing, 2007), cover leadership, strategy, setting direction, and fostering innovation and creativity.

Susan Carol Curzon, in *Managing Change: A How-To-Do-It Manual for Librarians* (London: Facet Publishing, 2006), covers planning, decision making, and other issues related to change in library services and programs.

Sharon Markless and David Streathfield, in *Evaluating the Impact of Your Library* (London: Facet Publishing, 2006), provide multiple strategies and tools to assess the impact of programs.

Robert D. Stueart and Barbara B. Moran's *Library and Information Center Management* (7th ed., Westport, CT: Libraries Unlimited, 2007) is a comprehensive book on planning, coordinating, and other management techniques.

G. Edward Evans and Patricia Layzell Ward's *Beyond the Basics: A Management Guide for Library and Information Professionals* (New York: Neal-Schuman, 2003) is mostly about management but encourages program directors to consider their work in the context of the institutions they serve.

Jo Bryson, in *Managing Information Services: A Transformational Approach* (Aldershot, Hampshire, UK: Ashgate, 2006), provides advice about planning and managing programs so that they fit their environments.

Peter Hernon and Nancy Rossiter, in *Making a Difference: Leadership and Academic Libraries* (Westport, CT: Libraries Unlimited, 2006), cover theories, perspectives, and strategies for library work in that setting.

Marianne Broadbent and Ellen S. Kitzis, in *The New CIO Leader: Setting the Agenda and Delivering Results* (Boston: Harvard Business School, 2005), advise on how CIOs should organize and lead IT programs.

Gregory S. Smith, in *Straight to the Top: Becoming a World-Class CIO* (New York: Wiley, 2006), presents detailed advice on how to succeed as a CIO.

Karl D. Schubert, in *CIO Survival Guide: The Roles and Responsibilities of the Chief Information Officer* (New York: Wiley, 2004), provides insight into needed leadership skills.

Mark Lutchen, in *Managing IT as a Business: A Survival Guide for CEO's* (New York: Wiley, 2004), discusses how to link IT to corporate strategy.

David E. McNabb, in *Knowledge Management in the Public Sector: A Blueprint for Innovation in Government* (New York: M.E. Sharpe, 2006), and Niall Sinclair, in *Stealth KM: Winning Knowledge Management Strategies for the Public Sector* (New York: Butterworth-Heinemann, 2006), discuss strategies for starting and developing knowledge management programs in government.

Helpful Books on Leadership and Program Development

Many other books may be of use because they explore leadership and program development themes of interest to archivists and records managers. Particularly helpful for new leaders and managers are these three titles:

Thomas J. Neff and James M. Critin, *You're in Charge: Now What? The 8 Point Plan* (New York: Three Rivers Press, 2005).
Michael Watkins, *The First 90 Days: Critical Success Strategies for New Leaders at All Levels* (Boston: Harvard Business School Press, 2003).
Linda A. Hill, *Becoming a Manager: How New Managers Master the Challenges of Leadership* (Boston: Harvard Business School Press, 2003).

James M. Kouzes and Barry Z. Posner have written an outstanding series of books on leadership including: *The Leadership Challenge* (4th ed., San Francisco: Jossey-Bass, 2007), perhaps the best book in print on what it means to be a leader; *A Leader's Legacy* (San Francisco: Jossey-Bass, 2006), discusses the personal traits of leaders; *Encouraging the Heart: A Leader's Guide to Rewarding and Recognizing Others* (San Francisco: Jossey-Bass, 1999).

James MacGregor Burns has also written works of surpassing excellence and influence, including *Leadership* (New York: HarperCollins, 1978) and *Transforming Leadership: A New Pursuit of Happiness* (New York: Grove Press, 2003), on how effective leaders transform their organizations.

Warren Bennis is another writer who has achieved stellar status; particularly useful are *On Becoming a Leader: The Leadership Classic* (New York: Perseus Books, 2003), a reissue of a book written in 1989, perhaps the best book in print on the distinction between management and leadership; and Bennis and Robert J. Thomas, *Leading for a Lifetime: How Defining Moments Shape the Leaders of Today and Tomorrow* (Boston: Harvard Business School Press, 2007), focusing on integrity, adaptive capacity, and engaging other people.

Other good titles include:

Robert L. Dilenschneider, in *Power and Influence: The Rules Have Changed* (New York: McGraw-Hill, 2007), suggests that leaders need to "accept, adapt, accelerate."

Robert M. Galford and Regina Fazio Maruca, in *Your Leadership Legacy: Why Looking Toward the Future Will Make You a Better Leader Today* (Boston: Harvard Business School Press, 2006), argue that envisioning the legacy you want to leave helps shape your leadership style.

Michael A. Roberto's *Why Great Leaders Don't Take Yes for an Answer: Managing for Conflict and Consensus* (Philadelphia: Wharton School Publishing, 2005) covers decision making, managing conflict, and building consensus.

Justin Menkes, in *Executive Intelligence: What All Great Leaders Have* (New York: Collins, 2005), describes a set of individual skills that effective leaders use to make decisions, accomplish tasks, and move their organizations to greatness.

Mark Gerzon, in *Leading Through Conflict: How Successful Leaders Transform Differences into Opportunities* (Boston: Harvard Business School Press, 2006), discusses the leader's role in bridging gaps and bringing people together.

Jay A. Conger and Ronald A. Riggio's *The Practice of Leadership: Developing the Next Generation of Leaders* (San Francisco: Jossey-Bass, 2006) is a collection of essays by a number of authors on exemplary leadership practices.

Another important vein of literature contends that the heart of leadership is being attuned to the emotions, needs, and motivations of individual employees:

Daniel Goleman, in *Emotional Intelligence: Why It Can Matter More Than IQ* (New York: Bantam Books, 1996), introduces the concept of emotional intelligence—how we handle ourselves and our relationships.

Daniel Goleman, Richard Boyatzis, and Annie McKee, in *Primal Leadership: Realizing the Power of Emotional Intelligence* (Boston: Harvard Business School Press, 2002), discuss how to implement the concept.

Richard Boyatzis and Annie McKee, in *Resonant Leadership* (Boston: Harvard Business School, 2005), discuss "mindfulness, hope, and compassion."

The ethical and moral aspects of leadership are increasingly important to leaders of archives programs, and to program executives generally. Some helpful works include these:

Doug Lennick and Fred Kiel, *Moral Intelligence: Enhancing Business Performance and Leadership Success* (Philadelphia: Wharton School Publishing, 2005), on leading from moral principles.

Bill George, *Authentic Leadership: Rediscovering the Secrets to Creating Lasting Value* (San Francisco: Jossey-Bass, 2003), on concern for employees and customers.

Bill George and Peter Sims, *True North: Discover Your Authentic Leadership* (San Francisco: Jossey-Bass, 2007), on "the internal compass that guides you successfully through life."

Joanne B. Ciulla, *Ethics: The Heart of Leadership* (New York: Greenwood Press, 2004), on the moral relationship between leaders and followers.

Linda K. Trevino and Katherine A. Nelson, *Managing Business Ethics: Straight Talk About How to Do It Right* (4th ed., New York: Wiley, 2006).

These are some other books that are worth reading because they cover what leaders should avoid:

Barbara Kellerman, in *Bad Leadership: What It Is, How It Happens, Why It Matters* (Boston: Harvard Buisness School, 2004), covers such factors as incompetence and rigidity.

Stanley Finkelstein, in *Why Smart Executives Fail and What You Can Learn from Their Mistakes* (New York: Portfolio, 2003), provides multiple explanations of why executives fail.

Three related books provide guidance on changing and developing programs and organizations:

John P. Kotter, *Leading Change* (Boston: Harvard Business School Press, 1996), a very influential book on the steps or stages of change.

John P. Kotter and Dan S. Cohen, *The Heart of Change: Real-Life Stories of How People Change Their Organizations* (Boston: Harvard Business School Press, 2002), stories about how people implemented Kotter's ideas.

Dan S. Cohen, *The Heart of Change Field Guide: Tools and Tactics for Leading Change in Your Organization* (Boston: Harvard Business School Press, 2005), with detailed checklists, charts, and other guidance on how to lead through the stages of change.

Jim Collins' works on how businesses succeed and stand the test of time are very insightful, including *Built to Last: Successful Habits of Visionary Companies* (with Jerry I. Porras) (New York: Harper Business, 1997); *Good to Great: Why Some Companies Make the Leap . . . and Others Don't* (New York: Harper Collins, 2001); and *Good to Great and the Social Sectors* (Boulder, CO: Jim Collins, 2005), on how to apply the *Good to Great* principles from the 2001 book to the nonprofit sector.

Other good titles include these:

Michael Fullan, in *Leading in a Culture of Change* (New York: Wiley, 2007), discusses leadership competencies, including setting a vision and keeping on top of the change process.

Lawrence Hrebiniak, in *Making Strategy Work: Leading Effective Execution and Change* (Philadelphia: Wharton School, 2005), discusses the link between planning and execution.

Ronald A. Heifetz and Marty Linsky's *Leadership on the Line: Staying Alive Through the Dangers of Leading* (Boston: Harvard Business School Press, 2002) covers how to make hard choices.

Several other books provide insight on how to move programs ahead:

Gary L. Neilson and Bruce A. Pasternack, in *Results: Keep What's Good, Fix What's Wrong, and Unlock Great Performance* (New York: Crown Business, 2005), diagnose organizational effectiveness and advise on building "resilient" organizations.

Paul C. Light, in *The Four Pillars of High Performance: How Robust Organizations Achieve Extraordinary Results* (New York: McGraw-

Hill, 2005), draws on lessons from the RAND Corporation to describe success factors.

Gary Hamel, in *Leading the Revolution* (Boston: Harvard Business School Press, 2000), discusses the process of change and stresses that it can be initiated from the middle of an organization, not just from the top.

Tom Kelley, in *The Ten Faces of Innovation* (New York: Currency Doubleday, 2005), draws on the experiences of the design firm IDEO to explain how to mesh the talents of innovative people.

William E. Fulmer, in *Shaping the Adaptive Organization: Landscapes, Learning, and Leadership in Volatile Times* (New York: AMACOM, 2000.), describes how to create an "adaptive culture."

Stephen C. Harper, in *The Forward-Focused Organization* (New York: AMACOM, 2001), connects leadership and strategy and explains how they can be used to shape organizations.

Edward E. Lawler III and Christopher G. Worley, in *Built to Change: How to Achieve Sustained Organizational Effectiveness* (New York: Wiley, 2006), maintain that organizational effectiveness requires being change-adept.

Lowell L.L. Bryan and Claudia L.I. Joyce's *Mobilizing Minds: Creating Wealth from Talent in the 21st Century Organization* (New York: McGraw Hill, 2007), is useful on managing complexity, organizational design, and worker satisfaction.

Tom Davenport, in *Thinking for a Living: How to Get Better Performance and Results from Knowledge Workers* (Boston: Harvard Business School Press, 2005), offers insights into how to motivate professionals.

The focus in this section is mostly on leadership rather than management. But several books that connect leadership and management, often by stressing the concept of *execution*, which connects the two, are useful to consider. Three books authored or co-authored by management consultant Ram Charan blend advice about execution, follow-through, and getting results:

Larry Bossidy and Ram Charan, *Execution: The Discipline of Getting Things Done* (New York: Crown Business, 2002).

Bossidy and Charan, *Confronting Reality: Doing What Matters to Get Things Right* (New York: Crown Business, 2004).

Charan, *Know-How: The 8 Skills That Separate People Who Perform from Those Don't* (New York: Crown Business, 2007).

Loren B. Belker and Gary S. Topchik's *The First Time Manager* (5th ed., New York: AMACOM, 2005) is packed with good advice as well.

A very useful series of books, written by authors who are, or were, associated with the Gallup Organization, draws on surveys of employee interests, motivations, and needs and includes the following:

Marcus Buckingham and Curt Coffman, *First, Break All the Rules: What the World's Greatest Managers Do Differently* (New York: Simon and Schuster, 1999), on the need to value and motivate people.

Marcus Buckingham and Donald O. Clifton, *Now, Discover Your Strengths* (New York: Simon and Schuster, 2001), on how to identify and leverage strengths.

Marcus Buckingham, *Go Put Your Strengths to Work: Six Powerful Steps to Achieve Outstanding Performance* (New York: Free Press, 2007), with additional guidance on how to capitalize on strengths.

Rodd Wagner and James K. Harter, *12: The Elements of Great Managing* (New York: Gallup Press, 2006), a very systematic and useful approach, focusing on what employees want and need to succeed.

Marcus Buckingham also wrote *The One Thing You Need to Know About Great Managing, Great Leading, and Sustained Individual Success* (New York: Free Press, 2005), on the approaches that effective leaders and managers follow.

NOTES

1. A useful introduction is provided in: McAfee, Andrew. 2006. "Enterprise 2.0: The Dawn of Emergent Collaboration." *Sloan Management Review* 47 (Spring): 21–28.
2. For an overview of some of these issues, a useful source is: Benedict, Karen M. 2003. *Ethics and the Archival Profession: Introduction and Case Studies.* Chicago: Society of American Archivists.
3. Some of these issues, particularly "transition in" for a new leader, are covered in Neff, Thomas J. and James M. Citrin. 2005. *You're*

In Charge: Now What? The 8 Point Plan. New York: Three Rivers Press.

4. An excellent model for defining program direction skills—and the skills needed by practitioners generally—is the new statement by ARMA International, *Records and Information Management Core Competencies* (2007). Available at: www.arma.org/competencies (accessed October 30, 2007).

5. Several useful new insights into management can be found in: Hamel, Gary. 2007. *The Future of Management*. Boston: Harvard Business School Press; and Pfeffer, Jeffrey. 2007. *What Were They Thinking? Unconventional Wisdom About Management*. Boston: Harvard Business School Press.

About the Editor and Contributors

Bruce W. Dearstyne is Adjunct Professor at the College of Information Studies, University of Maryland, where he served as a professor for eight years, teaching in the areas of archives, records management, and information management. Prior to that, he was for many years a program director at the New York State Archives. He is the author of several books and nearly 100 articles on the topics of archives and records management. He holds a BA in history from Hartwick College, and a PhD in history from Syracuse University. He is a certified archivist and a Fellow of the Society of American Archivists.

*

Eugenia K. Brumm, PhD, CRM, FAI, is Director in the Legal Operations Consulting area at Huron Consulting Group. Dr. Brumm has been in the records management field for 20 years as a practitioner, consultant, and academic. She has developed several records management programs from scratch that included the development of policies and procedures, retention schedules, and records center operations and has implemented records management software and large-scale document imaging operations. Dr. Brumm holds an MS in library science, an MA in Slavic languages, and a PhD in library and information science from the University of Illinois. She is the author of *Managing Records for ISO 9000 Compliance*, published by ASQ Quality Press, and has published in *ARMA Records Management Quarterly, Information Management Journal, Quality Progress, Records and Retrieval Report, Information Management Review, Document Management*, and other publications. She has received numerous professional awards for her innovative work, including the prestigious Britt Literary Award in 1996 and 2006, the Christine Zanotti Award in 1997, and the Emmet Leahy Award in 2004. She was inducted as a Fellow of ARMA International in 2006.

Diane K. Carlisle, **CRM**, has over 25 years of experience in the field of records and information management. Her primary specialties are records management strategy development, business process reviews, and the creation and use of international and national level standards in the development of records and information management policy and practices. She is a charter member of the ISO committee that developed the international records management standard and continues her work in the development of international standards. Before joining Baker Robbins & Company, Diane was Director of Professional Resources at ARMA International, where she established the Standards Development Program, provided subject matter expertise in the development of ARMA's educational products and services, and authored articles on records management topics. Before that, she was a consultant with Millican & Associates where she developed retention policies and schedules for Department of Energy sites, and an internal consultant for US WEST where she developed strategy and policy for the independent subsidiaries of the corporation, as well as training programs for US WEST employees. Diane holds an MLIS in library and information science from the University of Denver and an MBA from the University of Phoenix. She is a 2003 recipient of the ARMA International Distinguished Service Award, and a 2006 recipient of the ARMA International Britt Literary Award.

Carol E. B. Choksy, **PhD**, **CRM**, **PMP** is an adjunct lecturer at the School of Library and Information Science, Indiana University, Bloomington, Indiana, where she teaches strategic intelligence, management, and records management. She is also CEO of IRAD Strategic Consulting, Inc., a records management consultancy. Her experience in records management consulting includes nearly every industry including federal, state, and local government and NGOs and every phase of the life cycle, from planning to death certificates and archives. Dr. Choksy is a certified records manager (CRM) and a project management professional (PMP). She is currently president of ARMA International.

Peter Emmerson is a director and principal consultant of Emmerson Consulting Limited. He has more than 40 years' experience as a practitioner and as a consultant in archives and records management. One of the United Kingdom's leading records professionals, he co-founded Emmerson Consulting with Elizabeth Parker in 1998. He was previously Head of Barclays Bank's Records Services business from 1987 to 1999. Peter is a graduate of the University of London and holds the Diploma in Archives Studies of that university. He began his professional career with the National Archives of Rhodesia, returning to the United Kingdom in 1976 to join British Steel's archives and records management team. He edited and co-authored *How to Manage Your Records* (Cambridge: ICSA Publishing, 1989). He is Chair of the Society of Archivists beginning in September 2007, a past president of the International Records Management Council and a former chairman of the Society of Archivists Records Management Group. He is a member of the U.K. delegation to ISO TC46/SC11, the subcommittee responsible for ISO 15489, the international records management standard. Peter was nominated on four separate occasions for the Emmett Leahy award.

James E. Fogerty is Head of Documentary Programs at the Minnesota Historical Society, and directs the Society's Oral History Office. He has directed archives and oral history projects for individual corporations, and on issues relating to agriculture, the environment, the recreation industry, and the medical device industry, and with a number of immigrant communities. Fogerty is a Fellow of the Society of American Archivists, and served on its Governing Council and on the Council of the Oral History Association. He chaired the Oral Sources Committee of the International Council on Archives, and is currently a member of its Business Archives Section. He has authored numerous articles, especially on the development of oral history and archives in business.

Mark A. Greene has been Director of the American Heritage Center (AHC), University of Wyoming (UW), since August 2002. The AHC is UW's archives, manuscript repository, and rare book library. He began his career as archivist of Carleton College, followed by 11 years as the curator of manuscripts at the Minnesota Historical Society, and tenure as head of research center programs for the Henry Ford Museum in Dearborn, Michigan. Mark has published over a dozen articles on archival matters in the United States, Canada, Sweden, and the United Kingdom. He has been editor of one of the three U.S. archival journals. He is a national workshop instructor in the archival field, and a leader in the Society of American Archivists, where he has served on the Governing Council and chaired the manuscripts repositories section, the congressional papers roundtable, and the committee on archival education and professional development. In 2002 he was named an SAA Fellow. He was elected SAA's vice president/president-elect in 2006 and became president in 2007.

Edie Hedlin served for ten years as the Director of Smithsonian Institution Archives, retiring in 2005. Prior to that she held multiple positions with the National Archives and Records Administration, served as a consultant to major organizations including the World Bank and European Bank for Reconstruction and Development, and was the first corporate archivist for Wells Fargo Bank. She began her archival career on the staff of the Ohio Historical Society and has served on the staff of the National Historical Publications and Records Commission. Dr. Hedlin holds a master's degree and a PhD in history from Duke University. She is a past president of the Society of American Archivists and a founding member of the Academy of Certified Archivists. Her publications and speaking engagements focus on business, government, electronic records, and general archives management issues.

Tanya Marshall is an assistant state archivist with the Vermont State Archives. She started her career with the state of Vermont in 2003, first as temporary archivist and then as coordinator of the Vermont Judicial Records Program. Since 2005 she has been responsible for developing the state's records appraisal program. Ms. Marshall earned a master's degree in library science from the University of Maryland, with a concentration in archives, records and information management, and completed all coursework for a doctorate in information science. She has presented papers at conferences of the Society of

American Archivists, New England Archivists, and Mid-Atlantic Regional Archives.

Philip F. Mooney has been Director of the Archives Department of The Coca-Cola Company since 1977. Before joining Coca-Cola, he was an archivist at the Balch Institute for Ethnic Studies in Philadelphia and at Syracuse University. A Fellow of the Society of American Archivists, he has been a frequent speaker at archival meetings, and he has authored numerous articles on the subject of business archives in the United States. Among his publications are chapters in *The Records of American Business* (1977) and *Leadership and Administration of Successful Archival Programs* (2001). He has also taught a workshop on Business Archives for the Society of American Archivists for over 20 years. In his role as archivist for The Coca-Cola Company, he has conducted numerous interviews for radio and television including three segments on the *Today Show* and appearances on the History Channel, the Food Network, and CNN. Phil holds an undergraduate degree from Boston College and a master's degree in history from Syracuse University.

Gregory Sanford has been Vermont State Archivist since 1982. He is a past president of the New England Archivists (1988–1989) and member of the steering committee of the Council of State Coordinators (now the Council of State Archivists) (1993–1996). He was coordinator of the Oral History Program at the Massachusetts Institute of Technology (1977–1978), and was assistant director of the George D. Aiken Oral History Project at the University of Vermont (1976–1977 and 1978–1981). He was recipient of the New England Archivists Distinguished Service Award in 2002. His Continuing Issues initiative was recognized by the Society of American Archivists through the 2002 Hamer-Kegan Award, the first Web presentation to be so honored.

Kelvin Smith recently retired as Head of the Accessions Management Unit and Records Management Consultant in the Records Management and Cataloguing Department of the National Archives of the United Kingdom. He spent all his career (beginning in 1967) with the National Archives (formerly the Public Record Office) and during that time was awarded a BA by the Open University. His particular specializations include records appraisal and archiving, records management standards, and the promotion of records management in government. Most recently he drafted the Lord Chancellor's Code of Practice on the Management of Records under Freedom of Information and developed Model Action Plans for compliance with the code. He also published *Freedom of Information: A Practical Guide to Implementing the Act* (Facet Publishing, 2004), *Planning and Implementing Electronic Records Management* (Facet Publishing, 2007), and *Public Sector Records Management: A Practical Guide* (Ashgate, 2007). As well as being a regular presenter of records management issues at conferences, workshops and seminars, he has undertaken frequent assignments in developing countries, mainly in East and Southern Africa, on behalf of the International Records Management Trust, and is Honorary Secretary of the Association of Commonwealth Archivists and Records Managers.

Leon Stout is Head of Public Services and Outreach for the Eberly Family Special Collections Library at the Penn State University Libraries. From 1974 to September 2001, he served as Penn State's university archivist and holds the academic rank of Librarian, Special Collections. He is now responsible for the development and administration of public services and outreach programs for all three archival and rare book units in Special Collections. He also teaches in the library studies and history programs, and is a frequent guest lecturer on campus history and architecture. He received his bachelor's and master's degrees in history from Penn State and the master of library science degree from the University of Pittsburgh. He is the author of a number of articles on archival topics and Penn State history, and wrote the state assessment report, *Historical Records in Pennsylvania*, for the Pennsylvania Historical and Museum Commission. He is a frequent presenter at archival meetings, and has been a consultant to colleges and universities, governmental archives, corporations, and historical societies. Originally appointed by Governor Casey in 1989, he continues to serve as a member of the Pennsylvania State Historical Records Advisory Board and was appointed in 2003 to the U.S. National Historical Publications and Records Commission and chairs its Executive Committee. He has served as chair of the Mid-Atlantic Regional Archives Conference and he has served terms as treasurer, vice president, and president of the Society of American Archivists, the professional body representing nearly 5,000 archivists and manuscript curators across North America. In 1996, he was named a Fellow of the society, its highest individual award.

Christine Ward is New York State Archivist and Assistant Commissioner for Archives and Records as well as Chief Executive Officer of the Archives Partnership Trust. She has been with the New York State Archives since 1981 and served as Director of Operations, Chief Archivist for Archives Operations and Research Services, and Archives' Preservation Officer. Prior to coming to the state archives, she held the position of manuscripts librarian at the Albany Institute of History and Art. She is a member of the Council of State Archivists and the Society of American Archivists where she has chaired numerous committees and task forces. In 1993, she was named a Fellow of the society, their highest professional honor. She has taught graduate and continuing education courses and is a regular participant on panels and sessions at professional meetings on issues relating to preservation management for libraries and archives and administration and strategic development for cultural institutions. She recently co-edited a joint publication of the Council of State Archivists and the National Governors' Association on managing governors' records. She is a Fellow of the State University of New York at Albany's College of Arts and Sciences and in 2005 received the State University of New York at Albany's Distinguished Public Service Award.

Index

Page numbers followed by the letter "t" indicate tables.

A

A*CENSUS, 3, 8–9
Academy of Certified Archivists (ACA)
    Managing Archival Program, 15–16
Academy of Management Journal, 317
Academy of Management Review, 317
Adams, Azad, 318
Adizes, Ichak, 256
Adkins, Elizabeth, 129
Administration. *See also* Leadership;
    Management.
    experience, learning from, 98–101,
    131
Adobe Portable Document Format
    (PDF), 237
AIIM International, 54, 63t, 64t, 65t, 67
Alan K. Simpson Institute for Western
    Politics and Leadership, 152
Ambacher, Bruce, 252
American Archivist, 252, 317
American Association for State and
    Local History, 278
American Crystal Sugar Company, 117,
    125
American History Center. *See* Wyoming,
    University of, American History
    Center (AHC)
American Library Association, 142
American National Standards Institute
    (ANSI), 32, 45, 48–51, 62t–64t
American Society for Quality (ASQ), 32
Analysis, Selection, and Implementation
    Guidelines Associated with
    Electronic Document Management
    Systems, 64t
Andersen, Elmer, 130
Anderson, Karen, 318
Andersen Corporation, 124
Archival programs. *See also* Pennsylva-
    nia State University Archives
    changing needs, 5
    development, 4, 124–127
    disaster preparedness, 13
    employees, 107–109, 139
    experience, learning from, 98–101, 131

    external funds, 270–271, 277
    planning, 110–112, 143, 170–173
    reports, 188
    resources, 19–20
    retention reviews, 113
    strategies, 21–22, 303–307
Archives. *See also* Barclays Bank;
    Corporate archives; Standards
    audiovisual productions, 195–196
    change and, 5, 7, 12, 94–96
    collection policy, 10, 123–127, 148–
    149
    corporate, 71–74
    defined, 1–2
    electronic information, 17–19, 71–74
    evidence repository, 72–74
    exhibitions, 194–195
    future trends, 313–317
    infrastructure, 100
    institutional context, 5, 16, 116–119
    leadership skills, 22
    marketing and public relations, 95,
    102–106, 117–119, 128–133
    measurement, 20, 303–305
    media partnership, 128–133
    mission, 271–272
    oral history, 123–127
    outreach, 128–133
    planning and priorities, 9, 110–112,
    143
    processing policies and procedures,
    145–146
    productivity, 173–175
    promotion, 254
    storage facilities, 6, 100, 139
    traits, 153–156
"Archives Month," 12
Archivists
    faculty guidelines, 146–148
    mission, 166–167
    opportunity and adaptation, 115–116,
    128–133
ARMA. *See* Association of Records
    Managers and Administrators
    (ARMA) International

Arthur Anderson, 70
ASCII, 238
Association of Records Managers and
    Administrators (ARMA) Interna-
    tional, 1
    Emmett Leahy Award, 36–37
    Information Management Journal, 35
    International Education Foundation,
        21–22
    International Standards Task Force,
        2007, 13
    Iron Mountain Award for Excellence,
        304
    ISO 9000 Task Force, 32
    ISO 15489-1, 57, 59, 71–72
    Local Association of Records
        Managers and Administrators
        Chapters, 84–85, 89
    standards, 47–48, 54, 62t–65t, 67
Association of Research Libraries
    (ARL), 246
    Libraries' Management Review and
        Analysis Program, 246
Audiovisual productions, 195–196
Australian National Standard (AS 4390),
    58, 67
*Authentic Leadership: Rediscovering the
    Secrets to Creating Lasting Value*
    (George), 322

B

"Baby Boomer," 8
*Bad Leadership: What It Is, How It
    Happens, Why It Matters*
    (Kellerman), 322
Bakken, Earl, 124–125
Barclays Bank
    business realities, 96–98
    Central Records Store (CRS), 98–101
    changes, 94–96
    "doers," 102–106
    employees, 107–109
    entrepreneurial approach, 106–107
    facility needs, 100, 103–106
    future, managing, 110–112
    Group Archives Unit (GAU), 96, 100,
        111
    history of, 92–94
    human factor, 107–109
    Manchester facility, 98–101
    Records Management Projects Unit
        (RMPU), 101–102, 106–107, 111

Records Services Section, 92, 99
    retention reviews, 113
Barclays Bank International (BBI), 93
Barclays Dominion, Colonial and
    Overseas (DCO), 93
Barclays National Records Centre
    (BNRC), 101
Bearman, David, 252
*Becoming a Manager: How New
    Managers Master the Challenges
    of Leadership* (Hill), 320
Belker, Loren B., 325
Bellman, Geoffrey M., 155, 157
Benedict, Karen, 129, 318
Bennis, Warren G., 263, 265, 293, 297,
    320–321
Best practices, 14
*Beyond the Basics: A Management
    Guide for Library and Information
    Professionals* (Edward), 319
Blair, Gerald M., 142
Booz Allen Hamilton, 302–303
Bossidy, Larry, 300, 324
Boyatzis, Richard, 298, 322
British Standards Institute (BSI), 48, 61t,
    67
Broadbent, Marianne, 319
Brown, Tom, 252
Bruemmer, Bruce, 129
Brumm, Eugenia K., 32
Bryan, Lowell L. L., 324
Bryson, Jo, 319
Buckingham, Marcus, 296, 325
Budget strategies, 19–20, 43, 270–271
Buffet, Warren, 120
*Built to Change: How to Achieve
    Sustained Organizational
    Effectiveness* (Lawler and
    Worley), 324
*Built to Last: Successful Habits of
    Visionary Companies* (Collins),
    323
Burns, James MacGregor, 295, 320

C

California Management Review, 317
Canada (Library and Archives of)
    (LAC), 11
Carucci, Ron, 150
Ceeney, Natalie, 7
Center for Digital Government, Digital
    States Award, 304

Center for Electronic Records, 173
Central Records Store (CRS), 98–101
Certifying professionals, 14
  ACA expectations, 15–16
  ICRM expectations, 16–17
Chapman-Smith, V., 271
Charan, Ram, 300, 324–325
Chief Executive Officer (CEO), 14, 76,
  156, 198, 294
Chief Financial Officer (CFO), 41–43,
  76
Chief Information Officer (CIO), 5, 18,
  223, 260, 305
China, 121, 243
Choo, Chun Wei, 308
*CIO Survival Guide: The Roles and
  Responsibilities of the Chief
  Information Officer* (Schubert),
  319
Citrin, James M., 305
Ciulla, Joanne B., 322
Clifton, Donald O., 325
CNN, 73
Coca-Cola Company, 191, 199–200
Code of Federal Regulations (CFR), 33
Code of Practice on the Management of
  Records, 237
Coffman, Curt, 325
Cohen, Dan S., 302, 323
Collection policy, 123–127, 140, 148–
  149
Collins, Jim, 154, 302, 304, 323
Computer-Assisted Retrieval (CAR)
  system, 39, 249–250
*Confronting Reality: Doing What
  Matters to Get Things Right*
  (Bossidy and Charan), 324
Conger, Jay A., 321
*Consider the Source: Historical Records
  in the Classroom* (Daniels), 270,
  278
Constantini, Jo Ann M., 127
Continuing Issues, 218–220, 224
Corporate archives
  business plan integration, 189–190
  collection development, 123–127
  development of, 184–187
  exhibitions, 194–196
  failure of, 186–187
  identifying objectives, 119–120
  leadership factor, 201–203
  legacy, 126

marketing, 117–119, 128–133, 187–
  189, 195–198
measuring, 134
mind-set, 127–128
opportunity, seizing, 128–133
outreach, 128–133
partnering, 121–124, 128–133
product enhancement, 125–127
public relations, 196–197
publications, 192–194
relationships, 74–77, 95, 102–106,
  198–199
revenue, 120–122, 127–128
value of, 199–201
Council of State Archivists, 4–6
  guidelines, 13
  Report of the Blue Ribbon Panel, 20
Covey, Stephen, 85
Cox, Richard J., 21–22, 262
Craig, Barbara L., 157
Critin, James M., 320
Curzon, Susan Carol, 319
Customer friendly, 9

D

Daniels, Julie, 269, 278
Daniels-Howell, Todd, 155
Davenport, Thomas, 309–310, 324
Dean, Howard, 225
Dearstyne, Bruce W., 221, 318
DePree, Max, 298
*Developing Leadership in Information
  Services* (Roberts and Rowley),
  318
Digital information technology, 4
Digital Object Store, 238–239
Digital records, 6, 17–19, 70. *See also*
  Seamless Flow Programme;
  Standards
  Center for Digital Government,
    Digital States Award, 304
  Computer Assisted Retrieval (CAR)
    system, 39
  Freedom of Information Act (FOIA),
    18, 75, 232, 236–237
  redaction, 236–238
*Digital Records Conversion Process:
  Program Planning, Requirements,
  Procedures, The*, 62t
Dilenschneider, Robert L., 321
*Directory of Corporate Archives in the
  United States and Canada*, 183

DoD 5015.2-STD *Design Criteria Standards of Electronic Records Management Software Application*, 52–53, 61t
Dollard, Charles, 252
Drucker, Peter, 85, 119, 127
Duranti, Luciana, 37

E

E-discovery, 13
The Effective Executive (Drucker), 85
The 8th Habit: From Effectiveness to Greatness (Covey), 85
Electronic records, 4, 6, 17–19. *See also* ISO (International Organization for Standardization); Seamless Flow Programme; Standards
Center for Digital Government, Digital States Award, 304
evidence, 216
preservation, 240–241
Procedures and Issues for Managing Electronic Messages as Records, 65t
program roles, 314
Electronic Records Archives (ERA) Project, 53
Electronic Records Management System (ERMS), 53, 239–240
Electronic Records Online (EROL), 231
E-mail records, 56, 74–75
Emmett Leahy Award, 36
Emotional Intelligence: Why It Can Matter More Than IQ (Goleman), 321
Encouraging the Heart: A Leader's Guide to Rewarding and Recognizing Others (Kouzes and Posner), 320
Enron, 70
Enterprise Project Management Office (EPMO), 223–224
Entrepreneurial approach, 106–107
Erie Canal: New York's Gift to the Nation, The, 282
Erie Canal Time Machine, 282
Esposito, Jackie, 255, 258
Establishing Alphabetic, Numeric, and Subject Filing Systems, 62t
Ethics: The Heart of Leadership (Ciulla), 322
Ethics and the Archival Profession:

Introduction and Case Studies (Benedict), 318
Evaluating the Impact of Your Library (Markless and Streathfield), 319
Evans, G. Edward, 319
Execution: The Discipline of Getting Things Done (Bossidy and Charan), 324
Executive Intelligence: What All Great Leaders Have (Menkes), 321
Exhibitions, 194–196

F

Filippelli, Ronald, 245
Finch, Elsie Freeman, 129
Finkelstein, Stanley, 322
Firestone Tire and Rubber Company, 184
First, Break All the Rules: What the World's Greatest Managers Do Differently (Belker and Topchik), 325
First, Break All the Rules: What the World's Greatest Managers Do Differently (Buckingham and Coffman), 325
First 90 Days: Critical Success Strategies for New Leaders at All Levels, The (Watkins) 320
Fogerty, James E., 153–154
"Folksonomy Effect," 74
Forde, Helen, 10
Forward-Focused Organization, The (Harper), 324
Four Pillars of High Performance: How Robust Organizations Achieve Extraordinary Results, The (Light), 323–324
Framework for Integration of Electronic Document Management Systems and Electronic Records Management Systems (AIIM), 64t
Freedom of Information Act (FOIA), 18, 75, 232, 236–237
Fullan, Michael, 323
Fulmer, William E., 324
Functional Requirements for Electronic Records Management Systems, 61t

G

Galford, Robert M., 321
Gates, Bill, 70, 120
Geda, Carolyn, 252

General Mills, 124, 132
Generic Metadata Management Store (GMMS), 229–230
George, Bill, 322
George Washington University, 32
Georgia State Archives, 9
Gerzon, Mark, 321
Go Put Your Strengths to Work: Six Powerful Steps to Achieve Outstanding Performance (Buckingham), 325
Goleman, Daniel, 321–322
Good to Great (Collins), 323
Good to Great: Why Some Companies Make the Leap . . . and Others Don't (Collins), 323
Good to Great and the Social Sectors (Collins), 323
Google, 194
"Google Effect," 74
Gow, Kay F., 84
Graco, Inc., 125–126
Gracy, David, 129
Great Northern, 117
Greene, Mark, 119, 142
Greenfield Village, 137
Gubernatorial records, 214

H
H. B. Fuller, 124
Hackman, Larry J., 270, 308
Hagley Museum and Library, 120, 123
Hamel, Gary, 324
Harper, Stephen C., 324
Harter, James K., 309, 325
Harvard Business Review, 317
Harvard Business School, 120, 295
Hearst Education Fund, 271
Heart of Change: Real-Life Stories of How People Change Their Organizations, The (Kotter and Cohen), 323
Heart of Change Field Guide: Tools and Tactics for Leading Change in Your Organization. The (Cohen), 323
Hebard, Grace Raymond, 138
Heifetz, Ronald A., 323
Henry Ford Museum, 137
Herb, Steven L., 258
Herdon, Peter, 319

Hill, Linda, A., 294, 320
History Day, 140, 275
History Happened Here, 274–275
Holland Patent Central School, 277
Holly, Ed., 143
Honeywell, 117
House Government Operations Committee, 216
Hrebiniak, Lawrence G., 312, 323
Hubbard, Stanley S., 133
Hubbard Broadcasting, 129–130
Hudson-Fulton-Champlain Quadricentennial, 282
Hurricane Katrina, 13, 78

I
Implementing Electronic Document and Record Management Systems (Adams), 318
Information and Image Management (Ricks and Gow), 84
Information and Records Management: Document-Based Information Systems (Robek), 318
Information Management Journal (ARMA), 35, 317
Information professionals, role of, 291–294
Information technology (IT), 12–13. *See also* Seamless Flow Programme; Standards
departments, 72, 76, 80
objectives, 82–83
records information and, 41–42
Institute of Certified Records Managers (ICRM)
Emmett Leahy Award, 36–37
expectations, 16–17
"The Handbook for Candidates (ICRM), 2006," 16
International Multifoods, 117
International Organization for Standardization. *See* ISO (International Organization for Standardization)
INTERPARES project, 37
Interuniversity Consortium for Political and Social Research, University of Michigan, 252
Intraprise, 117–119
Iraqi National Museum, 73
Iron Mountain Award for Excellence (ARMA), 304

ISO (International Organization for
    Standardization), 45, 48, 60t
  accrediting body, 53–54
  development process, 50–53
  ISO 9000, 32, 40, 49, 60t
  ISO 15489-1, 57–59, 71–74
  ISO 15489-2, 59
  ISO 23081, 59
  ISO TC 46/SC11, 58
  ISO TC 171, 58, 60
  standards tables, 60t–65t

J

JP Morgan Chase, 282
Jefferson, Thomas, 208
Jimerson, Randall, 10–11
JITC (Joint Interoperability Test
    Command), 52
Johnson, Edward, R., 246
Jones, Tim, 131
Joyce, Claudia L. I., 324
Joyce, William, 138
Journal of Leadership Studies, 317

K

Kanter, Rosabeth Moss, 308
Karan, Donna, 120
Kellerman, Barbara, 322
Kelley, Tom, 324
Kiel, Fred, 322
Kitzis, Ellen S., 319
*Knowledge Management in the Public
    Sector: A Blueprint for Innovation
    in Government* (McNabb), 320
Kotter, John P., 301, 323
Kouzes, James M., 298, 310–311, 320
Kraft Foods Inc., 191
Kurtz, Michael J., 22, 318

L

Lauren, Ralph, 120
Lawler, Edward E., 295, 324
Leader to Leader, 317
Leader's Legacy, A (Kouzes and Posner),
    320
Leadership
  A*CENSUS, 3, 8–9
  allies, development of, 168–170
  assessment, 178–181
  becoming a leader, 293–294
  building and managing relationships,
    74–77, 95, 306–307

challenges, 138–141, 298–299
communications, 71–74, 291–293
confidence, 310
contextual, 27–30
decision making, 299
defined, 2, 137–138
employee development and, 41–42,
    83–85, 107–109, 170–173
execution, 300–301
evaluating, 173–175
future, 313–317
goals, 81–82, 164–166
learning adaptive mode, 308–310
media partnership, 128–133
mission, 166–167
models for strong programs, 301–303
network building, 307–308
organizational environment, 87–88
planning and priorities, 81–83, 110–
    112, 143, 170–173
presence, 30, 34–35
program development, 124–127
project management, 86–87, 223–224
purpose, clarity and consistency,
    296–297
relationships, 40–43, 74–77, 95
risk taking, 29, 36–39
return on investment (ROI), 37–38
role of, 26, 31–34, 69–71, 137–138,
    291–294
shared meaning, 297
skills, 14–17, 22, 31–34
staff productivity, 173–175
strategy, 21–22, 35–36, 78–80, 303–
    306
teaching, 30–31
traits, 153–156
transforms, 295–296
varieties of, 294–295
vision, 30–31, 36–39, 81, 141–144
Leadership, 317
Leadership (Burns), 320
*Leadership and Administration of
    Successful Archival Programs*
    (Dearstyne), 318
*Leadership & Organization Development
    Journal*, 317
Leadership Challenge, The (Kouzes and
    Posner), 320
*Leadership on the Line: Staying Alive
    Through the Dangers of Leading*
    (Heifetz and Linsky), 323

Leadership Quarterly, 317
Leading Change (Kotter), 323
Leading for a Lifetime: How Defining Moments Shape the Leaders of Today and Tomorrow (Bennis and Thomas), 321
Leading in a Culture of Change (Fullan), 323
Leading the Revolution (Hamel), 324
Leading Through Conflict: How Successful Leaders Transform Differences into Opportunities (Gerzon), 321
Legacies, 282
Legacies Project, 277
Legal Acceptance of Records Produced by Information Technology Systems, 63t
Legal discovery, 13, 74
Legislative records, 213–214
Lennick, Doug, 322
Liberty High School, New York City, 277
Libraries' Management Review and Analysis Program, 246
Library and Archives of Canada (LAC), 11
Library and Information Center Management (Stueart and Moran), 319
Light, Paul C., 323–324
Lillehei, C. Walton, 124–125
Linard, Laura, 120
Linsky, Marty, 323
Littauer Education Fund, 271
Lloyd, Margaret, 144, 146, 156
Local Association of Records Managers and Administrators (ARMA) Chapters, 84–85, 89
Local Government Records Management Grants Program, 276–278
Local Government Records Management Improvement Fund, 271, 274, 276, 281
Local Government Records Management Improvement Law, 271
Lutchen, Mark, 319

M
3M Company, 117, 125
Maguire, Sheridan, 144, 146, 156
Making a Difference: Leadership and

Academic Libraries (Herdon and Rossiter), 319
Making Strategy Work: Leading Effective Execution and Change (Hrebiniak), 323
Management. *See also* Administration; Leadership
assessment, 178–181
differs from leadership, 292–294
goals, 16–17
skills, 15–16, 22, 31–34
style, 175–181
Management Learning: The Journal for Managerial and Organizational Learning, 317
Management Skills for Archivists and Records Managers, (Shepherd and Anderson, 318
Managing Archival and Manuscript Repositories (Kurtz), 318
Managing Archives: Foundations, Principles, and Practice (Williams), 318
Managing Business Ethics: Straight Talk About How to Do It Right (Trevino and Nelson), 322
Managing Change: A How-To-Do-It Manual for Librarians (Curzon), 319
Managing Electronic Messages as Records, 63t
Managing in the Information Age (Prentice), 318
Managing Information Services: A Transformational Approach (Bryson), 319
Managing IT as a Business: A Survival Guide for CEO's (Lutchen), 319
Managing Records for ISO 9000 Compliance (Brumm), 32
MARC records, 145–146
Markless, Sharon, 319
Maruca, Regina Fazio, 321
Maryland, University of, 221
Massachusetts Institute of Technology, 211
Masters of Library Science (MLS), 221
McCormick, Teri, 129–131
McGregor, Douglas, 245
McKee, Annie, 298, 322
McNabb, David E., 320
Mech, Terrence F., 151

Media partnership, 128–133
Medtronic, 124
Meissner, Dennis, 119
Mellon Fellowship, 264
Menkes, Justin, 321
Metadata, 229–230
Mid-Atlantic Regional Archives
  Conference (MARAC), 252
Midwest Archives Conference, 137
Minnesota Historical Society (MHS),
  116–118, 123, 125–126
  leadership, 153–156
  media partnership, 129–133
  "Minnesota Method," 119
Minorities, 8
Mobilizing Minds: Creating Wealth from
  Talent in the 21st Century Organi-
  zation (Lowell and Joyce), 324
Moore, Thomas L., 141, 154
Moral Intelligence: Enhancing Business
  Performance and Leadership
  Success (Lennick and Kiel), 322
Moran, Barbara, 319
MoReq (Model Requirements for the
  Management of Electronic
  Records), 53, 61t
Morgan Stanley v. Coleman, 72
Moss, Michael, 128
Municipal records, 215–216

N
National Archives, United Kingdom, 7,
  9–10, 61t, 67. See also Seamless
  Flow Programme; United
  Kingdom National Archives
  (TNA)
  background, 227, 228t, 231
National Archives and Records Adminis-
  tration (NARA), 252–253
  Center for Electronic Records, 173
  Machine Readable Branch, 173
  Mission statement, 259
  standards, 52, 67
National Archives of Canada, 252
National Association of Government
  Archives and Records Administra-
  tors (NAGARA), 4
National Association of Government
  Communicators, 278
National Council for History Education,
  278
National Historical Publications and

Records Commission (NHPRC),
  4, 145
  grant, 149, 216, 251, 253
National History Day, 275
National Information Standards Institute,
  67
Naugler, Harold, 252
Neff, Thomas J., 305, 320
Neilson, Gary L, 302–303, 323
Nelson, Katherine A., 322
Networking, 307–308
New CIO Leader: Setting the Agenda
  and Delivering Results, The
  (Broadbent and Kitizis), 319
New England Archivists' Distinguished
  Service Award, 209
New York State
  Board of Regents, 272–273, 283–286
  Cultural Education and Museum Act,
  284
  Division of the Budget, 272–273, 287
  document-based questions (DBQs),
  279–280
  Education Commissioner, 272
  Education Department, 272–273,
  278–279
  Executive Office, 287–289
  Library, 269, 280
  Museum, 265, 280
  Office for Technology, 288
  Office of Higher Education, 280
  P–16 Regents' education reform plan,
  283–286
  Thruway, 274–275
  University of the State of New York
  (USNY), 273, 280
New York State Archives. See also New
  York State
  Archives Partnership Trust, 271, 274,
  282
  budget, 6, 270
  Educational Uses grant, 276–277
  fee-based revenue, 6, 270
  Legacies Project, 277
  Local Government Records Manage-
  ment Grants Program, 276–278
  Local Government Records Manage-
  ment Improvement Fund, 271,
  274, 276, 281
  mission, 271–272
  Office of Cultural Education, 269,
  285

publications and promotions, 274–
279
teacher training, 280–283
use reporting, 5
Nonprofit organizations, 122–124
Northern Westchester-Putnam Teacher
Center, 277
Northwest Airlines, 117, 125–126
Norton, Andrew, 150
Now, Discover Your Strengths
(Buckingham and Clifton), 325
Nuclear Regulatory Commission (NRC),
38

O
OAIS. *See* Open Archive Information
Systems (OAIS)
Office of General Counsel (OGC), 168
*On Becoming a Leader: The Leadership
Classic* (Bennis), 293, 320–321
One Bank. *See* Barclays Bank
*One Thing You Need to Know About
Great Managing, Great Leading,
and Sustained Individual Success,
The* (Buckingham), 325
O'Neil, Dennis, P., 297
Online information, 18
Online Public Access Catalog (OPAC),
141
Open Archive Information Systems
(OAIS), 235
Oral history, 123–127
Organizational environment, 87–88

P
Pasternack, Bruce A., 302–303, 323
Peavey, Frank, 130
Penn State, 247–278, 256, 258, 260–261
Land Grant University, 247
Pennsylvania State University Archives
assessing program, 245–247
central administrative files project,
249–250
computer assisted retrieval (CAR),
249–250
EASY system, 253–254
electronic records, 252–254
Historical Collections and Labor
Archives (HCLA), 243–245
Nittany Lion, 258
Outreach, 247–248
Penn State Blue Band, 258

Penn State Room, 244–247
Public Services and Outreach, 245
Records Management Advisory
Committee, 251, 260
records management and university
archives, 250–252
"Statiana Alcove," 244
university, service to, 248–250
"Peter Principle," 33–34
Pfeffer, Jeffrey, 310
Pillsbury, 124
*Planning and Implementing Electronic
Records Management*, (Kelvin),
318
Posner, Barry Z., 298, 310–311, 320
*Power and Influence: The Rules Have
Changed* (Dilenschneider), 321
*Practice of Leadership: Developing the
Next Generation of Leaders, The*
(Conger and Riggio), 321
Prentice, Ann E., 318
Preserving the Past, 258
*Primal Leadership: Realizing the Power
of Emotional Intelligence*
(Goleman, Boyatzis, and McKee),
322
Procter & Gamble, 191
Project management, 86–87
Enterprise Project Management
Office (EPOM), 223
Province of Victoria, 67
Public Administration Review, 317
Public records, 220–224
Public relations, 102–106, 196–198
intraprise, 117–119
marketing, 190–195, 254
media partnerships, 128–133
Publications, 192–194, 275–279

Q
Qing Dynasty, 244
Quaker goldsmiths, 92

R
RAND Corporation, 18
Records
defined, 2, 5
evidentiary, 5
gubernatorial, 214
legislative, 213–214
municipal, 215–216
public records, 220–224

Records and information management (RIM), 32
Records Center Operations, 65t
Records management. *See also* Barclays Bank; Corporate archives; Standards
building relationships, 40–43, 74–77, 95, 102–106
change, 5, 7, 12, 94–96
Code of Practice on the Management of Records, 237
communications, 71–74, 291–293
digital records, 6, 17–19, 62t
disaster preparedness, 13
employees, 83–85, 107–109, 139
faculty guidelines, 146–148
future trends, 313–317
Human Resources Department, 77
initiatives, 34–35
innovations, 36–39
ISO 9000, 32, 40, 49, 60t
ISO 15489-1 standard, 57, 59, 71–72
ISO 15489-2 standard, 58–59
ISO TC 46/SC11, 58
ISO TC 171, 58, 60
leadership, 14–17, 22, 26–28, 81–83, 153–156
learning, 131
mastery of the field, 28–30
measurement, 20, 303–305
mission, 271–272
planning, 81–83, 110–112, 143, 170–173
program development, 9, 56–57, 70, 124–127
processing policies and procedures, 145–146
process-oriented standards, 50–51
Records Management Advisory Committee, 251
resources, 19–20
role of leader, 31–34, 291–293
storage facilities, 6, 100, 139
strategy, 21–22, 35–36, 78–80
teaching, 30–31
university archives and, 250–252
Records Management—Part 1, 57–59
Records Management Advisory Committee, 251
Records Management Responsibility in Litigation Support, 65t

Records of American Business, The (Moss and Richmond), 128
Redaction of records, 236–238
Relationship building and managing, 74–77, 95, 102–106
Researching the History of Your School (Roe), 276
Resonant Leadership (Boyatzis and McKee), 322
Results: Keep What's Good, Fix What's Wrong, and Unlock Great Performance (Neilson and Pasternack), 302–303, 323
Richmond, Leslie, 128
Ricks, Betty, R., 84
Riggio, Ronald, 321
Robek, Mary F., 318
Roberto, Michael A., 151, 299–300, 321
Roberts, Sue, 318
Rockefeller Archive Center (RAC), 169–170
Roe, Kathleen, 276
Rogers, Paul, 153
Rossiter, Nancy, 316
Rowley, Jennifer, 318
Royal Bank of Canada, 118
Russell, Keith, 151

S
Sarbanes-Oxley Act (2002), 7, 12–13, 21, 70, 78, 112
Schellenberg, Theodore R., 245
Schubert, Karl D., 319
Seamless Flow Programme. *See also* Electronic records
appraisal and selection, 229
assessment, 232–234
background, 227, 228t, 229
benefit analysis, 239–240
business change and training project, 94–96, 231–235
delivery and presentation, 230
Electronic Records Online (EROL), 231
Freedom of Information Act, 18, 75, 232, 236–237
management and security, 231
metadata and cataloguing, 229–230
modernizing government, 229
National Archives transfer, 230

Open Archive Information Systems
(OAIS), 235
pilot transfer, 238–239
preservation and maintenance, 230
process model, 228f
public web search and resource
discovery, 229
records transfer, 235–236
redaction, 236–238
technology watch, 230
September 11, 2001 terrorist attacks, 13
7 Habits of Highly Effective People, The
(Covey), 85
*Shaping the Adaptive Organization:
Landscapes, Learning, and
Leadership in Volatile Times*
(Fulmer), 324
Sheldon, Brooke, E., 143
Shepherd, Elizabeth, 318
Shipton, Clifford, 245, 257
Sims, Peter, 322
Sinclair, Niall, 320
Skupsky, Donald, 37
Slade, William, 209–210, 217
Sloan Management Review, 317
Smith, Gregory S., 305, 319
Smith, Kelvin, 318
Smithsonian Center for Archives
Conservation (SCAC), 169
Smithsonian Institution Archives (SIA),
164–166, 168–169, 173
Smythe, Elizabeth, 150
Snelling, Richard, 216
Society of American Archivists (SAA), 1
A*CENSUS, 3, 8–9
"Archives Month," 12
Automated Records and Techniques
Task Force, 252
awards, 278
Congressional Papers Roundtable,
154
Distinguished Service Award, 304
electronic information/records issues,
19
external reviews, 138
Hamer-Kegan Award, 209
leadership, 137, 158–159
management skills, 15–16, 22
meeting, 246
members, 183
Presidential Address, 10–11
public relations workshop, 129

Soo Line Railroads, 117
Soviet Union, 121
Spitzer, Eliot, 286–287
St. Lifer, Evan, 149
Standards
accrediting body, 53–54
consensus, 51
defined, 47–48
development of, 14, 46–47, 54–55
education of, 47
electronic records management, 40,
48–51, 58–65
evaluating of, 55–56
importance, 45–46
policies and procedures, 57–58, 65t
process-oriented, 50–51
scope, 51–53
Submission Information Package
(SIP), 235
use of, 56–57
Web sites, 66–67
Standards Developing Organizations
(SDOs), 54–56
State of State Records The (Council of
State Archivists), 4–6
*Stealth KM: Winning Knowledge
Management Strategies for the
Public Sector* (Sinclair), 320
Stephens, Denise, 151
Stewart, Thomas A., 153
Stout, Leon, J., 253
*Straight to the Top: Becoming a World-
Class CIO* (Smith), 319
Strategic Management Journal, 317
Strategic planning, 78–83, 110–112
Streathfield, David, 319
Stueart, Robert D., 319
Submission Information Package (SIP),
235
Sutton, Robert I., 310
Sverdloff, Brent, 120

T
Teaching with Historical Records, 276,
281
Ten Faces of Innovation, The (Kelley),
324
*Thinking for a Living: How to Get Better
Performance and Results from
Knowledge Workers* (Davenport),
324
Thomas, Robert J., 263, 265, 297, 321

Throughout the Ages, 282
"Top Leader Behaviors That Set Apart
    Exceptional Senior Leaders,"
    (O'Neil), 297
Topchik, Gary S., 325
*Transforming Leadership: A New Pursuit
    of Happiness* (Burns), 320
Trevino, Linda K., 322
*True North: Discover Your Authentic
    Leadership* (George and Sims),
    322
12: The Elements of Great Managing
    (Wagner), 325

U

UBS Warburg v. Zubulake, 70, 72
United Kingdom National Archives
    (TNA), 7, 9–10, 61t, 67. *See also*
    Seamless Flow Programme
    background, 227, 228f, 229–231
    impact assessment, 232–235
    modernizing government, 229
University Art Museum, Wyoming,
    University of, American History
    Center (AHC), 139
University of the State of New York
    (USNY), 273
University of Vermont Special Collec-
    tions, 209
U.S. Department of Defense, 52

V

Verizon, 277
Vermont
    Buildings and General Services/
        Public Records Division, 211,
        221, 223
    Constitution, 209, 219
    Council of Censors, 215–216
    Enterprise Project Management
        Office (EPOM), 223–224
    Public Records Commission, 210,
        220–224
    Public Records Division, 210–212,
        221–224
    Public Service Award, 209
    Secretary of State, 208
    State Papers Division, 208, 211
Vermont Information Strategy Plan
    (VISP), 216
Vermont State Archives
    Division of Public Records, 224

    gubernatorial records, 214
    history of, 208–212
    legislative records, 213–214
    municipal records, 215–216
    Public Records Commission, 222–
        224
    records based information, 217–220
    State Chief Information Officer
        (CIO), 223
    statutory authority, 220–222
    Vermont Statues Annotated, 215–216,
        221
Veysey, Laurence R., 245
Victoria Electronic Records Strategy
    (VERS), 61t
*Vital Records: Identifying, Managing,
    and Recovering Business-Critical
    Records*, 64t

W

Wagner, Rodd, 309, 325
Ward, Patricia Layzell, 319
Washington, George, 208
Watkins, Michael, 320
Web site, 66–67, 200, 218, 229–230, 282
Welch, Jack, 299
Welch, Susy, 299
Wells Fargo Bank, 164–166
Western Trails, 140
"What Leaders Do," (Welch and Welch),
    299
White, Herbert, 143
*Why Great Leaders Don't Take Yes for an
    Answer: Managing for Conflict
    and Consensus* (Roberto), 321
*Why Smart Executives Fail and What You
    Can Learn from Their Mistakes*
    (Finkelstein), 322
Williams, Caroline, 318
Williams, Robert, 37
Wilson, Ian E., 11
Workforce, 7–8
World Bank, 164
Worley, Christopher G., 295, 324
Wyoming, University of, American
    History Center (AHC)
    challenges, 156–157, 138–141
    decision making, 149–153
    history, 137–138
    leadership, 138–141, 153–156
    managing change, 144–149
    vision, 141–144

Y

Yahoo!, 194
Yale, 244
Your Leadership Legacy: Why Looking
Toward the Future Will Make You
a Better Leader Today (Galford
and Maruca), 321
You're in Charge: Now What? (Neff), 320